EXPLAINING
AMERICA

By Garry Wills

CHESTERTON

POLITICS AND CATHOLIC FREEDOM

ROMAN CULTURE

JACK RUBY

THE SECOND CIVIL WAR

NIXON AGONISTES

BARE RUINED CHOIRS

INVENTING AMERICA

CONFESSIONS OF A CONSERVATIVE

AT BUTTON'S

EXPLAINING AMERICA

EXPLAINING AMERICA: THE FEDERALIST

Garry Wills

DOUBLEDAY & COMPANY, INC.

GARDEN CITY, NEW YORK

1981

Library of Congress Cataloging in Publication Data

Wills, Garry, 1934-
   Explaining America.

   (His America's political enlightenment)
   Includes indexes.
   1. Federalist. I. Title. II. Series.
JK155.W54   320.973

ISBN: 0-385-14689-2
Library of Congress Catalog Card Number: 79-6542
Copyright © 1981 by Garry Wills
All Rights Reserved
Printed in the United States of America
First Edition

Table of Contents

Plan of the Series

This book is a successor to *Inventing America: Jefferson's Declaration of Independence*, which argued that Jefferson's draft of the Declaration (as opposed to the document the Congress issued) was influenced by eighteenth-century Scottish concepts of the moral sense.

Since the Congress excised the characteristically Scottish elements from Jefferson's draft, the question arises whether any other political thinkers of our early national period were influenced by the Scottish Enlightenment. This book answers that question in the affirmative, so far as Madison and Hamilton are concerned, by tracing their debt to Hume's political essays.

Though The Federalist defends the Constitution with a theory of government, the Constitution is not itself a theoretical statement, but a practical instrument of rule. Whether it reflects any single theory will be the subject of my next book, *Building America: The Constitution*. A fourth volume, *Judging America: The Supreme Court*, will complete a series with the general title *America's Political Enlightenment*.

Prologue

Many people, wanting to explain America's Constitution to themselves or others, turn first to The Federalist; and, within that book, turn first to No. 10. As they should. And not only for explaining *American* politics. Lord Acton, in his inaugural address as Regius Historian at Cambridge, called the debates of "the most enlightened states in the American union" worth those of nearly all other "constituent assemblies" taken together. America's deliberations are "paramount in the literature of politics." He was referring to the arguments, state by state, over what constitution to adopt internally; and, more important, what Articles to conclude with each other (for a start); then what federal constitution, finally, to settle on.

In "the most enlightened states" Acton surely included New York and Virginia, famous for their struggles to ratify the federal Constitution—struggles that elicited the best writings of a Virginian and two New Yorkers who shared the name "Publius." Their efforts were directed, immediately, to ratification by New York; but the essays produced were also used in Virginia's convention against the ablest critics of this plan for government, Patrick Henry and George Mason.

America's first entirely developed art was political literature, the oratory and pamphleteering that shaped our early history. The eighteenth century was a time of great political urgencies greatly expressed. Johnson and Burke, "Junius" and Bolingbroke, Paine and Cobbett thundered, protreptic or admonitory. And Americans were in the front rank of this literary movement. Jefferson is the rival of Junius, on whom he modeled his first works (*Inventing*, 80–1). John Adams can grumble as instructively, at times, as Dr. Johnson. Yet nothing, even in the Revolution of the 1770s, called out more eloquence and ingenuity than the debates of 1787-8 over ratification of the federal Constitution. If history had retained only the arguments of Richard Henry Lee and Patrick Henry, later ages would wonder how the Constitution ever got itself adopted, after taking such a splendid verbal pounding. If James Wilson's defense of the Constitution were preserved as well, the scales would be balanced, a case for the Constitution securely made. But The Federalist presents us with the spectacle of rhetorical and analytic overkill.

The authors pass governments in review, adopting this good feature, rejecting that flawed part; scanning the entirety of politics through the focus of the Philadelphia Convention. Fired off three a week, the essays overwhelmed response. Who, given ample time, could have answered such a battery of arguments? And no time was given. As soon as one was digested, there were two more in the coffee house. In the Philadelphia *Freeman's Journal* an antifederalist writer grumbled: "Publius has already written 26 Numbers, as much as would jade the brains of any poor sinner . . . so that in decency he should now rest on his arms, and let the people draw their breath for a little" (December 12, 1787). But Publius was just getting his second wind after twenty-six essays. The "Numbers" appeared in four of the five New York City papers, prompting this lament to the *New-York Journal:* "We take McLean to read Publius in the best edition, and he gives us two at a time; and Childs for the daily news and advertisements, but they are curtailed—and we are disappointed —for the purpose of serving up the same Publius at our expense. Loudon we take for his morality and evangelic sentiments; but here again we are imposed upon by being made to pay for the very same Publius, who has become nauseous by having been served up to us no less than in two other papers on the same day" (January 1, 1788).

The eighty-four essays (printed in book form as eighty-five) are, among other things, a marvel of mental energy. Two men turned out seventy-one of these essays in just over six months (the run of papers from No. 6 through No. 77, minus Jay's one contribution in this span)—essays as trenchant in thought as they are graceful in expression. Hamilton, the begetter of the whole scheme, was lightning fast with his quill, assuming a dizzying variety of classical names. No one, on either side of the Atlantic, turned out more pamphlets of high quality than Hamilton. But in The Federalist he outdid even himself. And Madison, slower to write and speak, drew on the deep reserves of learning acquired in preparation for the Philadelphia Convention of 1787. Though Hamilton was busy with his law firm, and Madison with his duties in the Continental Congress, these men found time to compose their essays while maneuvering with friends and foes during a time of distraction and debate. As Douglass Adair notes (*Fame*, 53), the great project went forward, for over a year, at an average of a thousand well-chosen words every day. It is enough to make all other writers on politics despair.

But the time of closest collaboration was simply the climax of long years spent coming to rough agreement on the need for a stronger central government. All three men had reached this conclusion during the course of the revolutionary war, and the experience of the Confederate Congress had confirmed it. All three were especially intent on giving Congress the power to regulate trade, on opposing the separate states' power to issue paper money. Madison and Hamilton had especially close ties in this endeavor, dating from their joint service in the congresses of 1782–3, their attendance at the Annapolis Convention of 1786, and their joint call for a federal convention next year (where both men would be active delegates). Later differences have obscured their basic agreement on priorities and tactics in the national crisis of the 1780s. Hamilton went on to the Treasury, and Madison to the presidency; but if they had both died in the summer of 1788, their countrymen might justifiably suppose they had accomplished the great work for which they were born—and had accomplished it as a team.

Although Hamilton initiated and outlined the project "Publius" would complete, Madison wrote the paper most praised for its brief cogency. It compresses in little space a line of argument he had been elaborating in notes and speeches directed to, or arising from, the Constitutional Convention's debates. And who, after all, could bring more authoritative skill to the Constitution's explication than the man who drew up its first draft in Philadelphia and frustrated its best critics in Richmond? Even Robert

Dahl, a shrewd critic of Madison's thought, acknowledges his many skills:

> Madison, however, had the rare gift—doubly rare among political leaders—of lucid, logical and orderly exposition of his theoretical argument; perhaps in no other political writing by an American is there a more compactly logical, almost mathematical piece of theory than Madison's The Federalist, No. 10 (*Preface to Democratic Theory*, 5).

Here, it would seem, we have an explanation that really explains —not only authoritative but clarifying. Madison had both the right and the ability to explain the document of which he has long been called the father.

All this seems obvious; which just makes the essay's history more mysterious. No. 10 was not used to explain America until comparatively recently; and since then it has been used most effectively to attack the Constitution it was trying to defend. Despite many references to the paper's lucidity, there has been great confusion over *what* it says, and *how* what it says can apply either to the Constitution itself or to the government formed on its base. The explanation itself calls for explaining.

The nineteenth century's best expounders of our political system, Tocqueville and Bryce, managed their task without any help at all from the tenth paper. Douglass Adair, after a survey of the entire literature on No. 10, reached the astonishing conclusion that before 1913 "practically no commentator on The Federalist or the Constitution, none of the biographers of Madison, had emphasized Federalist 10 as of special importance for understanding our 'more perfect union'" (*Fame*, 75–6).

The year 1913 changed all that because it saw the publication of Charles Beard's *An Economic Interpretation of the Constitution*. Beard treated Madison as an economic determinist, indeed as his own forerunner—but on the other side of the barricades. Madison was for him what Calhoun would later be called, the Marx of the ruling class. Trying to make a constitution in Philadelphia, Madison was dealing with men who were themselves on the make, men who wanted their ventures protected. It was for their benefit that Madison invented his argument against majority rule. The real mystery of The Federalist is that, having done this, Madison wrote and published a description of the *way* he did it. Beard's Madison explains the game so well that he gives the game away. In this view, it was lucky for Madison that Federalist 10 did not get much attention at the outset; it might have defeated his own purpose. Madison had given a privileged few the weapons for controlling "the landless proletariat" (Beard, 157).

Beard first put Federalist 10 in the center of constitutional debate, where it has remained ever since. Moreover, he seemed to solve one problem that has plagued discussion of the paper. The checks Madison puts on factious majorities would encumber virtuous majorities as well. Or, to state the same thing conversely, a minority of skilled "proles" could in time use the weapons forged to repress the majority of their brethren. Indeed, no matter how one defines the "good guys" in Madison's eyes—whether as propertied or virtuous or whatever—why should we presume they will monopolize the use of checks and controls, which are available to anyone who acquires skill in using them? If you hand everyone a six-gun, does that give an edge to the good guys or to the bad guys? It depends, obviously, on how many troops there are on either side. The six-gun's machinery is unbiased; why did Madison suggest that only the bad guys' guns would jam?

Beard's answer was straightforward. In society as it actually existed in 1787, the privileged few were in a position to seize the first jobs in the *judiciary*. Since justices were the only officers with life tenure, and since the framers had carefully arranged for "judicial control" over legislation (163), they could have things their way for all the foreseeable future.

Yet Beard also had a fallback position. Even if the judiciary should someday come into different hands, so that active protection of privilege was no longer possible, the system of checks would still serve the propertied class. In a society "where the field of private property is already extended to cover practically every form of tangible and intangible wealth" (155), a deadlocked government serves owners' interests almost as well as one rigged in their favor. Government continues to help them just by doing nothing.

Beard's reading of Madison has affected all subsequent discussion. This is true not only of those who were Beard's ideological allies—J. Allen Smith, for instance, and Vernon Parrington—but even of comparatively neutral bystanders. The latter might not agree with Beard's politics; but they often felt that he got *Madison's* politics right. Adair could write in 1951 that Beard's "interpretation still governs to a remarkable degree the contemporary view of Federalist 10, Madison, and the Constitution" (76). Five years after that statement, Robert Dahl confirmed it in his analysis of No. 10. As we shall see, Dahl had another quarrel to pick with Madison; but he shows, in passing, that he thought Beard had a good quarrel going too. He tells us that Madison elaborated a "protective ideology for the minorities of wealth, status, and power" (*Preface*, 30). He "wished to erect a political system that would guarantee the liberties of certain minorities whose advantages of status, power and wealth would, he thought, probably not be tolerated indefinitely by a constitutionally untrammeled majority" (31). In Dahl's view it is lucky, given Madison's aims, that Madison's scheme just did not work.

Another school of thought, too, made a virtue of the fact that Madison's form of government does not seem to work. Next after Beard's economic interpretation of the paper, the pluralist reading has been the most influential in modern times. If Madison's machinery is neutral in itself, not distinguishing between factious and virtuous blocs, he must have wanted government to be ineffective—just what Beard maintained in his fallback position. But the pluralists, led by Harold Laski, did not see in this a design to protect a single minority. They assumed that Madison wanted to leave the field open for other agencies to participate— voluntary, corporate, benevolent, or whatever. Limited government promotes a wide range of social activities; its citizens do not conceive social life as narrowly *political* in all aspects. Paul F. Bourne has traced (in *Perspectives in American History*, 1974) the broad impact Laski's reading of Madison had in the 1920s, especially on Walter Lippmann.

The pluralists argued that Madison planned the best of governments because it delivers the *least* possible government. But their general praise of social groupings left out that typical American institution, the political party. Exponents of the party system have always been uncomfortable with Madison's tenth paper. E. E. Schattschneider (in *Party Government*, 1942) described Madison's war on parties:

> It was hoped that the parties would lose and exhaust themselves in futile attempts to fight their way through the labyrinthine framework of the government, much as an attacking army is expected to spend itself against the defensive works of a fortress (7).

For Schattschneider, No. 10 was an injury to which No. 51 added insult. Madison splintered *society* in No. 10 to prevent majority faction. Then, having done so, he went further in No. 51 and splintered *government*—a kind of "fail-safe" insurance to abort any organized political program:

> What is more amazing, however, is that the second argument destroys the first. Madison's defense of federalism annihilates his defense of the separation of powers. If the multiplicity of interests in a large republic makes tyrannical majorities impossible, the principal theoretical prop of the separation of powers has been demolished (9).

This is a lament James MacGregor Burns took up, twenty years later, in *The Deadlock of Democracy* (1963). According to Burns, either No. 10 is wrong, which makes No. 51 necessary; or No. 10 is right, which makes No. 51 not only superfluous but destructive of what No. 10 accomplished:

> Why would not any popular majority representing such a variety of interests perforce become so broad and moderate in its goals as never to threaten any major or even minor or individual interest? Why was it necessary to have what Madison called "auxiliary precautions" of checks and balances built right into the frame of government? (21).

Madison, in this view, having taken pains to keep majorities virtuous, then made sure the virtuous majority would not be able to accomplish any of its goals. It was left for Madison's friend, Jefferson, to see through the self-defeating aspects of No. 51 and base his "strategy of majority rule" (40) on *social* checks as opposed to *institutional* hedges. Burns, you see, agrees with No. 10 only as a way of attacking the constitutional machinery of checks that The Federalist in general was meant to defend. Like Beard, but for his very different reason, he will agree with Madison in order to undo Madison's work. Those who favor party reform leading to ideologically "responsible" parties in America tend to follow Schattschneider and Burns in thinking No. 10 should be saved only as a weapon against No. 51—that is, as a weapon against the Constitution itself, which includes the offending checks that "deadlock" government.

So far, then, after the long sleep of No. 10, busy activity around it has given us three main readings of great influence: the economic, the pluralist, and the partisan. The only one of these that was entirely favorable—the pluralist—was framed in the twenties, when certain liberals did not *want* government to work. Bourne shows how close the Lippmann of *Public Opinion* was to Herbert Hoover's first view of government's role. This reading has now become the heritage of right-wing libertarians.

The most important and devastating modern treatment of No. 10 has the fewest political axes to grind. Not that Robert Dahl is himself "value free." Indeed, he agrees with important elements in the other analysts' position. Like Beard, he thinks Madison was carrying the property owners' water for them—but he is more interested in logical than in ideological flaws. Like the pluralists, he believes in a kind of distributed sovereignty and "polyarchy"—but he thinks pluralists can find little real or lasting comfort in The Federalist. Like Schattschneider and Burns, he thinks social diversity more important than governmental divisions; and he does not fear increased partisan activity—so he might be expected to smile on No. 10 and scowl at No. 51.

But Dahl is one of those who has given the study of politics a more rigorous method, and his analysis of No. 10 is a model of cool disassembly. No one has asked so meticulously, not why Madison said this or that, but *what* he said in No. 10. It is true that Dahl first compliments Madison on his "lucid, logical, and orderly exposition" (*Preface*, 5); but then he patiently shows that we are being served up a kind of lucid and logical nonsense.

Madison purports to build a system that, well tended, will be tyranny-proof. Dahl says we cannot apply the relevant test— whether it escapes tyranny in fact—unless we have a clear definition of tyranny. The only essential definition Dahl can extract from Madison is the following: Tyranny is severe deprivation of natural rights (6). But that definition depends upon another, which is not forthcoming. We cannot know what tyranny is till we know what natural rights are—*all* natural rights, since deprivation of *any* can deliver us to tyranny.

Pressed at all, this line of thought would take us into the difficulty of insuring philosophical unanimity on the nature of right. No wonder Madison prefers an operational "definition" of tyranny that is really just a loose statement of one condition for its existence: Tyranny is the concentration of all governmental power in the same hands. But power *can* be benignly concentrated, just as it can be dispersed in evil systems; so Madison's operational definition is just a statement of probability (17).

Grant the probability, what then? Madison says that concentration of power can be prevented by separating the branches and giving them mutual checks. Yet these checks, short of violence, depend on a system of threats based on social approbation —and the same inhibitions can be exercised in other ways (e.g., through elections). So the checks are not sufficient in some cases, and not needed in others. Madison keeps trying to solve mechanically a problem that is not one of sheer mechanics. Adherence to one governmental process will not reveal the nature of right, of the good society—or of "faction" as opposed to those things. The use of an operational definition eludes the problem it cannot solve; but the maneuver is feckless. One talks about the machinery for accomplishing something not to be talked about.

Dahl's analysis is close and incisive—it leaves Madison no way out. The idea that extent of territory will improve politicians and prevent electoral abuse is "extremely dubious and probably false" (16). No. 51 does not help us understand No. 10 since the former's propositions, on scrutiny, "seem to dissolve before our eyes like the Cheshire cat" (20). Indeed, "the Madisonian style of argument provides no satisfactory answers to the fundamental questions it raises" (21). Dahl has to flesh out Madison's definition of tyranny even to show its uselessness, since "Madison's own definition is a trivial one" (24). The mere effort to put Madison's case in syllogistic form (since his own semblance of logical procedure is rhetorical) reveals a line of thought "so deeply ambiguous that it is difficult to know precisely how to do justice to the argument" (12). Dahl can only conclude that Madison's effort at compromising the republican principle to

protect the few has given us a product in which "the explicit
and implicit terms of the compromise do not bear careful analysis" (31). The more thoroughly he examines Madison's argument,
the more convinced (and convincing) he becomes that it is "shot
through with assumptions and arguments that do not stand up
under criticism" (90), that "his nice distinctions were at bottom
arbitrary" (106).

One could hardly ask for a challenge more thorough or basic;
and, naturally, defenders of Madison have tried to rescue him
from Dahl. But no such effort holds the field—for a very good
reason. Grant Dahl his assumptions (reasonably enough, since
they are the current assumptions of his profession), and the critique is unanswerable. That is why Dahl's treatment of No. 10
has had an impact on the scholarly world of our time that almost
equals Beard's in his day—which means that No. 10 has gone
from bad to worse in its time of "resurrection" and prominence.
At least Beard thought Madison was shrewd.

Nor is Dahl's analysis a mere exercise in logic-chopping, as
some have said (or hoped). He raises, in the most pointed way, a
series of questions that go to the heart of Publius' task. Dahl's
claim that Madison is working from an operational nondefinition
of tyranny gives us an important clue to follow. Calling one procedure the cure for tyranny may be a reflection of the Enlightenment's fascination with social machinery externally imposed,
with the magic of technique.

But is the ethos of a system entirely, or even mainly, determined by its governing processes? If not, how can one be sure
that a change in mechanics will change the ethos? And if one
cannot be sure of that, then tyranny can perdure on adoption of
Madison's system, just as freedom can emerge without it. Dahl, a
student of comparative governments in the world today, sees
that free and repressive governments are not neatly sorted out
by Madison's norms. Admittedly, this judgment must be relative,
since no scheme works entirely as Madison prescribed—including
our own. Madison thought the principal check would be *on* the
Congress *by* the Congress, through bicameralism. Not only is
that not the case; the Congress has not, for some time, been the
principal wielder of day-to-day power. The executive branch
offers better candidates for that role: the President, the bureau-

cracy, the military establishment, or some combination of the three. And the executive had no internal check at all in Madison's scheme.

By the test of experimental success, Madison's analysis is made to look irrelevant. The legislative chambers not only fail to perform the task assigned them; insofar as they differ in character at all (and are therefore in a position to check each other), they reverse the functions assigned them. The House of Representatives was to be the "radical" chamber, cooled and made stable by conservative senators. Yet the House has for some time been the most "conservative" part of the whole federal establishment.

Nor, according to Dahl, is this simply an accident. It reflects the framers' basic misunderstandings about the country for which they crafted a government; so that

> the constitution they created has survived not because of their predictions but in spite of them. Madisonian theory provided a brilliant and enduring defense—one is tempted to say rationalization—of the rules they set up. We have seen in what respects the Madisonian approach is deficient. More relevant to our present purposes is the extent to which the members of this historic assemblage did not know what they were doing. . . . The men at the Convention misunderstood the dynamics of their own society. They failed to predict correctly the social balance of power that was to prevail even in their own lifetime. They did not really understand that in an agrarian society lacking feudal institutions and possessing an open and expanding frontier, radical democracy was almost certain to become the dominant and conventional view, almost certain to be conservative about property (141–2).

What claim is left, then, for Madison's praised and demolished essay No. 10? It is wrongheaded in its motive, time-bound in its assumptions, inconsistent in its arguments, inapplicable in Madison's own time, misleading in ours. Insofar as America has avoided the dangers Madison foresaw, it has done so despite him, by the very methods he denounced—by the organization of political parties, the growth of the executive, the development of what he would have called (with alarm) direct democracy. It seems clear, then, that anyone trying to explain America in Madison's terms will end up wide of the mark.

Despite a strange reverence for Madison's No. 10, Paul Bourne rightly notes that the "political scientist's Madison" has for long been a rather bedraggled figure, his argument in disarray, his defenders unable to agree on any remedy for this situation. But the possibility remains that Madison looks rather shabby to us because he has been shabbily treated, by history or historians or both. It is this possibility I mean to explore.

EXPLAINING
AMERICA

PART ONE

THE "HAMILTONIAN" MADISON

ONE

Annapolis

Legislators, therefore, ought not to trust the future government of a state entirely to chance, but ought to provide a system of laws to regulate the administration of public affairs to the latest posterity.

—Hume, 1.3.105

James Madison arrived at the Annapolis Convention on September 4, 1786. He tried, always, to come early for such meetings. He was no orator, to sway men. He depended on homework, knowledge of the terrain, time spent preparing himself and others. Besides, he had to leave himself temporal margins, allow for the sudden onslaught of fatigues so crippling he considered them a form of epileptic seizure. Ever since his dangerous experiment in sleeplessness while a student at Princeton, he had become a strict economist of his energies. This would make the frail man with the sunken eyes and sickly air outlive his healthier contemporaries—and outlive them in more than longevity. It also made him seem cold, rather shriveled, to those not let into the magic circle of his affections. But his friends knew how firmly he must control what Edmund Pendleton called "your crazy [shattered] constitution" (*JM*, 3.172).

He knew how to get things done before things began. But the Annapolis Convention seemed beyond even his organizing skills. He had opposed the scheme, though later historians would attribute it to him. He had missed its predecessor, the Mount Vernon Conference of 1785, when his political foe, Governor Patrick Henry, neglected to inform him of the convening date (*JM*, 8.324)—the best way to disarm a man who depends on preparation as thoroughly as Madison did. This Annapolis Convention held little promise of accomplishment; and anything it did to regularize the confederate states' commerce might work against Madison's own plan—the strengthening of the Continental Congress.

In fact, by one of the ironies of history, James Madison was for all his political life a consistent opponent of revisionary conventions, though his own greatest fame would come from the Constitutional Convention held in Philadelphia one year after the Annapolis Convention. As a member for Virginia at the Confederate Congress of 1783, he had joined Alexander Hamilton in opposing the "partial conventions" of states trying to settle their own commercial and boundary disputes. Madison, with his national outlook, thought all these concerns should be channeled through the Congress itself: "Mr. Madison and Mr. Hamilton disapproved of these partial conventions, not as absolute violations of the Confederacy, but as ultimately leading to them & in the meantime exciting pernicious jealousies [suspicions]" (*JM*, 6.425). When Hamilton substituted a plan for a general convention, to supersede the partial meetings, Madison did not support him. He felt the nation must build on what unity it had; departure from the Congress would just add to centrifugal pressures on the Confederation. After the Philadelphia Convention had come up with the Constitution's draft, he opposed any further conventions before ratification; and he wrote one of his more impassioned Federalist papers (No. 49) to oppose revisionary conventions, called periodically or ad hoc, after ratification.

Attendance at Annapolis did not signify any change in Madison's attitude toward partial conventions. He desponded enough of congressional action to wish, in 1786, for the general convention he had rejected three years earlier. But delegates to Annapolis—even if they all showed up, which was unlikely— could address themselves only to commercial ties among the states. So Madison wrote to Jefferson, in the weeks preceding the Annapolis meeting:

> Many Gentlemen both within & without Congs. wish to make this Meeting subservient to a Plenipotentiary Convention for amending the Confederation. Tho' my wishes are in favor of such an event, yet I despair so much of its accomplishment at the present crisis

that I do not extend my views beyond a Commercial Reform. To speak the truth I almost despair even of this (*JM*, 6.96).

Why, if Madison was so diffident about the Annapolis meeting, was he considered its originator through most of our history —in fact, until 1954, when Julian Boyd sifted the matter with characteristic thoroughness (*TJ*, 9.204–8)? One reason, clearly, was Madison's leading role in the Philadelphia Convention—toward which Annapolis was seen, in retrospect, as pointing the way. It was thought he carried out a grand strategy, dating back almost two years before the Philadelphia Convention; though Edmund Cody Burnett noticed the odd fact that Madison was not "talking up" his plan even on the eve of the Annapolis meeting, when he made a leisurely summer tour of New York and Philadelphia on his way to Annapolis (*JM*, 9.119).

But the main cause of confusion was historians' early treatment of the Annapolis meeting as a "fallback" annex to Madison's motion, in the Virginia House of Delegates, for a strengthened Confederate Congress. Though John Tyler introduced the Annapolis plan, it became the custom for historians to treat Tyler (father of the future President) as Madison's cat's-paw in this. Boyd, however, shows that Tyler had voted against Madison's original plan; and Madison said that friends of his plan chose to do nothing rather than pass it in the weakened form. It was at this point that Tyler, instead of "doing nothing" with the friends of the plan, brought forward his own scheme. Tyler's relatives always claimed he was the plan's true author, and Boyd has vindicated them. (Tyler—a charming fellow who managed to remain the friend of Patrick Henry and Thomas Jefferson, which would seem an impossible feat—opposed the Constitution that later grew out of his own motion for a partial conference.)

Madison's principle of arriving early had its supreme demonstration in Annapolis, where he took up lodgings a full week before the sessions began, though he expected little from the effort. In a larger sense, his whole summer tour had been a preparation for the conference—it was three years since he had sat in the Confederate Congress, and this man whose health forbade hard traveling needed to test the winds and sound men's minds. He stopped off in Princeton to confer with his old teacher, the political catalyst John Witherspoon.

What he heard and saw on this trip was bound to discourage him. His own earlier strictures against partial conferences were being used, not only against the meeting itself, but against Madison's state and region. Rufus King was writing, in June:

> It is doubtful what the real sentiments of Virginia are on the question of commercial powers. This is certain, that the proposition for the Annapolis convention, which originated in the Assembly of Virginia, did not come from the persons favorable to a commercial system common to all the States, but from those, who in opposition to such a general system have advocated the particular regulations of individual States. [If King had more than regional suspicion to go on here, he was closer to the role of Tyler than better-informed historians would for a long time be.] The merchants through all the States are of one mind, and in favor of a national system. The planters in the Southern States are divided in their opinions and it is to be feared that the majority is against the only plan, which can insure the prosperity and honor of the confederacy (Burnett, *Letters*, 8.389–90).

These suspicions in the North were answered from the South. During this same period Madison received, from the Congress in New York, James Monroe's letters tracing a conspiracy to extrude the South from the Confederation:

> It is manifest here that Jay & his party in Congress are determin'd to pursue this business [negotiations with Spain for rights to the Mississippi] as far as possible, either as the means of throwing the western people & territory without the Govt. of the U.S. and keeping the weight of population & govt. here [in New York], or of dismembering the govt. itself, for the purpose of separate confederacy (*JM*, 9.104–5).

When Shays's Rebellion occurred, right after the Annapolis gathering, Henry Lee saw that, too, as part of a Northern conspiracy: "The insurgents are taking all the necessary arrangements to prepare for the last appeal. Their ostensible object is the revision of the constitution but they certainly mean the abolition of debts public & private, a division of property & a new government founded on principles of fraud & inequity, or re-connexion with G.F." (*JM*, 9.144). Madison accepted this interpretation of the rebellion and passed it on to his father: "They profess to aim only at a reform of their Constitution and of certain abuses in the public administration, but an abolition of debts public & private, and a new division of property are strongly suspected to be in contemplation" (ibid., 154).

All through this period, the Confederation was falling apart; the Annapolis meeting was not the kind of effort that could knit things together again; it would become another symptom of decline. Madison knew, by the time he reached Annapolis, that most states would not be sending delegates. The sessions were to be held in the senate room of the State House—at that time a place more honored than the Philadelphia chamber where the Declaration of Independence had been signed. Washington, in a gesture that carried his fame around the world as Cincinnatus, had surrendered his army in that room.

Only eleven others joined Madison in Annapolis—they could meet in a room at George Mann's Inn (the place where Washington had been entertained the night before his resignation). The meeting, shadowy enough to begin with, was a kind of mock half attempt at half measures. Only three states were officially represented. Yet there were men of real stature in the group. John Dickinson came from Delaware. He had drafted most documents of the preindependence Congresses; and Madison had watched him receive an honorary degree at the end of his first year at Princeton. From New Jersey came William Churchill Houston, Madison's former tutor at Nassau Hall. John Witherspoon, on his arrival in America, had made Houston, a recent graduate, his curator of philosophical apparatus—which meant that the precious orrery of Rittenhouse was his to protect (*Inventing*, 100–2). Neither Witherspoon nor Houston could know they were charged with the keeping of an even greater national treasure in James Madison.

The meeting with Houston at Annapolis was a forecast of the Princeton gathering Madison would find, to his pleasure, at the Constitutional Convention. Nine Princeton graduates would be present in Philadelphia (as opposed to three from Harvard and four from Yale). Houston, appointed to the Philadelphia meeting in 1787, would be unable to attend because of poor health; but he supported the draft that emerged from it, which indicates that his sympathies were with Madison at the Annapolis gathering of 1786.

What could this small dinner table full of men do at Annapolis? Obviously not what they were commissioned to do—iron out commercial conflicts among the states. The very model for this meeting—the conference of Virginia and Maryland representatives held the year before at General Washington's home—worked against any Annapolis mandate. Maryland, one party to the Mount Vernon meeting, refused to send delegates to Annapolis. Madison recognized in that state's objections his own fear of partial conferences. He wrote to Jefferson: "Maryd. or rather her Senate negatived an appointment because they suppose the measure might interfere with the plans or prerogatives of Congs." (*JM*, 9.96 and 9.50).

Even the Mount Vernon conference had lacked a quorum of Virginia delegates (after Henry failed to inform Madison and Randolph of the meeting's site and date). That meeting, too, could not fill the formal room at Gadsby's Tavern in Alexandria; it was retired to General Washington's home. Madison, as a member of the committee in the House of Delegates for considering plans that emanated from Mount Vernon, joined others in ignoring the lack of a three-man quorum on Virginia's part (Brant, 2.386). He would not, therefore, worry that three signers of anything that might emerge from Annapolis would be speaking unofficially for their states (Tench Coxe for Pennsylvania, Alexander Hamilton and Egbert Benson for New York). Madison would later expand the mandate of the Philadelphia Convention in Federalist No. 40. (One of the reasons he feared conventions was his awareness that they can take on a life of their own and go beyond what was originally intended.)

But how could the maimed affair at Annapolis be inflated beyond comic dimensions? Even the local paper only noticed the delegates' "arrival" on the day they adjourned (September 14). As the first arrivals waited for others to trickle in, there was some discussion of giving up any effort to convene. The affair could be made to look ridiculous. But another early arrival, Abraham Clark from New Jersey, brought with him a state commission that went beyond the commercial disputes that others were addressing. Clark and Madison had worked together in committee at the 1783 Congress; their presession conversations in Annapolis must have touched on the New Jersey instruction. Since the Convention was itself so powerless, that document of a state legislature came as close as anything to an official call for more serious measures. The Convention, by a maneuver attributed to Madison and Hamilton, used Clark's credentials as its main piece of business, passing on New Jersey's call in the formal address to Congress. The Annapolis address, drafted by Hamilton, quotes the text carried by Clark, urging delegates "to consider how far a uniform system in their commercial regulations and *other important matters,* might be necessary to the common interest and permanent harmony of the several States . . . effectually to provide for the exigencies of the Union" (*AH,* 3.687; italics in original). Then the proposal is advanced under New Jersey's colors:

> In this persuasion your Commissioners submit an opinion, that the idea of extending the powers of their Deputies, to other objects, than those of Commerce, which has been adopted by the State of New Jersey, was an improvement on the original plan, and will deserve to be incorporated into that of a future Convention . . . (688).

In closing, Hamilton borrowed from the excerpt of New Jersey's instruction he had quoted, asking for a plenary convention "to devise such further provisions as shall appear to them necessary to render the constitution of the Federal Government adequate to the exigencies of the Union" (689).

Madison, who had expected little from the meeting, accomplished a great deal *because* it could be diverted from its original object. If the conference had been able to propose specific plans for commercial regularization, any call it might have issued for further convenings would have been hostage to debate on those commercial proposals; indeed, the more adequate the measures recommended, the more ominous they would have seemed to those opposing further grants of power to Congress. In that way, a "successful" Annapolis Convention would just have created resistance to any plan for revision of the Articles.

There is no detailed account of the semiformal proceedings in Annapolis; but Madison's early position on the ground, his opportunity to talk with each arriving delegate, and his influence with Edmund Randolph, the vain and showy leader of his own delegation, gave him the kind of leverage he exercised in most committee situations. John Dickinson was elected chairman of the meeting. The young Tench Coxe, a financial theorist of Hamilton's school and scope, would support any plan for powers to stabilize the Confederation's economy. Egbert Benson, Hamilton's colleague from New York, kept the brief minutes.

Two of the twelve delegates had been born off the American continent—Saint George Tucker (now a Virginia delegate) in Bermuda, and Alexander Hamilton on Nevis in the British West Indies. By coincidence, they were both heroes of the siege at Yorktown, where Tucker was wounded. Tucker would continue the proud Virginia tradition of legal scholarship, succeeding George Wythe in the oldest academic chair of law in America and succeeding Edmund Pendleton as chief justice on the state's supreme bench.

Hamilton was another of Madison's acquaintances from the Confederate Congress, where, as members of the same committee, they worked for stronger funding measures in 1782 and 1783 (*AH*, 3.199–200, 340–4) and were united in defense of the French alliance (ibid., 294–6). Temperament would finally tell when they clashed in the first Washington Administration; but their relations to this point were cordial, and based on mutual respect. When Hamilton was criticized for acting to move Congress in panic from Philadelphia to Princeton, he turned naturally to Madison for defense (*JM*, 7.213–15), which Madison was happy to supply (ibid., 382–3).

Hamilton was slight like Madison, but vibrant where the other swayed or seemed ready to collapse. Gilbert Stuart shows the instinctive lean of Madison on the nearest prop in his Annapolis portrait, where the gray eyes are shaded under the prominent arc of his brow. There was an elfin look to Madison. Balding from youth, he still looked boyish in old age—a gnome prematurely (and uncomfortably) wise, weighting his sentences as if to give ballast to his toy body. Hamilton's eyes were exposed—they seemed almost to meet and collude at the point where his nose pinched abruptly back into his brow. His intelligence seemed on the surface, coming at you, aiming narrowly along the pointed nose at taller men whose measure he soon took. Trumbull captured Hamilton's robin-breasted perch, as if poised for flight, in the National Gallery portrait. Everything about him was active and outgoing. Not even an official representative at Annapolis, nor on the drafting committee, he nonetheless managed to write the call for a national convention that became the final meaning of the Annapolis Convention.

Madison knew how touchy Edmund Randolph, Virginia's attorney general and the official leader of his own delegation, could be. Randolph, handsome and well meaning, was a southern John Hancock, without great mental ballast. He was typically hesitant about the call for a convention. When he finally went to Philadelphia, he would offer the Virginia Plan for a Constitution, then oppose the draft that emerged; blow hot and cold in Virginia; explain himself in ways that just confused things further; and end up pleading *for* ratification. One gets a sense of his mind at work in the explanation he offered for this course of conduct:

> Should the people of America surrender these powers, they can be paramount to the constitutions and ordinary acts of legislation, only by being delegated by them. I do not pretend to affirm, but venture to believe, that if the confederation had been solemnly questioned in opposition to our constitution, or even to one of our laws, posterior to it, it must have given away. For never did it obtain a higher ratification, then a resolution of assembly in the daily form (Letter to the House of Delegates, October 16, 1787).

Ask not for context. It makes no better sense there. Though Randolph was trying to explain his *opposition* to the Constitution, Madison wrote, in his January letter to Washington: "It is generally understood here that the arguments contained in it in favor of the Constitution are much stronger than the objections which prevent his assent."

Clarity and vigor were things Randolph feared; and Hamilton radiated both. Besides, Randolph was a stickler for office—he would insist, as governor, on proposing Madison's Virginia Plan in Philadelphia. Hamilton had no official standing in Annapolis, where his state did not even produce a quorum of delegates. The tradition recorded by John T. Morse, Hamilton's biographer, fits the character of all three men—Randolph shied at the plain speaking of Hamilton's first draft in Annapolis; but Hamilton briskly defended it; till Madison took him aside and said, "You had better yield to this man, for otherwise all Virginia will be against you" (Brant, 2.386). Hamilton softened his language, somewhat, and all twelve "commissioners" signed it. Madison returned to Philadelphia in the company of Hamilton and Tench Coxe (Mitchell, 1.367). An historic alliance was taking shape.

TWO

Nassau Hall

The question is not concerning any fine imaginary republic, of which a man may form a plan in his closet.
—Hume, 1.7.126

Madison shared Hume's low regard for the mere closet theorist.
He gladly admitted in The Federalist that the 1787 Constitution
showed "deviations from that artificial structure and regular
symmetry, which an abstract view of the subject might lead an
ingenious theorist to bestow on a Constitution planned in his
closet or in his imagination" (37.238). Later he plays down the
difficulty of drafting certain kinds of tax law by saying: "A skillful individual in his closet, with all the local codes before him,
might compile a law on some subject of taxation for the whole
union, without any aid from oral information . . ." (56.380).

Yet Madison left his mark on America largely by his devotion
to closet study of theoretical works. He was not a soldier-scholar
like Hamilton, an empirical scientist like Benjamin Franklin
(and, to some extent, Thomas Jefferson); not a parliamentarian
like Samuel Adams, an orator like Patrick Henry, a magnetic
leader like George Washington. He made his way, at point after
point, because he knew more than others about the issues being
debated in the Congress, in the Virginia legislature, in the convention, in the House of Representatives. Douglass Adair calls
Madison's course of self-education on the range of confederacies,
completed before the Philadelphia Convention, "probably the
most fruitful piece of scholarly research ever carried out by an
American" (*Fame*, 134).

Madison was a bookish fellow who recalled with pleasure his
discovery (at age twelve) of Addison's smooth and moralizing
essays. That occurred shortly after Madison went to school with

Donald Robertson, who boarded his scholars at the plantation of
a Presbyterian divine, Robert Innes—for Madison, a heady experience, gladly recalled; he stayed with Robertson for five years
(from age eleven to sixteen). The tutor was a product of the
Scottish Enlightenment at its peak. Educated at Aberdeen and
Edinburgh, he came to America in 1752—just six years before
Jefferson's teacher, William Small, set sail from Aberdeen (*Inventing*, 177–8). The excellence of Robertson's academy made
local families of the established church patronize this Presbyterian with a preacher's license—especially the Taylor family, at
whose plantation Robertson lived during his first years in America. By the time Madison attended the school, John Taylor of
Caroline was there, whose views on federal union would later
compete with Madison's own; and John Tyler had just left the
man who later opposed Madison on the desirability of an Annapolis Convention (thus advancing his old classmate, unwit-
tingly, to the stage of his real fame at Philadelphia).

Madison received from Robertson as good a fundamental
schooling in languages, logic, and mathematics as was to be had
in Virginia—much better, for instance, than Jefferson had received at the same stage from William Douglas of Glencairn.
When Madison returned to his father's estate, Montpelier, after
his five years with Robertson, Madison père hired a tutor for his
own children—Thomas Martin, a zealous young graduate of
Princeton. Martin was beginning his ecclesiastical career—as a
more famous Princeton graduate, Philip Fithian, later would at
Nomini Hall—as a resident teacher of young children. Madison
was the classroom exception, a boy old enough to share Martin's
own enthusiasms and memories of study at Nassau Hall.

When it came time for college, Madison's father rejected the
two most obvious courses—education in England, which the
James River oligarchy prized, or at the colony's own William and
Mary, a school of no distinction now that William Small was
gone. Instead, Madison would go to Martin's alma mater. This
was a decision made easier for the elder Madison by a visit from
Martin's brother, Alexander, who had graduated from the Col-
lege of New Jersey in 1756. Alexander Martin, a prominent
North Carolina lawyer, had opposed the Regulator uprisings as
King's Attorney of Rowan County. He, too, recommended Nas-

sau Hall to the young James Madison (whom he would oppose at the Philadelphia Convention seventeen years later, as one of the pre-Witherspoon Princetonians who fought the Constitution).

Madison rode up to Princeton with the Martin brothers in 1769. He was entering a college that was in the process of remaking—from a good (and highly religious) school to an even better (and highly political) school. Not that Princetonians had been apolitical in the Stamp Act days of the middle sixties. Opposition to the king and the established church came easily to the "New Side" Presbyterians of the Great Awakening's aftermath. As Carl Bridenbaugh teaches us, many were involved in the opposition to attempts at bringing an Anglican bishop to America.

Yet the very zeal of the college and its advocates had split the Presbyterian community. The search for a successor to Dr. Samuel Finley, the college's fifth president who died in 1766, developed into a struggle between the Old Side and the New Side Presbyterians, each scheming to advance its own man (V. L. Collins, *President Witherspoon*, 1.75 ff.). This scheming went forward even after Witherspoon had been called from Scotland, since Witherspoon at first declined. But a Princeton man visiting in Scotland—Benjamin Rush, who would give Thomas Paine the title for his pamphlet, *Common Sense*—persuaded this defender of Thomas Reid's commonsense philosophy to come to America.

Witherspoon, though first put forward by the New Side, was supposed to be a compromise candidate. It was an odd role for a man more at home with controversy than with compromise. Old Siders could take comfort in his fight for King against Pretender in Scotland's uprising of '46, when he was imprisoned for his pains. New Siders would approve his leadership of the puritanical "Populars" cause in Scotland, which opposed the Moderates who made common cause with godless folk like David Hume and lax institutions like the theater (Mossner, *Hume*, 336–7, 356, 368). Witherspoon was best known for satirizing the worldly and aesthetic preoccupations of many Enlightenment preachers. In *The Moderator* (1757) he made fun of the three Humes—Henry Home (Lord Kames), the jurist and aesthete whose writings had tremendous impact on the young Jefferson; David Hume, the

scoffer at miracles; and John Hume, their cousin, the minister
who dared to write plays for the secular stage:

> On a little name, which has produced three great
> heroes to support the declining glory of Britain:
> An impious J[udge], a wicked sceptic sage,
> A stage-playing priest; O glorious NAME and Age!

Despite Witherspoon's misgivings over the "worldly" aspect of
the Scottish Enlightenment, his strictures were blunted by time.
In America he softened his early distrust of Hutcheson's aesthetic approach to morality (Collins, 1.28). No author is mentioned so often in Witherspoon's *Lectures on Moral Philosophy*,
published in 1800 (3, 4, 5, 11, 16, 17, 24, 25, 26, 68, 82, 90, 129).
Ironically, after his satirical assaults on Lord Kames, his own
ethic most resembled Kames's—accepting the moral sense as a
separate faculty (as Hutcheson argued), but insisting that reason
and duty need more emphasis than Hutcheson gave them (*Inventing*, 203–5). Witherspoon's position is stated briefly in the
following sentence: "Though there is no occasion to join Mr.
Hutchinson [sic] or any other, in their opposition to such as
make reason the principle of virtuous conduct, yet I think it must
be admitted, that a sense of moral good and evil, is as really a
principle of our nature, as either the gross external or reflex
senses, and as truly distinct from both as they are from each
other" (*Lectures*, 17). Witherspoon concentrated his distrust of
aestheticism on Shaftesbury (4, 7, 11, 19, 24, 68), and was free to
elevate the importance of Hutchesonian benevolence (52, 56)
and unalienable rights (56; cf. *Inventing*, 231–7). In epis-
temology, he remained the bitter opponent of Hume and the
champion of Thomas Reid's "commonsensical" self-evident truths
(*Lectures*, 39; cf. *Inventing*, 182–91).

Madison was plunged into the controversies of the Scottish
Enlightenment the minute he entered Nassau Hall. These
thinkers were being studied elsewhere on the American continent, but nowhere more intensely than at Princeton: Douglass
Adair—who discovered Madison's debt to Hume in his doctoral
dissertation of 1943—was increasingly impressed by the Scottish
contribution to America's intellectual formation:

At Princeton, at William and Mary, at Pennsylvania, at Yale, at

King's, and at Harvard, the young men who rode off to war in 1776 had been trained in the texts of Scottish social science . . . Princeton, for example, where nine members of the Constitutional Convention of 1787 graduated, was a provincial carbon copy, under President Witherspoon, of Edinburgh . . . The great names in this sudden flowering of the Scotch intellect are David Hume, Francis Hutcheson, Adam Smith, Thomas Reid, Lord Kames, and Adam Ferguson. Their books formed the core of the moral philosophy course at Princeton, and it was in these works treating of history, ethics, politics, economics, psychology, and jurisprudence, always from the modern and enlightened point of view, that Madison received his "very early and strong impressions in favor of Liberty both Civil & Religious" (*Fame*, 95, 96, 128).

Adrienne Koch gives us a similar picture of the atmosphere at Princeton: "Witherspoon had studied with David Hume, Adam Smith, and Thomas Reid. The Scottish Enlightenment in moral philosophy and social scientific areas, therefore, became a philosophic must for the students at old Nassau Hall" (*Madison's Advice*, 9).

By the middle of the eighteenth century, the Scottish theory of moral sense as a separate faculty was, as Perry Miller called it, "the most formidable tendency in contemporaneous moral speculation" (*Errand into the Wilderness*, 238). It touched even those Americans who did not have Scottish mentors. Hutcheson's works, for instance, had a profound influence on America's most original moral thinker, Jonathan Edwards: "When Edwards turned to Hutcheson, he found a logic that followed his own, almost to the end" (ibid., 243). Hutcheson's optimism about man's tendency toward benevolence jarred slightly with the Edwards view of fallen man—just as it did with Witherspoon's doubts about the Moderates. But in his dissertation on the *Nature of True Virtue* Edwards agreed with Hutcheson that virtue "is the beauty of the qualities and exercises of the heart," so that "true virtue most essentially consists in benevolence to being in general." Clyde Holbrook rightly concludes that Edwards "was not willing to travel the whole road with Hutcheson, but it is clear, both here [in *Original Sin*] and in the *True Virtue*, that he had drawn upon him and coveted his support wherever appropriate to his own views" (Yale, *Works of Edwards*, vol. 3, 75). That describes, as well, the attitude of Dr. Witherspoon at Princeton.

Witherspoon was probably the most influential teacher in the entire history of American education. His pupils included a president of the United States and a vice-president, twenty-one United States senators and twenty-nine members of the House, twelve state governors, fifty-six state legislators, and thirty-three judges (of whom three sat on the Supreme Court). His students were everywhere in the Revolutionary Army—in the ranks and in command (eleven captains, six majors, four colonels, ten lieutenant colonels). An equally prestigious list could be drawn up of college founders and teachers, Presbyterian ministers and successful authors, trained by him (Collins, 2.222–30).

Witherspoon was a born, if improbable, leader—rational yet skittish, austere and egotistical at the same time, stately and eccentric. His captivity while fighting against the Pretender had left him with a nervous disorder that made him jump about, and twitch alarmingly, like Dr. Johnson. He tended to faint when excited—falling right out of his pulpit once (ibid., 2.231). But his force of character kept eighteenth-century Tom Joneses in line, and his students affected his own Scottish accent, answering "Brawly, brawly, Dr. Wotherspoon" when he asked them how they were (2.219, 232). Hume said that Presbyterians were all Whigs, and this was so superlatively true of Witherspoon that a story was told of him as far away as North Carolina: When a man seeking shelter was told "I allow no man to sleep under my roof but a whig," the traveler said, "Then let me rest here in peace, for I graduated under Witherspoon" (2.228).

The scholarly life's social aspects, its peculiar male giddiness and common-room ribaldry, were an important part of Madison's three years at Princeton. Shy and reclusive (despite Dolly's late reform of his celibate habits), he forged intense friendships at Princeton that lasted through his life. When he arrived at the college, the Well-Meaning Club, founded by a "town boy" in 1765, had just been disbanded; but it would rise again in Madison's first year with that town boy's favorite term for its new title—the Cliosophic Society. Madison no doubt came to know William Paterson, the Princeton attorney who had delivered his class address in 1763 as a "cliosophic" oration. Paterson

was a kind of campus legend (see Julian Boyd's sketch of him in
Eighteen from Princeton, 3). At Philadelphia Madison would engage him in intellectual battle when Paterson countered the Virginia Plan with his own New Jersey Plan. There are times when
the Constitutional Convention must have looked like a reunion
of Princetonians.

Madison did not belong to "Clio"—as did Aaron Burr, whose
years at Princeton overlapped his own—but to the rival American
Whig Society, formed (in the year of his arrival) to revive the
defunct Plain Dealing Club. Madison entered the war of rhym-
ing insults between the clubs; less from merit, it seems, than
from friendship with the two class poets—Philip Freneau, whose
scurrilous journalism in support of Madison's Republicans later
earned George Washington's reference to "that rascal Freneau";
and Hugh Henry Brackinridge, who would still be using hudri-
brastic verse as a weapon against the Cincinnati when Madison
had become a sedate Confederate congressman. These two
friends were men of action as well as words—Brackinridge would
go west to have a bookman's adventure on the frontier; Freneau
became a Revolutionary privateer on runs to the West Indies, and
spent a period of hideous confinement in a British prison ship.
The young Madison had his moment of literary swagger with
these friends, and retained a warm feeling for them long after
political passions had made both of them a wealth of enemies.

As one might expect at the solemn Dr. Witherspoon's school,
the Whig and Clio societies were not devoted entirely to merry
pranks. Philip Fithian, who followed Madison at Princeton,
wrote a famous list of student antics that ranged from "Darting
Sun-Beams upon the Town-People" to "ogling women with the
Telescope" (part of William Houston's "apparatus" put to unin-
tended use). But Fithian included in his list, as well, the "giving
each other names and characters." The Whigs gave secret names
(usually taken from classical heroes) to their members, and expected them to live up to these titles. Our understanding of later
appeals to virtue among one's peers is deepened if we remember that some Revolutionary heroes had assumed the mantle
of Brutus or Cato in their college days. James McLachlan points
out that no one thought it odd or stilted for Joseph Warren to
put on a toga before mounting the pulpit in Old South Church to

give the Massacre Day oration in 1775. American engravings of
the elder Pitt in a toga, paintings of Washington as Cincinnatus,
busts of Franklin as a Roman senator—all these are expressions
of the classical zeal for republican virtue that we shall find at the
very heart of The Federalist.

When Madison was asked, in the Confederate Congress, to
draw up the list for a congressional library, it is not surprising
that the Scottish Enlightenment was heavily represented on that
list. In the very first and most inclusive category, the Law of Nature, he includes the canonical treatises of his time—Wolff, Grotius, Pufendorf. That was to be expected. But he also includes
two Scottish works, Hutcheson's *System of Moral Philosophy* and
Adam Ferguson's *Institute of Moral Philosophy,* along with the
book on natural-law principles by Hutcheson's Swiss disciple,
Burlamaqui (*JM,* 6.66–7). Locke is not included here but—where
one expects him, as part of the "trinity" of commonwealthmen
(Sidney, Harrington, Locke)—in the more limited category of
Politics (ibid., 85; cf. *Inventing,* 171). Here Ferguson appears
again, for his *History of Civil Society* (86). Other Scots in this
category include Hume, for the political essays (87)—his history
came earlier in the list (80), along with his friend Robertson's
history of Scotland (82); Adam Smith's *Wealth of Nations* (86);
and John Millar's *Ranks in Society* (86). Lord Kames is absent,
as he would be from the mature Jefferson's libraries (*Inventing,*
201). Other favorites of Jefferson appear on the list—Rapin de
Thoyras's *History of England* (80) and William Petty's *Political
Arithmetic* (87).

Naturally, Dr. Witherspoon's resentment of David Hume
just whetted his students' interest in him. When Madison's friend,
William Bradford, decided to study English history, he did not
turn to Rapin de Thoyras, the Whig champion, or Smollett, the
other Scot who had written that story, but to Hume (*JM,* 1.103).
Bradford already knew his Hume well enough to quote from
memory (therefore inaccurately) the *Inquiry Concerning Human Understanding* (ibid., 73). He did not have to give a source
for his citation when writing to his friend from Princeton. (The
passage quoted is the one Adair considered the basic premise of
Scottish sociology—*Fame,* 111.)

When Madison undertook his typically thorough preparation

for service in the Confederate Congress, he knew the financing of the Revolution would take up much of his time. He studied the economic works of Hume, and wrote his first important essay, "Money," to argue with one proposition from the Scot's "On the Balance of Trade" (*JM*, 1.303). But the principal impact of Hume is traced by Adair in The Federalist essays. He finds clear evidence of borrowing from five different essays—"Idea of a Perfect Commonwealth," "Of Parties in General," "Of the First Principles of Government," "Of the Independence of Parliament," and "Parties of Great Britain" (*Fame*, 98–104). Geoffrey Marshall discovered, independently of Adair, the tie between No. 10 and the "Perfect Commonwealth" essay (*Philosophical Quarterly*, 4.14, 1954, 225–6).

Even turns of phrase reflect Madison's close reading of his model—"aliment" in No. 10, taken from Hume's own discussion of faction (*Fame*, 103–4); or the way a society is "broken" as a way of baffling faction (ibid., 102). One passage in No. 10 is especially close to a Humean original: When Madison distinguishes the faction arising from attachment to leaders from one based on attachment to persons (10.59), the division seems meaningless until one sees how slavishly Madison has copied Hume, who made a special category for the Scottish Jacobites' attachment to persons. Analyzing the Madison and Hume passages, Adair concludes that No. 10 was phrased rather misleadingly at this point "because Hume's book was open on the table beside him" (*Fame*, 105; cf. diss. 266).

Following Adair's lead, I hope to show that there are many other passages of Hume absorbed into Madison's analysis. And even this early we might note a more general influence of Hume's essays on the style, organization, even the length of the Federalist papers. Granted, Addison was the source of most essay style in the eighteenth century, and had been an early favorite of Madison. Nonetheless, Hume added a special quality to the polemic literature of his day. Addison had written from a psychological viewpoint—"typing" Whig and Tory, gently teasing or encouraging his types. By the time Hume wrote, a harsher air of polemic had entered the literature. Junius and Bolingbroke lashed and scolded. Hume's essays were written to counter Bolingbroke's *Craftsman* papers (*Essays*, Green-Grose intro., 41,

44–5). Hume tells us what qualities he considered a foil for his own contributions:

> Lord BOLINGBROKE's productions, with all their defects in argument, method and precision, contain a force and energy which our orators scarcely ever aim at; though it is evident, that such an elevated stile has much better grace in a speaker than in a writer, and is assured of more prompt and more astonishing success (1.13.173).

Hume came to make up for Bolingbroke's defects in "argument, method and precision." Though he meant, here and in his history, to shed "the plaguey prejudices of Whiggism" (Green-Grose, 73), his essays were distinguished by their impartial, scientific, "disinterested" air. His condemnation of faction and parties has the appearance, at least, of being evenhanded, and he makes a flourish of methodical procedure: "I would only persuade men not to contend, as if they were fighting *pro aris & focis* [Bolingbroke's phrase], and change a good constitution into a bad one, by the violence of their factions" (1.3.109).

Publius, as author of The Federalist, comes before us as an impartial judge, without any special role or stake in the transactions at Philadelphia. In this posture, Madison (of all people) pretends to have no "inside knowledge" of what went on in the Philadelphia Convention (37.233, 237; 43.296), or of Virginia's history (52.358), or of Southern attitudes on slavery (54.367). So judicious is the approach that, as Martin Diamond notes of No. 39, Madison seems to add weights now to one arm of a balance, now to the other, fidgeting it toward perfect equilibrium. This almost finicky air of looking now to one side, now to the other, is Hume's in essays like "Whether the British Government Inclines More to Absolute Monarchy, or to a Republic" (1.7) or "Of the Protestant Succession" (2.15).

Another mark of this scientific approach is what might be called the bifurcative method: There is a choice—one of two—and then that one is split into two and a further choice made, and so on. The best example of that in The Federalist is No. 10:

> There are two methods of curing the mischiefs of faction: the one by removing its causes; the other, by controlling its effects.

> There are again two methods of removing the causes . . .
> (10.58).

When that branch proves a dead end, Madison returns to the other (controlling its effects) and considers two cases: minority faction, and majority. How to control a factious majority?

> By what means is this object obtainable? Evidently by one of two only (10.61).

Hume uses this method—and with him, too, it has a certain useless flourish of thoroughness. (Madison's passage on removing the causes of faction is not really anything that would be contested; he just wants to make his procedure seem almost mechanically fair).

> Opinion is of two kinds, to wit, opinion of INTEREST and opinion of RIGHT . . .
> Right is of two kinds, right to POWER and right to PROPERTY . . . (1.4.111; cf. 1.3.100–4).

Like Hume's essays, the Federalist papers are shorter than *Craftsman* essays, more impersonal and scientific than *Spectators* —fond of Latinate distinctions, methodically exhaustive, coolly describing their own "candor" (1.4, 10.57, 54.367, 61.412).

Hume's essays were praised and blamed for their scientific claims—and so were those of Madison. A correspondent to the *New-York Journal* mocked those claims with the suggestion that Publius "next have resort to *conic sections*, by which he will be enabled with greater facility, to discover the *many windings* of his favorite system" (January 7, 1788). The man whose tutor tended Rittenhouse's scientific machinery could not take that entirely as an insult. Madison spoke French reluctantly, all his life, since he pronounced it with a Scottish burr picked up from Robertson and Witherspoon. But in other ways, which he could not (and would not have wanted to) hide, his very thinking had a Scottish accent from the start.

THREE

Opinion

> It may farther be said, that, though men be much gov-
> erned by interest; yet even interest itself, and all
> human affairs, are entirely governed by *opinion*.
> —Hume, 1.7.125

If some essays by Madison remain difficult to interpret, No. 49 is
clear, and clearly a scandal. Dahl, referring to its arguments,
does not even bother to refute things so "patently invalid or
highly inconclusive" (*Preface*, 14). It is not surprising that, for a
long time, the paper was attributed to Hamilton. Some admirers
of Madison would still like to fob it off on his partner in the enterprise. Not only does Madison pick an argument, here, with
Jefferson; he seems to depart from all the Jeffersonian ideals of
democracy.

The state of the argument at No. 49 is this: Madison is on his
way to proving (in No. 51) that the only way to keep the three
main departments of government separate is to divide the most
powerful branch internally. But first he argues (in No. 48) that
mere separation of the legislature from the other departments
is not sufficient, in a republic, to keep it in check. Then he
dismisses the idea of a special commission—whether called ad
hoc, as Jefferson proposed (No. 49), or periodically, as the Pennsylvania constitution provided (No. 50)—to police the boundaries of separation.

Madison respectfully differs from Jefferson, giving five arguments against resort to such a body of constitutional review.

1. In Jefferson's plan, two branches could prevent the commission's formation, even if great offenses occurred.
2. The option of calling the commission would encourage peo-

ple to be too critical of their government because (this is the showstopper) people on the lookout for defects in government will lose their *awe of government*.

3. The opportune moment for constitution-making, during and just after the Revolution, has passed.

4. The same popularity that gives the legislature an edge in the government would give it the edge in any commission.

5. Indeed, membership on the commission would probably overlap with that of the most dangerous branch, so the putative "crooks" in any constitutional violation would also be the cops.

6. Another showstopper: The very turmoil that might justify calling the commission would prevent its insulation from popular unrest. An aroused populace should not be heeded, only a calm one: "It is the reason of the public alone that ought to control and regulate the government. The passions ought to be controled and regulated by the government" (49.343).

The offending second argument should be looked at in its entirety:

In the next place, it may be considered as an objection inherent in the principle, that as every appeal to the people would carry an implication of some defect in the government, frequent appeals would in great measure deprive the government of that veneration, which time bestows on everything, and without which perhaps the wisest and freest governments would not possess the requisite stability. If it be true that all governments rest on opinion, it is no less true that the strength of opinion in each individual, and its practical influence on his conduct, depend much on the number which he supposes to have entertained the same opinion. The reason of man, like man himself is timid and cautious, when left alone; and acquires firmness and confidence, in proportion to the number with which it is associated. When the examples which fortify opinion, are *antient* as well as *numerous*, they are known to have a double effect. In a nation of philosophers, this consideration ought to be disregarded. A reverence for the laws, would be sufficiently inculcated by the voice of enlightened reason. But a nation of philosophers is as little to be expected as the philosophical race of kings wished for by Plato. And in every other nation, the most rational government will not find it a superfluous advantage, to have the prejudices of the community on its side (49.340).

Most of us, I venture, grew up with the generalization that Madison and the framers distrusted governmental power. Yet here he inculcates an almost abject trust in it. The people must be encouraged to think their government is "antient" and deserving of "reverence." Beard accused the authors of The Federalist of using "the sanctity and mystery of the law as a foil to democratic attacks" (*Economic Interpretation*, 161), and this passage seems to vindicate his charge.

It might be argued that America's governments were not ancient when Madison wrote—indeed, the federal government was not even in place. But that just gives more urgency to the task, once government is in place, of getting it an *undisturbed* antiquity as soon as possible. The less ancient it is in itself, the more one must leave it alone, let it *acquire* a stable past. If this passage were shown to anyone only vaguely acquainted with eighteenth-century literature, it is safe to bet it would be attributed to Edmund Burke. Who else argued so eloquently for the foundation of government on "the prejudices of the community," since "the voice of enlightened reason" is an insufficient support?

The third argument against Jefferson is hardly less disturbing to modern democrats. Madison says the state constitutions were formed during the patriotic time of union against an external foe, a time of "enthusiastic confidence of the people in their patriotic leaders," when internal discord was forsworn for the duration. That is a description some historians would argue with; but what concerns us here is Madison's *use* of his description. Encouraging discussion of a constitution, once adopted, runs "the danger of disturbing the public tranquility by interesting too strongly the public passions" (49.340). "Interesting" here means "engaging" (see Glossary). Madison seems to believe that the people should not be listened to when they care deeply. Does that mean they *can* speak only when they would not *bother* to? Jefferson said that the Revolution itself was the work of generous passion. In the famous Head and Heart letter, the Heart accuses the Head in these words: "If our country, when pressed with wrongs at the point of the bayonet, had been governed by it's heads instead of it's hearts, where would we have been now? hanging on a gallows as high as Haman's. You begin to calculate and to compare wealth and numbers: we threw up a few pulsations of our warmest blood; we supplied enthusiasm against wealth and numbers; we put our existence to the hazard, when the hazard seemed against us, and we saved our country" (*TJ*, 10.451). If Jefferson is right, then by Madison's norms the state constitutions should not have been framed at such a passionate moment.

Madison's sixth argument seems to foreclose the very possibility of reforming governments. He has maintained that the popularity of the legislature would give it impunity, since review boards reporting to the people would find its affections already engaged. But what if the legislature loses its popularity, does something so flagrantly wrong and unappealing that it will "admit no specious [attractive] colouring"? Then it should be vulnerable—which is the catch. When it is not too popular to be attacked successfully, it is so unpopular that attack would unsettle the whole frame of government:

> In such a posture of things, the public decision might be less swayed by prepossessions in favor of the legislative party. But still it could never be expected to turn on the true merits of the question. It would inevitably be connected with the spirit of pre-existing parties, or of parties springing out of the question itself. It would be connected with persons of distinguished character and extensive influence in the community. It would be pronounced by the very men who had been agents in, or opponents of the measures, to which the decision would relate. The *passions* therefore not the *reason* of the public would sit in judgment (49.343).

Can we trust nothing we were told about Madison through the years? He is credited with putting faction to constructive use, since he admitted its causes could not be eliminated. Let ambition contend with ambition, we read in No. 51, to reach a kind of equilibrium through properly umpired competition. But here we are warned not to disturb the government—even when its acts admit of no plausible defense, no "colouring" of the public purpose—because that might "bring the passions into play." Now he is saying, or seems to be, that since we cannot eliminate the causes of passion, we must do nothing. Here, indeed, is government—or, rather, nongovernment—by deadlock.

Perhaps Madison means only that *constitutional* questions should not be settled at a time of popular unrest. That would

allow normal political disputes to go forward by the interplay of
competing interests, all mutually checked and balanced. It is
only when "redefining the system" of checks that the populace is
not to be heeded if clamorous. But the test of a system is its handling of important matters, not unimportant ones. Madison has
shaped an hypothesis where the supreme branch of government
is acting without any cover of plausible right, and yet recourse to
the people is interdicted. In a desperate situation, the desperate
remedy is to do nothing. Elsewhere he has said that only the
people have the right to establish a constitutional system; but
now he adds a qualifier—the people can do it only when they are
calm. Who is to decide the degree of calm necessary to consider
grave constitutional failures? Is the best sign of danger in-
souciance?

I dwell on this paper because it needs dwelling on. It gives
better support to the criticisms of Beard and Burns than do the
passages they adduce. (Beard cites No. 49, but only its introductory thesis, not any of its six arguments, where the real dead-
lock-theory "dynamite" is.) Besides, it is not to be supposed
that Madison lightly differed from his intellectual companion,
Thomas Jefferson, or that he did not take Jefferson's proposal
seriously and make his argument against it equally serious and
considered. Granted, Madison is going to say (in No. 51) that a
bicameral legislature will be less likely to violate the separation
of powers, will therefore *need* less policing. But that does not
cancel the fact that he opposed a constitutional commission because of its tendency to engage the popular passions, to make
citizens look for defects in their government instead of reverenc-
ing it, to put the people in charge of their own affairs. If that is
not anti-Jeffersonian, what is?

But so far, in these comments on No. 49, I have overlooked a
word not entirely clear in its force—a dangerous procedure, as
we shall find, in dealing with The Federalist. I mean the word
"opinion" as used in Madison's second argument against Jefferson:

> If it be true that all governments rest on opinion, it is no less true
> that the strength of opinion in each individual, and its practical
> influence on his conduct, depend much on the number which he
> supposes to have entertained the same opinion (49.340).

Students of eighteenth-century political theory are familiar with the idea that government rests on property, or contract, or divine right, or consent, or benevolence. But where did this confident maxim about *opinion* as government's basis come from? We cannot even tell, at a first reading, what the introductory clause has to do with the rest of the sentence. Is the introductory "if" concessive (*though* governments rest on opinion, *nonetheless* . . .) or inferential (*since* governments rest on opinion, *then* . . .)?

Madison's use of "opinion" elsewhere in The Federalist does not throw much light on this sentence. In fact, his use of the word in No. 10 would seem to make nonsense of our passage in No. 49. There he seems to make opinion the basis of *faction*, which is at odds with government in the large and best sense. One "cure" for faction, he notes (by way of completeness), would be to remove its causes "by giving to every citizen the same opinions, the same passions, and the same interests" (10.58). But this is impracticable: "As long as the reason of man continues fallible, and he is at liberty to exercise it, different opinions will be formed . . ." Opinion, you see, is the result of reason's fallibility; if all knew perfectly, they would agree. So far No. 10 is in accord with No. 49, where opinion and prejudice are contrasted with "enlightened reason." But, having said that it is the job of government to *control* faction, how can he also say that government rests on the opinions that *fuel* faction? In No. 49, remember, opinion is attached to "antient" things as a kind of unquestioning reverence.

One of Hume's essays used by Adair to explicate Madison's No. 10 is the 1742 "Of the First Principles of Government" (1.4). Adair does not cite the opening of that paper, which poses the question of rule in a way that was customary with Hume: How do rulers exact obedience? (1.4.110; cf. 2.12.444–5). This is not accomplished by force, since the whole body of the community can outweigh the ruling few if resort is had to brute strength. The answer Hume gives is the one Madison adopts: "It is, therefore, on opinion only that government is founded" (1.4.110; cf. *History,* 5.59.274; Giarrizzo, 21–8). The similarity of the two maxims is backed by a similarity of context. Hume goes on to say that "opinion of right"—the citizens' presumption of legitimacy— is demonstrated in "the attachment which all nations have to their ancient government, and even to those names which have had the sanction of antiquity. Antiquity always begets the opinion of right" (1.4.110).

Opinion in Hume is a "prepossession," a judgment in place, considered apart from any evidence that brought people to it (*History*, 4.41.10 and 4.43.117). Such opinion often effects what it purports to describe:

> The tenth legion of CAESAR, and the regiment of PICARDY in FRANCE were formed promiscuously from among the citizens; but having once entertained a notion, that they were the best troops in the service, this very opinion really made them such (1.21.255).

The shrewd legislator expects opinion to do much of his work for him:

> When a man is prepossessed with a high notion of rank and character in the creation, he will naturally endeavour to act up to it, and will scorn to do a base or vicious action, which might sink him below that figure which he makes in his own imagination (1.11.151).

When Hume says that government is founded on the people's opinion of right and opinion of interest, he means that the ruled will stay docile to government only so long as they feel that they *ought* to obey and that obeying will serve their *advantage*. This, he claims in his essay "Of the Original Contract," is the true meaning of government by consent: "When we consider how nearly equal all men are in their bodily force, and even in their mental powers and faculties, till cultivated by education; we must necessarily allow that nothing but their own consent could, at first, associate them together, and subject them to any authority" (2.12.444–5). For him, legitimacy is derived from the people, not so much in theory as in fact. He states this in terms that could be mistaken for Locke's:

> The people, if we trace government to its first origin, in the woods and desarts, are the source of all power and jurisdiction, and voluntarily, for the sake of peace and order, abandoned their native liberty, and received laws from their equal and companion (445).

Yet Hume regularly rejected what he called the "selfish system" of Locke (*Enquiry*, 267) and called his political writings "despicable" (*History*, 6.71.320). And he goes on, in this very place, to attack the notion of tacit consent and the Lockean contract.

> I may now ask, upon what foundation the prince's title stands? Not on popular consent surely: For though the people willingly acquiesce in his authority, they never imagine, that their consent made him sovereign. They consent; because they apprehend him to be already, by birth, their lawful sovereign (2.12.453; cf. *History*, 6.71.314).

Their *opinion* of legitimacy, however derived, is what makes them acquiesce, creating legitimacy.

For Hume, society did not begin with Locke's hypothetical individual in the state of nature but in the affective life of the family (*Treatise*, 486; cf. *Inventing*, 285–6). Such tribal life can exist without formal government—a conclusion "verified in the *American* tribes, where men live in accord and amity among themselves without any establish'd government" (*Treatise*, 540). But conquest, trade, and refinement call for specialization and division of labor, to be justified by the utility of political and commercial arrangements:

> What necessity, therefore, is there to found the duty of allegiance or obedience to magistrates on that of fidelity or a regard to promises, and to suppose, that it is the consent of each individual, which subjects him to government; when it appears, that both allegiance and fidelity stand precisely on the same foundation, and are both submitted to by mankind, on account of the apparent interests and necessities of human society? (2.12.455).

Hume ends this essay, "Of the Original Contract," with an appeal to common opinion: "If scarce any man, till very lately, ever imagined that government was founded on compact, it is certain that it cannot, in general, have any such foundation" (2.12.400). Hume can make such an appeal because he believes in a shared moral sense, acting uniformly to pursue and promote happiness (*Inventing*, 208–11). He expressly connected this teaching with rejection of Locke's contract in the *Treatise of Human Nature*:

> Lest those arguments shou'd not appear entirely conclusive (as I think they are) I shall have recourse to authority, and shall prove, from the universal consent of mankind, that the obligation of

submission to government is not deriv'd from any promise of the subjects. Nor need any one wonder, that tho' I have all along endeavour'd to establish my system on pure reason, and have scarce ever cited the judgment even of philosophers or historians on any article, I shou'd now appeal to popular authority, and oppose the sentiments of the rabble to any philosophical reasoning. For it must be observ'd, that the opinions of men, in this case, carry with them a peculiar authority, and are, in a great measure, infallible. The distinction of moral good and evil is founded on the pleasure or pain, which results from the view of any sentiment, or character; and as that pleasure or pain cannot be unknown to the person who feels it, it follows, that there is just so much vice or virtue in any character, as every one places in it, and that 'tis impossible in this particular we can ever be mistaken (546–7).

For Hume, "opinion of right" is based on the moral sense, setting the *end* of society in an intercourse of kind offices, while "opinion of utility" renders judgment on the *means* to that end (*Inventing*, 196–8).

Hume's doctrine on opinion is maintained, not only in his *Treatise* and *Essays,* but in his most popular work of the period, his *History of England.* He concludes his controversial (i.e., sympathetic) treatment of Charles I's death with this passage:

If ever, on any occasion, it were laudable to conceal truth from the populace, it must be confessed, that the doctrine of resistance affords such an example, and that all speculative reasoners ought to observe, with regard to this principle, the same cautious silence, which the laws in every species of government have ever prescribed to themselves. Government is instituted in order to restrain the fury and injustice of the people, and being always founded on opinion, not on force, it is dangerous to weaken, by these speculations, the reverence which the multitude owe to authority, and to instruct them beforehand, that the case can ever happen when they may be freed from their duty of allegiance (5.59.274).

A passage like that makes us understand why Jefferson so bitterly disliked Hume's *History.* But it makes all the more mysterious Madison's use of Hume's doctrine on opinion as the basis of government. Adair traced Hume's influence on the concept of faction in No. 10. Madison, it might be said, extracted that teaching from the more general setting of Hume's politics. But when we see him arguing, from Hume's doctrine on opinion, for reverence to the established order, we begin to wonder if he knew what he was letting himself in for. Did he use Hume with full knowledge of the consequences? If he did, we must attribute to him a line of thought at odds with his reputation. But if he did not, then his claim as a serious political thinker is considerably reduced. Either way, the prospect is not comforting. If he embraced Hume's views, he is less the democrat than we thought. If he simply toyed superficially with them, then he is less the thinker. So far, at least, a look at the Humean sources for No. 49 leaves "the political scientist's Madison" deeper in trouble and more philosophically bedraggled.

FOUR

Corruption

I am led into this train of reflection, by considering
some papers wrote upon that grand topic of *court
influence and parliamentary dependence*, where, in my
humble opinion, the country party, besides vehemence
and satyre, shew too rigid an inflexibility, and too great
a jealousy [fear] of making concessions to their adversaries.

—Hume, 1.6.118

Adair notes that Madison copies almost slavishly Hume's description of attachment to leaders and attachment to persons.
This concept of emotional attachment to one's rulers shows up,
as well, in No. 49. The legislative branch cannot be checked by
review commissions because there are bound to be "prepposses-
sions in favor of the legislative party" (49.342; cf. 49.341). What
is the basis for such attachment? Madison answers, in a description of the legislators:

> Their connections of blood, of friendship, and of acquaintance, em-
> brace a great proportion of the most influential part of the society.
> The nature of their public trust implies a personal influence among
> the people, and that they are more immediately the confidential
> guardians of the rights and liberties of the people. With these ad-
> vantages, it can hardly be supposed that the adverse party would
> have an equal chance for a favorable issue (49.342).

We don't customarily talk of affection for our representatives in
America—indeed, Hamilton has been criticized for using that
concept in his infamous speech before the Philadelphia Convention (see Chapter Nine). But Madison assumes that friendship
and acquaintance, even "connections of blood," will enter into
prepossessions favoring the legislative branch.

Odd as this talk may sound to us, it was very prominent in Scottish thinking about politics. Since sociability held men together, one would expect it to have great force in their politics. Hume describes "*affection* to wisdom and virtue in a *sovereign*" (1.4.111) and says that faction can carry a man beyond himself, in noble obstinacy or ignoble vice: "The same social disposition of mankind is the cause of these contradictory appearances" (ibid.). The wisdom of Elizabeth I appears in her care to retain the *affection* of her subjects (*History*, 4.41.14–15, 37; 4.43.104; 4.44.177).

Hume believed that "the social Passions are by far the most powerful of any, and that even all the other Passions receive from them their chief Force and Influence" (1.11.154). Opinion is dispersed as by contagion, making even distant followers feel closely united to their leaders. Hume notes the paradox of greater generosity where there is less interest (1.9.135):

> By parties from affection, I understand those which are founded on the different attachments of men toward particular families and persons, whom they desire to rule over them. These factions are often very violent; though, I must own, it may seem unaccountable, that men should attach themselves so strongly to persons, with whom they are no wise acquainted, whom perhaps they never saw, and from whom they never received, nor can ever hope for any favour. Yet this we often find to be the case, and even with men, who, on other occasions, discover no great generosity of spirit, nor are found to be easily transported by friendship beyond their own interest. We are apt to think the relation between us and our sovereign very close and intimate (1.8.133).

Hume was intrigued by the dynamics of social action, the psychological interplay between leaders and followers:

> 'Tis difficult to penetrate into the thoughts and sentiments of any particular man; but 'tis almost impossible to distinguish those of a whole party, where it often happens, that no two persons agree precisely in the same maxims of conduct. Yet I will venture to affirm, that it was not so much PRINCIPLE, or an opinion of indefeasible right, which attached the TORIES to the ancient royal family, as AFFECTION, or a certain love and esteem for their persons. The same cause divided ENGLAND formerly between the houses of YORK and LANCASTER, and SCOTLAND between the families

of BRUCE and BALLIOL; in an age, when political disputes were but little in fashion, and when political *principles* must of course have had but little influence on mankind. The doctrine of passive obedience is so absurd in itself, and so opposite to our liberties, that it seems to have been chiefly left to pulpit-declaimers, and to their deluded followers among the vulgar. Men of better sense were guided by *affection;* and as to the leaders of this party, 'tis probable that *interest* was their chief motive, and that they acted more contrary to their private sentiments, than the leaders of the opposite party. Tho' 'tis almost impossible to maintain with zeal the right of any person or family, without acquiring a good-will to them, and changing the *principle* into *affection;* yet this is less natural to people of an elevated station and liberal education, who have had full opportunity of observing the weakness, folly, and arrogance of monarchs, and have found them to be nothing superior, if not rather inferior to the rest of mankind. The *interest,* therefore, of being heads of a party does often, with such people, supply the place both of *principle* and *affection* (1.9.142).

In No. 49 Madison recognizes the "enthusiastic confidence of the people in their patriotic leaders" (49.341) as a force "which stifled the ordinary diversity of opinions on great national questions" when the constitutions of the states were being drawn up. But now this same affection, given to the legislature, will make that branch uncheckable. In No. 63 he notes that popular affection will go naturally to the House of Representatives, forcing the Senate to compete for "the affections and support of the entire body of the people themselves" (63.431). In No. 57 he says that the affections felt for the representatives are bound to be reciprocated, at least initially: "They will enter into the public service under circumstances which cannot fail to produce a temporary affection at least to their constituents. There is in every breast a sensibility to marks of honor, of favor, of esteem, and of confidence, which, apart from all considerations of interest, is some pledge for grateful and benevolent returns" (57.385; for the basis of this language in moral-sense philosophy, see *Inventing,* 225–6). In No. 46 he says that the "prepossessions" in favor of nearer delegates will cause a "predilection" for state governments over the federal: With the former "will a greater proportion of the people have the ties of personal acquaintance and friendship, and of family and party attachments" (46.316). Once again we find a rich background in Hume for language that otherwise sits rather oddly in its place, or accords very little with what we expect from Madison. And if Madison's thought seems circular here, Hume labors under the same difficulty.

Why do I say the argument seems circular? Because, on the one hand, we have affectionate "prepossessions" favoring the rulers, a predilection that is to be encouraged, attaching people to their "antient" government. But, on the other hand, we are told that the legislature is dangerous precisely because of its popularity, its hold on the affections of the governed, which must not be engaged in constitutional review boards. Patriotic affection is both the desideratum and the danger, to be encouraged and repressed. Or, to put the problem another way: If government is based on popular opinion, and the legislature draws its strength from that, why should one *want* to check the legislature? If it voices the *opinion* on which the government is based, any check on that voice is subversive of the government's own basis and legitimacy.

The closer we look at No. 49, the more problems emerge from its scandalous simplicity. Robert Dahl criticized Madison for relying on "external" checks built into institutional features of the Constitution. He thought Madison neglected more important social forces for inhibiting deviant behavior:

> A contemporary social scientist would be inclined to assume that the prevailing type of family relationship, for example, would be at least as important a determinant of political behavior as the constitutionally prescribed system of government controls. Family structure, belief systems, myths, heroes, legitimate types of behavior in primary groups, prevailing or modal personality types, these and other similar factors would be crucial in determining the probable response of leaders and non-leaders and hence the probability of tyranny or non-tyranny (*Preface*, 18; cf. 22).

But we see that Madison, like Hume, *did* place great emphasis on family attachments, on affections, on ancient ties, on "opinion"-shaping things like Dahl's "myths" and "heroes." No. 49 argues in favor of the "prejudices" that keep men respectful of the law, the "opinion" that makes it binding. Madison advises us repeatedly to consult "the genius of the people," in ways that reflect Montesquieu's sociology of political types (see Chapter Twenty-one). But this encouragement of social forces making for docility is not what Dahl was looking for in Madison. He wanted social checks upon government itself, not social forces making the people *submit* to government. He came looking for what is commonly thought of as "Madisonian" ideas, and was quite right in not recognizing them in No. 49. So unrecognizable were they to him that he overlooked the fact that Madison *does* talk of social checks. He just talks about them "on the wrong side," as it were.

And that is the problem we shall find wherever Hume had an influence on Madison. We have been taught by recent scholars—Caroline Robbins, Bernard Bailyn, F. R. Pole, Gordon Wood, J. G. A. Pocock—to look for the Country party ideology of "Old Whigs" in America's Revolution. But on point after point Hume was the enemy of that ideology. His essays were written to refute one of the principal Country party spokesmen, Lord Bolingbroke. His "evenhandedness" of tone does not fully mask defense of the "Court" party's principles. No defender of Walpole himself, Hume nonetheless made the best case for Walpolism. This is apparent on all the major points of Court-Country debate in Hume's time—the legitimacy of opposition, the corruption of parliament, the frequency of elections, and parliamentary instruction.

In eighteenth-century England, opposition to the government still carried some taint of disloyalty. Since "King in Parliament" was sovereign, and the king could do no wrong, how could one oppose the government short of treason? The answer given by the Country party was that it was obedient to the permanent constitution, if not to the passing ministries. Hume, without demanding the passive obedience of theorists for absolute monarchy, stigmatized opposition as "faction" and argued that the presumption should always be in favor of obedience rather than opposition:

> Besides we must consider that, as obedience is our duty in the common course of things, it ought chiefly to be inculcated; nor can any thing be more preposterous than an anxious care and solicitude in stating all the cases, in which resistance may be allowed. In like manner, though a philosopher reasonably acknowledges, in the course of an argument, that the rules of justice may be dispensed with in cases of urgent necessity; what should we think of a

preacher or a casuist who should make it his chief study to find out such cases, and enforce them with all the vehemence of argument and eloquence? Would he not be better employed in inculcating the general doctrine, than in displaying the particular exceptions, which we are, perhaps, but too much inclined, of ourselves, to embrace and extend? (2.13.402).

Though Hume allows for particular resistance in the cases of Charles I and James II, he clearly does not envisage opposition as a normal course of conduct. This is his doctrine in the *History*:

Or should it be found impossible to restrain the licence of human disquisitions, it must be acknowledged, that the doctrine of obedience ought alone to be inculcated, and that the exceptions, which are rare, ought seldom or never to be mentioned in popular reasonings and discourses . . . Nor is there any danger, that mankind, by this prudent reserve should universally degenerate into a state of abject servitude. When the exception really occurs, even though it be not previously expected and descanted on, it must, from its very nature, be so obvious and undisputed, as to remove all doubt, and overpower the restraint, however great, imposed by teaching the general doctrine of obedience (5.59.274; cf. 6.71.310).

For Hume, who saw the force of personal attachment in the whole range of political ties, it was hard to distinguish government (always to be supported) from governors (who are opposable). On a parallel distinction between royal title and inheritance by blood, he wrote: "The generality of mankind never will enter into these [distinguishing] sentiments; and it is much happier, I believe, for society, that they do not, but rather continue in their natural prepossessions" (2.15.471).

Hume had as low an opinion of elections as did Dr. Johnson. He favored hereditary monarchy (1.3.100; 2.15.471–2).

But where no force interposes, and election takes place; what is this election so highly vaunted? It is either combination of a few great men, who decide for the whole, and will allow of no opposition: Or it is the fury of a multitude, that follow a seditious ringleader, who is not known, perhaps, to a dozen among them, and who owes his advancement merely to his own impudence, or to the monetary caprice of his fellows. Are these disorderly elections, which are rare too, of such mighty authority, as to be the only lawful foundation of all government and allegiance? In reality, there is not a more terrible event, than a total dissolution of government, which gives liberty to the multitude, and makes the determination or choice of a new establishment depend upon a number, which nearly approaches to the whole body of the people: For it never comes entirely to the whole body of them. Every wise man, then, wishes to see, at the head of a powerful and obedient army, a general, who may speedily seize the prize, and give to the people a master, which they are so unfit to chuse for themselves. So little correspondent is fact and reality to those philosophical notions [of the original contract] (2.12.448).

On the issue of corrupting the balanced constitution, Hume made a notorious defense of "placemen" and the use of ministerial money in elections, the two most serious complaints. On the instruction of delegates, which the Country party hoped would counter ministerial influence (Pole, *Political Representation*, 15–16), Hume's reaction was twofold. One strategy was to dismiss the issue as a fake one:

> I shall conclude this subject with observing, that the present political controversy, with regard to instructions, is a very frivolous one, and can never be brought to any decision, as it is managed by both parties. The country-party pretend not, that a member is absolutely bound to follow instructions, as an ambassador or general is confined by his orders, and that his vote is not to be received in the house, but so far as it is conformable to them. The court-party again, pretend not, that the sentiments of the people ought to have no weight with every member; much less that he ought to despise the sentiments of those he represents, and with whom he is more particularly connected. And if their sentiment be of weight, why ought they not to express these sentiments? The question, then, is only concerning the degrees of weight, which ought to be plac'd on instructions (1.4.113).

But Hume knew that some Country party leaders did want to exact binding pledges from candidates (Pole, 429); and he says that this, so far from preserving the mixed government, would expel the kingly element entirely and "reduce it to a pure republic" (ibid., 113):

> Were the members obliged to receive instructions from their constituents, like the DUTCH deputies, this would entirely alter the case; and if such immense power and riches, as those of all the

commons of GREAT BRITAIN, were brought into the scale, it is
not easy to conceive, that the crown could either influence that
multitude of people, or withstand that overbalance of property
(112).

It should be noted that this very paragraph is the one to which
Adair traces Madison's idea that, by extent of territory (making
instruction more difficult), "the force of popular currents and
tides is, in a great measure, broken" (113; cf. *Fame*, 102).

What was Madison's view of Hume's complex of ideas, so opposed to the Country party ideology Americans are supposed to
have adopted in the latter half of the eighteenth century? Obviously, Madison could not follow Hume in defense of a "mixed
government," with monarchy as one element of it (see Chapter
Eleven). But on specific points he is often closer to Hume than to
the opposition ideologues. We are beginning to see that he drew
most heavily on Hume's essays concerned with party—which
were directed against the very idea of opposition. Madison opposed parties and branded them with Hume's denigrating term
faction. In No. 49 Madison argues for a presumption of legitimacy in the government, one not to be disturbed by established
review boards, whose sanctioned opposition would "carry an implication of some defect in the government" (49.340) and might
disturb "the public tranquility by interesting too strongly the
public passions." He warned against such action *especially* when
the legislature was usurping. The review board, in that case,
"would inevitably be connected with the spirit of pre-existing
parties, or of parties springing out of the question itself"
(49.342).

Of course, Madison was defending the Philadelphia draft,
which included an amending process; so No. 49 grants "that a
constitutional road to the decision of the people, ought to be
marked out, and kept open, for certain great and extraordinary
occasions" (49.339). But Hume, too, said that extraordinary
abuses, carrying their own alarm, justified resistance to a Charles
or a James. The emphasis is on the extraordinary nature of such
opposition. In ordinary circumstances, faction and party are to
be discouraged.

On elections, Madison could not follow Hume, who allowed
that elections were necessary for supplying the republican com-

ponent of mixed government but denied them any role in the choice of a king. America would have no king; it would be a republic, not a mixed government. But Madison opposed the extreme Country party position, which—in attacking the septennial elections of Parliament's members—claimed that only *annual* elections would keep members adequately instructed by their constituents:

> I shall here perhaps be reminded of a current observation, "that where annual elections end, tyranny begins." If it be true, as has often been remarked, that sayings which become proverbial, are generally founded in reason, it is not less true that when once established, they are often applied to cases to which the reason of them does not extend. I need not look for a proof beyond the case before us (53.359).

The case before Madison in No. 53 is the biennial election of members to the most popular branch of the federal government. Madison defends this with a number of arguments that preclude "instruction." Representatives in the House must acquire knowledge that "can only be attained, or at least thoroughly attained, by actual experience in the station which requires the use of it" (53.362). This clearly means the representative is supposed to act beyond his instruction. Madison says that only experience on "the great theatre of the United States" (362) will inform a man on matters not knowable at the local level (where instructions can alone be issued). These matters embrace interstate relations, trade, and even a measure of action in foreign policy (363–4). Besides, the distance men travel will make it hard or impossible to return often for instruction, so "fit" men should be trusted, for longer periods, to act beyond instruction: "The distance which many of the representatives will be obliged to travel, and the arrangements rendered necessary by that circumstance, might be much more serious objections with fit men to this service if limited to a single year than if extended to two years" (364). Far from regretting this necessity imposed by distance, Madison argues in No. 10 that an extended republic removes the objection to a direct democracy, where the people are judges in their own case. Lack of instruction is vital to the ideal of representation Madison took from Hume (see Chapter Twenty-six):

The effect of the first difference [i.e., delegation rather than direct voting] is, on the one hand to refine and enlarge the public views, by passing them through the medium of a chosen body of citizens, whose wisdom may best discern the true interest of their country, and whose patriotism and love of justice, will be least likely to sacrifice it to temporary or partial considerations (10.62).

Obviously, the "chosen body" is trusted because of its patriotism and love of justice, not because of a pledge to the citizens taking the form of specific instruction. Here Madison is in direct conflict with the Country ideology, and in agreement with Hume.

But Madison goes even further in rejecting what recent scholars have taken to be the very essence of Country party thinking. Old Whigs in England claimed that the independence of Parliament, in its currently most powerful branch, the House of Commons, had been undermined by ministerial influence in the form of money and placemen. Hume denied that charge in his essay "Of the Independency of Parliament." Which side does Madison take on this issue?

Not only does Madison agree with Hume; he praises the British system in what might be called an imprudent way (a way some would think more typical of Hamilton). In No. 58 Madison argues that the popular branch will not be weakened by the Senate, because power over the purse will keep the House of Representatives powerful—like the House of Commons:

They [the representatives] in a word hold the purse; that powerful instrument by which we behold in the history of the British constitution, an infant and humble representation of the people, gradually enlarging the sphere of its activity and importance, and finally reducing, as far as it seems to have wished, all the overgrown prerogatives [technical term for royal power] of the other branches of the government . . . To those causes we are to ascribe the continual triumph of the British house of commons over the other branches of the government, whenever the engine of a money bill has been employed (58.394–5).

Nor is that an isolated reference to the British constitution as *escaping* the deep corruption Country ideologues ascribed to it. In No. 56, answering the claim that the ratio of constituents to representatives was too high, Madison relies on an argument *a fortiori*. The ratio of English voters to Members of Parliament was much higher, and the ministry wielded its "influence," yet the House of Commons stayed essentially independent.

> The experience of Great Britain which presents to mankind so many political lessons, both of the monitory and exemplary kind, and which has been frequently consulted in the course of these enquiries, corroborates the result of the reflections which we have just made . . . [In the House of Commons] there will be one representative only to maintain the rights and explain the situation of *twenty eight thousand six hundred and seventy* constituents, in an assembly exposed to the whole force of executive influence, and extending its authority to every object of legislation within a nation whose affairs are in the highest degree diversified and complicated. Yet it is very certain not only that a valuable portion of freedom has been preserved under all these circumstances, but that the defects in the British code are chargeable in a very small proportion, on the ignorance of the legislature concerning the circumstances of the people (56.382–3).

In the very next Number, Madison uses the very same argument to destroy a suspicion that the representatives will form a privileged class, unconcerned with the mass of men. Astonishingly, Madison says this did not occur to any great degree *even in England:*

> Is the doctrine [of representatives defending privilege] warranted by *facts?* It was shewn in the last paper, that the real representation in the British House of Commons very little exceeds the proportion of one for every thirty thousand inhabitants. Besides a variety of powerful causes, not existing here, and which favor in that country, the pretensions of rank and wealth, no person is eligible as a representative of a county, unless he possess real estate of the clear value of six hundred pounds sterling per year; nor of a city or borough, unless he possess a like estate of half that annual value. To this qualification on the part of the county representatives is added another on the part of the county electors, which restrains the right of suffrage to persons having a freehold estate of the annual value of more than twenty pounds sterling according to the present rate of money. Notwithstanding these unfavorable circumstances, and notwithstanding some very unequal laws in the British code, it cannot be said that the representatives of the nation have elevated the few on the ruins of the many (57.389).

That last clause expressly refutes the charge of corruption brought by the Country party. Madison admits faults in the British code—as, indeed, Hume did. But preserving "a valuable portion of liberty" is just what people like Bolingbroke said had *not* occurred.

The British constitution was not, in Madison's eyes, essentially corrupt. It did not allow the few to oppress the many. The independence of Parliament had not been undermined. On that essential *non*corruption Madison builds his *a fortiori* argument: "If it did not take place, despite shortcomings, even there, how much less chance does it have of infecting us, with our many comparative advantages?" Madison is taking, in 1788, the position Gordon Wood says was widely held at the beginning of the Revolution—that the British constitution was still essentially pure and binding for subjects on the mother island, but that Americans were left out of its protection (*Representation*, 4–11). That was a view widely shared; but it is a view that is supposed, among federalist authors, to be the preserve of Hamilton and Jay, the Anglophiles. Madison, as Jefferson's friend and ally, is most often thought of as a Francophile—and, in more recent times, as an American spokesman for England's opposition ideology. But on the most characteristic features of that ideology—the corruption of the British constitution, the need for instruction based on frequent and pledged elections, the presumption in favor of opposition—Madison is closer to Hume than to Bolingbroke. If this makes him an Anglophile, it is not the only way he resembles the Hamilton of popular stereotype.

FIVE

Construction

Now, where a pleader addresses himself to the equity
of his judges, he has much more room to display his
eloquence, than where he must draw his arguments
from strict laws, statutes, and precedents.
                                    —Hume, 1.13.167

Hamilton is generally considered the friend of strong central
government, focused in a vigorous executive; of implied powers,
to be spelled out of the Constitution by lax construings; of judicial review, as a check on popular legislatures. Madison, who
would later clash with him on some of these matters, is considered the champion of decentralized government, kept in bounds
by strict construction, with the popular branch allowed to prevail.

There is support for these positions in Madison's later writings,
but not in the period of The Federalist. The Virginia Plan he
submitted and argued for in Philadelphia was, in serious ways,
more centralizing in its scheme of government than the draft
adopted by the Convention. He proposed giving the federal
government a direct veto over state laws, a scheme resembling Hume's in the "Idea of a Perfect Commonwealth" (*JM*,
10.209–14). He wanted a stronger executive than the later draft
provided, and he argued for strengthening its powers even in
The Federalist (51.350). He wanted the judiciary to sit on a
council of revision with greater powers than the judicial review
of Hamilton's No. 78 (see Chapter Seventeen). Each of these positions, taken singly, is "Hamiltonian" in the popular sense.
Taken together, they show a drift of thought very different from
the one ascribed to Madison in most commentaries.

In light of his later history, the most surprising aspect of

Madison's thought as Publius is his advocacy of implied powers and broad construction. Hamilton's division of Publius' labors left to Madison the treatment of the federal government's general powers. That meant he must deal with the "necessary and proper" clause—which troubles strict constructionists to this day. The clause occurs in Section 8 of Article I, on the powers of Congress:

> To make all laws which shall be necessary and proper for carrying into execution the foregoing powers, and all other powers vested by this constitution in the government of the United States, or in any department or officer thereof.

In No. 44 Madison argues for the maximum power the phrase "necessary and proper" will allow. He not only opposes those who would exclude such a phrase but says it is the only form of grant that would meet the nation's needs. Without it, "the whole Constitution would be a dead letter" (44.303). In this Number Madison uses one of his ostentatiously methodical arguments, the exhaustive division: He says there were four, and *only* four, other courses the Convention might have taken on the subject:

1. The Convention might have limited the federal government to those powers expressly given in the document. But a similar limitation had crippled the Articles, whose weakness came from "construing the term *expressly* with so much rigour as to disarm the government of all real authority whatever" (44.303). An express grant was the wrong course precisely because it would call for strict ("rigorous") construction.

2. The Convention could have enumerated the powers that might be deemed necessary and proper. This is what Jefferson would claim had occurred in Philadelphia; but he had to misquote the Constitution to do so. In the memo criticizing Hamilton's bank scheme, the Constitution's mention of "foregoing powers" is quietly altered to read "enumerated powers":

> The second general phrase is "to make all laws *necessary* and proper for carrying into execution the enumerated powers" (*TJ*, 19.278; italics in original; strict constructionists prefer the adjective "necessary" to that which follows it).

In Jefferson's view, federal officers were checked by a document "intended to lace them up straitly within the enumerated powers" (ibid., 277). Grant even one power outside the express list and the whole Constitution falls apart:

> If such a latitude of construction be allowed to this phrase ["neces-sary and proper"] as to give any non-enumerated power, it will go to every one, for there is no one which ingenuity may not torture into a *convenience, in some way or other,* to *some one* of so long a list of enumerated powers (ibid., 278; italics in original).

That would be Jefferson's view, in 1791, and Madison would side with him. But in 1788, even when interpreting the phrase as at-tractively as he could for those suspicious of central power, Madison said that the Constitution did *not* enumerate all the leg-islative powers, *nor should it have done so:*

> Had the Convention attempted a positive enumeration of the powers necessary and proper for carrying their other powers into effect; the attempt would have involved a complete digest of laws on every subject to which the Constitution relates; accommodated too not only to the existing state of things, but to all the possible changes which futurity may produce (44.304).

Some may object, here, that Madison was defending in 1788 a Constitution without the Bill of Rights, the Tenth Article of which reserves nondelegated powers to the state or to the people. But "nondelegated," even in that Article, is not the same as "non-enumerated." Jefferson realized that. He does not rely on the Tenth Amendment in his fight against the bank; he argues from the nature of delegation itself—that the grant of a power to achieve an end does not involve a grant to any or all means to that end (*TJ,* 19.277). Yet that is precisely what Madison claims in No. 44, in terms even less circumscribed than Hamilton used, later, to propose the bank:

> For in every new application of a general power, the *particular powers,* which are the means of attaining the *object* of the general power, must always necessarily vary with that object; and be often properly varied whilst the object remains the same (44.304).

Jefferson answered Hamilton's more guarded statement of that view with this lament:

> It would reduce the whole instrument to a single phrase, that of in-

stituting a Congress with power to do whatever would be for the good of the U.S. and as they would be the sole judges of the good or evil, it would also be a power to whatever evil they pleased (*TJ*, 19.277).

3. Still another course open to the Convention would have been exclusion of powers deemed *un*necessary and *im*proper. But such exclusion would begin with the most outré abuses, by comparison with which any accidentally omitted abuse would look not only comparatively benign but (by the very fact of its omission) positively legitimated.

4. The last course open to the Convention was to remain silent on the matter of unnamed but necessary powers. That would create another problem, Madison claims, without really solving the one raised by the critics. For, even without this express mention of implied powers, the Constitution *by its nature* would still imply such powers:

> Had the Constitution been silent on this head, there can be no doubt that all the particular powers, requisite as means of executing the general powers, would have resulted to the government, by unavoidable implication (44.304).

Then why, if the Constitution possesses such powers without formal notice, get people "riled" by *putting* them on notice? Simply, says Madison, to remove any pretext for "drawing into question the essential powers of the Union" on some future occasion (305). No one can say they haven't been warned—that is the problem solved by what Madison calls the *only* appropriate course left open to the Convention.

Douglass Adair—writing in 1944, when he still despised Hamilton and when, as his editor admits (*Fame*, 27), he rather idolized Madison—saw that No. 44 gave John Marshall all the ammunition he needed to counter Madison's later attempts at a "strict construction" view of the Constitution (ibid., 33). Nor is the problem isolated, as Adair suggests, in No. 44. There are even stronger defenses of loose construction in Nos. 37 and 40.

Implied powers are spelled out by the construing art, so Madison refers to a single doctrine of implication-and-construction in No. 44. The Articles could not be made to work at all "without recurring more or less to the doctrine of construction or

implication" (44.303). Madison had "recurred to" implication
himself, in efforts to make the Articles function usefully (*JM*,
3.17, 72; cf. Brant, 2.108). If No. 44 deals with the implied-
powers side of this doctrine, No. 40 makes the more direct case
for latitude of construction.

In No. 40 Madison must face the accusation that the Convention exceeded the call given it by Congress. The Convention was
instructed to draw up amendments to the Articles, not to forge a
whole new government. But that objection depends on the way
you *construe* the call. And Madison tells us how to do that:

> There are two rules of construction dictated by plain reason, as
> well as founded on legal axioms. The one is, that every part of the
> expression ought, if possible, to be allowed some meaning, and be
> made to conspire to some common end. The other is, that where
> the several parts cannot be made to coincide, the less important
> should give way to the more important part; the means should be
> sacrificed to the end, rather than the end to the means (40.260).

The second rule in that passage, determining the grant of
power by the broad ends sought, not by the narrow means expressed, coincides with the interpretation of the "necessary and
proper" clause given in No. 44. Madison applies this rule of construction to the Philadelphia call by distinguishing the end proposed—a system "adequate to the exigencies of government and
the preservation of the Union"—from the means expressly given:
"revising the articles of confederation." Since the Convention
found that a mere confederacy would never be adequate to the
exigencies of government or the preservation of the Union, the
suggested means had to be jettisoned:

> Which was the more important, which the less important? Which
> the end, which the means? Let the most scrupulous expositors of
> delegated powers: Let the most inveterate objectors against those
> exercised by the Convention, answer these questions. Let them de-
> clare, whether it was of most importance to the happiness of the
> people of America, that the articles of confederation should be dis-
> regarded, and an adequate government be provided, and the Union
> preserved; or that an adequate government should be omitted, and
> the articles of confederation preserved. Let them declare, whether
> the preservation of these articles was the end for securing which a
> reform of the government was to be introduced as the means; or

whether the establishment of a government, adequate to the national happiness, was the end at which these articles themselves originally aimed, and to which they ought, as insufficient means, to have been sacrificed (40.260).

Not content with this grant of freedom to interpret, Madison adds two others. Since the Convention was called to change the Articles, who could say beforehand where the change should stop?

The State would never have appointed a Convention with so much solemnity, nor described its objects with so much latitude, if some *substantial* reform had not been in contemplation (40.261).

Furthermore, the proposed Constitution retains some Confederate features, just as the Articles had some national features (e.g., tax power reaching to the post office without intermediation of the states). One cannot say that the changes offered abandon the Articles *entirely*, offer an entirely new scheme for adoption:

The power of coinage has been so construed by Congress, as to levy a tribute immediately from that source [post offices] also. But pretermitting these instances, was it not an acknowledged object of the Convention, and the universal expectation of the people, that the regulation of trade should be submitted to the general government in such a form as would render it an immediate source of the general revenue? Had not the Congress repeatedly recommended this measure as not inconsistent with the fundamental principles of the confederation? Had not every State but one, had not New-York herself, so far complied with the plan of Congress, as to recognize the *principle* of the innovation? . . . The truth is, that the great principles of the Constitution proposed by the Convention, may be considered less as absolutely new, than as the expansion of principles which are found in the articles of Confederation (40.262).

Madison even anticipates the language of later construers when he says that a time of emergency will not brook "little ill-timed scruples," any "zeal for adhering to ordinary forms" (265). And he quotes his friend's Declaration of Independence on the right to "abolish or alter their governments" (265) that is always inherent in the people. That is: If the Convention exceeded its call, it did so on a principle which, if ratified by the people, can abolish any governmental call *or the very government itself*. This passage confirms the worst fears of those who criticize loose construction for remaking laws rather than interpreting them.

It could be urged that Madison was given a tough assignment in No. 40—to claim the Convention had not exceeded its powers when even the delegates at that Convention showed an awareness they were doing just that. One might suppose that Madison's rule of construction was tailored, for propaganda purposes, to this one task. That argument might be worth a hearing if Nos. 44 and 37 had never been written. In No. 44 Madison construes as widely as possible the "necessary and proper" grant —though he had every tactical reason, in that place, to minimize the federal power feared by opponents of the Constitution. There he was not constrained by propaganda goals.

Moreover, in No. 37—which launches the general exposition of the Constitution (after thirty-six Numbers devoted to the present Confederation and to confederacies in general)—Madison says the Constitution should be accepted because it can be defined in more adequate ways by later construings. This overture to the general argument involves a *captatio benevolentiae*. His audience should judge the Convention's efforts leniently. "A faultless plan was not to be expected" (37.232). The difficulties were great, the men involved were fallible. The most the Convention could do about its inevitable failings was "to provide a convenient mode of rectifying their own errors, as future experience may unfold them" (233). This is a reference to the amending power.

But construction as well as amendment must come to the aid of a faulty instrument: "All new laws, though penned with the greatest technical skill, and passed on the fullest and most mature deliberation, are considered as more or less obscure and equivocal, until their meaning be liquidated [clarified] and ascertained by a series of particular discussions and adjudications" (236). This remark occurs in the course of a long argument *a fortiori*. If it is difficult to be precise about gross distinctions, *how much more* difficult it is to deal with subtle distinctions, like the boundaries of jurisdiction in the Constitution:

> Not less arduous must have been the task [Madison, as usual, pretends he has to imagine what went on at the Convention] of marking the proper line of partition, between the authority of the gen-

eral, and that of the State governments. Every man will be sensible of this difficulty, in proportion, as he has been accustomed to contemplate and discriminate objects, extensive and complicated in their nature (234–5; cf. *JM*, 10.211).

Madison now traverses a kind of "chain of being" for things hard to distinguish.

1. The very instrument of distinction, the human mind, has different faculties whose "boundaries have eluded the most subtle investigations" (235).

2. Even the grosser divisions in the external world—not only between the great areas of inanimate, animate and animal life, but between species within those areas—test "the most sagacious and laborious of naturalists" (44.235). Madison is no doubt thinking of his own and Jefferson's disagreements with Buffon (see *JM*, 9.30, 52–3, 80–1; cf. *Inventing*, 284–6).

3. Different aspects of human institutions are even more difficult to sort out: "Experience has instructed us that no skill in the science of Government has yet been able to discriminate and define, with sufficient certainty, its three great provinces, the Legislative, Executive and Judiciary; or even the privileges and powers of the different Legislative branches" (235).

4. In the same way, "Legislators and jurists, have been equally unsuccessful in delineating the several objects and limits of different codes of laws and different tribunals of justice" (236).

5. Nor have the different kinds of law been finally established, "even in Great-Britain, where accuracy in such subjects has been more industriously pursued than in any other part of the world" (236).

6. And the jurisdiction of different courts is still fuzzily circumscribed (236).

7. Even the extent of single laws, "though penned with the greatest technical skill," must await "liquidation" by particular applications (236; cf. Hume, *History*, 1.11.469).

8. Not only are all these distinctions hard to perceive in themselves; the verbal distinctions that would correspond with them all have not been elaborated (236).

9. Even in the Bible, distinctions are hard to make because of its "cloudy medium" of human language (237).

In summary, the complexity of the matter to be dealt with, the fallibility of man's perceptions, and the unreliability of his verbal tools make it impossible to achieve even the approximations to precision found in other areas. The result is bound to lack final clarity, abstract symmetry, and "artificial structure" (238). Yet, just as the members of the Convention are presumed to have compromised their differences (237-9), so the various states should accept the result in a spirit of amity, trusting that further "liquidations" can be made by reasonable men. The ability of the men at the Convention to resolve their differences is a pledge of future adjudications in the spirit of compromise. Madison's appeal parallels that made by Gouverneur Morris when he drew up the covering letter for George Washington to sign in reporting the draft to the states for ratification: "The Constitution, which we now present, is the result of a spirit of amity, and of that mutual deference and concession which the peculiarity of our political situation rendered indispensible."

If the distinctions in the Constitution remain, of necessity, uncertain; if they await future "liquidation"; if the ratifiers are to trust each other that differences can be *worked out* within the framework offered; if these future discussions and adjudications are to be guided by a large spirit of compromise, not a niggling regard to the letter of this first attempt at legislation; if considerations like these are the starting point and norm of constitutional discussion—then Madison is arguing for a very adaptable and flexible instrument reflecting the needs of social man. This test of utility is what we might have expected from Madison's close reading of Hume. It not only makes him a defender of broad construction; it constitutes, in the conjunction of Nos. 44, 40, and 37, one of the most extensive and ingenious arguments for the idea of the Constitution as a "living document" responding to society's needs, not as a text frozen in the first approximations of those who compromised it into being. Hamilton would later argue that logic gave the *means* where it gave the *end*. Madison not only made that argument in No. 44, but in Nos. 37 and 40 he added a *moral* argument for reading the document of unity with a largeness of spirit. He out-Hamiltoned Hamilton.

PART TWO

THE "MADISONIAN" HAMILTON

SIX

Annapolis

The uncertainty of their life makes soldiers lavish and
generous, as well as brave: Their idleness, together
with the large societies, which they form in camps or
garrisons, inclines them to pleasure and gallantry: By
their frequent change of company, they acquire good
breeding and an openness of behaviour.
—Hume, 1.21.245

Hamilton traveled to Annapolis with Egbert Benson, older than
he but his follower. The other four delegates chosen to represent
New York did not think the trip worth their time. Governor Clinton did not want other states meddling with New York's independent customs policy. The state had fallen heir to the opprobrium expressed against Rhode Island when it refused Congress
the right to lay imposts. Though Beard and others would later
treat the effort to frame a constitution as "conservative" and
commercial in motivation, Madison probably thought he was
fighting a merchant selfishness, expressed in New York's tax upon
its neighbors, when he joined Hamilton in the effort to get the
Constitution ratified in Poughkeepsie (cf. *JM*, 8.280, 10.181, 194).

Hamilton knew his state would not have a quorum in Annapolis, but he had a certain tropism toward the desperate cause; he
did not mind acting alone. He was so clearly independent that
some thought him isolated—never truly American, this "bastard
brat of a Scotch peddler" (as John Adams called him) born on a
little rock in the Caribbean. Yet Hamilton had adopted New
York as his state before it declared independence, and he was
planning for the new country before it became a country. He
was one of the "young men of the Revolution" who, according to
Stanley Elkins and Eric McKitrick, spent their formative years in

the Continental Army. He never felt the divided loyalty—to state as well as nation—that stalled men like Samuel Adams in the backwaters of mere resistance once independence had been won.

Despite all this, Hamilton did seem to carry his own distances with him. Though charming, well liked, deeply loved by his family, he seemed always to be cutting a course somewhat mysterious to others if not to the man himself. Though a superb organizer and administrator, staff man to General Washington, general factotum as well as Secretary of the Treasury in the first national Administration, he would never be mistaken for a "company man." He seemed destined, in his moments of fulfillment, to stand alone, as when he leaped the palisades at Yorktown or turned and fired high at Weehawken. He reveals little of himself in his writings, and that little indirectly.

It is said that writers possess an inner landscape drawn from childhood experience or dream. If we wish to catch Hamilton remembering the islands of his youth, we must look carefully at a political metaphor like this:

> It is impossible to read the history of the petty Republics of Greece and Italy, without feeling sensations of horror and disgust at the distractions with which they were continually agitated, and at the rapid successions of revolutions, by which they were kept in a state of perpetual vibration, between the extremes of tyranny and anarchy. If they exhibit occasional calms, these only serve as short-lived contrasts to the furious storms that are to succeed. If now and then intervals of felicity open themselves to view, we behold them with a mixture of regret arising from the reflection that the pleasing scenes before us are soon to be overwhelmed by the tempestuous waves of sedition and party-rage. If momentary rays of glory break forth from the gloom, while they dazzle us with a transient and fleeting brilliancy, they at the same time admonish us to lament that the vices of government should pervert the direction and tarnish the lustre of those bright talents and exalted endowments, for which the favored soils, that produced them, have been so justly celebrated (9.50–1).

He is talking of Mediterranean republics, but remembering the Caribbean. Hamilton's first notable publication was his teen-age account of a storm ravaging the favored soil where his own bright talent seemed pent.

Hamilton was born on the tiny island of Nevis, where England kept its maritime court; the abrupt slope of its mountain toward the water made it hard to storm (though hard to farm as well). As a boy merchant Hamilton traded under the guns of St. Croix's fort (the same fort where his mother was imprisoned for lewd conduct by the man she married). When, as a student at King's College, Hamilton helped steal the British cannons from New York's Battery, he felt under him the contours of an island; he had grasped from early experience the logistics of harbor defense. He looked at New York, and even at England, in light of little Nevis:

> An insular situation, and a powerful marine, guarding it [England] in a great measure against the possibility of foreign invasion, supercede the necessity of a numerous army within the kingdom. A sufficient force to make head against a sudden descent, till the militia could have time to rally and embody, is all that has been deemed requisite (8.48).

It is not surprising that Hamilton showed a knowledge of fortification in The Federalist: "The nations of Europe are incircled with chains of fortified places, which mutually obstruct invasion" (8.44). By that time he had led a siege force himself at Yorktown. But it is surprising to find an eighteen-year-old student predicting, in 1775, the tactics that America could use to win a revolution:

> The circumstances of our country put it in our power, to evade a pitched battle. It will be better policy, to harass and exhaust the soldiery, by frequent skirmishes and incursions, than to take the open field with them, by which means, they would have the full benefit of their superior regularity and skill. Americans are better qualified, for that kind of fighting, which is most adapted to this country, than regular troops. Should the soldiery advance into the country, as they would be obliged to do, if they had any inclination to subdue us, their discipline would be of little use to them (AH, 1.158; cf. 1.275, 280).

That is from Hamilton's first popular pamphlet, The Farmer Refuted, published in 1775. He speaks, there, of New York as "our country." That phrase takes on special meaning when we look at the number of passages dealing with the West Indies. "The

Farmer" had claimed that the colonies' embargo would not hurt Great Britain; Hamilton answers that the West Indies are a way station for trade, subsisting off the continual influx of food and supplies, overpopulated with slaves working on one product, sugar. He sees this as the empire's weak point, and urges the colonies to direct all their pressure to it (ibid., 1.148–50; cf. 1.57, 60–2).

Hamilton's financial genius was part of a larger strategic sense that had a military center. He would have been a brilliant general. No wonder he chafed at Washington's "patronage," which kept him a mere staff officer endlessly writing letters. He sought a trivial occasion to quarrel with Washington; left his staff; begged and pulled strings to get a line command; finally had his moment in the very last battle of the war.

Hamilton reveals himself best when talking of others. One of his most autobiographical documents purports to be a eulogy to General Nathanael Greene, from a memorial service of the Cincinnati in New York. Hamilton exaggerates Greene's low birth (but not his own) to show what chances were given to talent by the war:

> It is an observation as just as it is common that in those great revolutions which occasionally convulse society human nature never fails to be brought forward in its brightest as well as in its blackest colors: And it has very properly been ranked not among the least of the advantages which compensate for the evils they produce, that they serve to bring to light talents and virtues which might otherwise have languished in obscurity or only shot forth a few scattered and wandering rays (*AH*, 5.348).

Greene, like Hamilton, won Washington's regard:

> He was not long there before the discerning eye of the American Fabius marked him out as the object of his confidence. His abilities intitled him to a preeminent share in the Councils of his Chief (ibid.).

In 1778, Hamilton watched Washington call staff meetings at which the commander's own inclination to harry General Clinton was overridden by Charles Lee and his supporters. Hamilton grumbled to his friends (*AH*, 1.510) and tacitly cheered on Greene, who urged attack. In the eulogy, Hamilton comes as close as one could, before the Cincinnati, to criticism of the sainted Washington:

> Tis enough for the honor of Greene to say that he left nothing unessayed to avert and to frustrate so degrading a resolution. And it was happy for America that the man, whose reputation could not be wounded without wounding the cause of his Country, had the noble fortitude to rescue himself and the army he commanded from the disgrace with which they were both menaced by the characteristic imbecility of a Council of War (349).

Greene, unlike Hamilton, escaped Washington's shadow with much of the war remaining to be fought:

> Hitherto we have seen the illustrious Greene acting in a subordinate capacity[,] the faint glimmerings of his fame absorbed and lost in the superior rays of a Washington. Happy was it for him to have been called to a more explicit station. Had this never been the case, the future historian perplexed between the panygeric of friends and the satire of enemies might have doubted in what colors to draw his true character. Accident alone saved a Greene from so equivocal a fate; a reflection which might damp the noble ardor of emulation and check the towering flight of conscious merit (350).

Greene's southern war of strikes and attrition is described with enthusiastic envy:

> [It] exhibits to our admiration a commander almost constantly obliged to relinquish the field to his adversary, yet as constantly making acquisitions upon him, beaten today[,] tomorrow without a blow compelling the conqueror to renounce the very object for which he had conquered and in a manner to fly from the very foe he had subdued (352–3).

Before saluting Greene, who died in bed after the war, Hamilton has to find a surrogate hero to give his story its natural climax:

> But before we take leave of a scene as honorable as it was advantageous to the American arms[,] it behoves us to stop for a moment to pay the tribute of merited applause to the memory of that Gallant officer who at the head of the Virginia line fell in this memorable conflict. More anxious to the last about his Country than himself, in the very agonies of departing life he eagerly inquired which of the contending parties prevailed and having learnt that his countrymen were victorious—He like another Epaminondas yielded up

his last breath in this noble exclamation. *Then do I die contented.*
Heroic Campbell how enviable was such a death! (358).

His own best friend in the army, John Laurens, had died such a
martyr's death, and Hamilton was caught up in the rhetoric that
made men like Nathan Hale perish with the eloquence of Addison's Cato. He read his classics with a romantic eye, jotting
scenes from Plutarch in the margin of his payroll book.

Some historians have amused themselves by guessing what
might have happened if Washington had fallen at Brandywine
or been captured at West Point. Could senior men have held the
army together? Or would a young genius seize the opportunity
and rise to the occasion? The parallel of another young artillery
officer, born on a foreign island, fired with the century's visions
from antiquity, suggests that the only American with the gifts
and the flaws of a Bonaparte was Hamilton. He had the right
combination of vision and grasp upon detail. No wonder Hamilton felt shadowed by Washington's gigantic steadiness. If there
is anything to my surmise, this aborting of a Napoleonic career is
among the many blessings Washington bestowed on his country,
just by being what he was, where he was.

Despite their later reputations, Hamilton was in many ways
more at home in the "new world" of his time than Madison.
Madison came from the wealthiest estate in Piedmont Virginia—
his father's two thousand acres and one hundred slaves out-
weighing Peter Jefferson's modest Shadwell plantation. Hamilton, born at a node of world commerce and affairs, was racing
with the age, headlong and prone to excess. Madison held back,
warning Hamilton to tone down his draft in Annapolis. For three
brief brilliant years the tortoise and the hare would work in har-
ness.

SEVEN

King's College

Political and religious divisions in the latter country
[Scotland], have been, since the [Glorious] *revolution*, regularly correspondent to each other. The PRES-
BYTERIANS were all WHIGS without exception:
Those who favoured *episcopacy*, of the opposite party.
—Hume, 1.9.142

The education of our revolutionary generation can be symbol-
ized by this fact: At age sixteen Jefferson *and* Madison *and*
Hamilton were all being schooled by Scots who had come to
America as adults. At sixteen Jefferson went to William and
Mary, where he met William Small, from whom he derived "my
first views of the expansion of science, and of the system of
things in which we are placed" (*Inventing*, 177–80). Madison, at
the same age, was finishing his course of study with Donald
Robertson. And Hamilton, in his sixteenth year, was sent to
America by Hugh Knox, the Princeton graduate who first appre-
ciated his literary gifts (*New Jersey Hist. Soc. Proceedings*, 69,
pp. 88–114).

Knox was a courageous man, ardent against slavery in his
parishes of the West Indies. He had begun life in America as an
easygoing preacher; but conversion led him to a deeper study of
theology at Princeton, where he stayed for further work with the
president, Aaron Burr. It is one of those quirks of history, one we
could hardly accept in fiction, that Knox sent Hamilton to die in
America at the hands of his own teacher's son.

Accepting a call to the little island of Saba, Knox did not yield
to West Indian lethargy. He kept his library up to date and fired
off his own contributions to presbyterian controversy, invariably
on the "moderate" side, rejecting harsher versions of predes-

tination. If Dr. Witherspoon opposed the aesthetic approach to religion, Knox would quote from Young's *Night Thoughts* in his sermon, "The Duty of Waiting for Our Great Change" (1768). He used the language of the Scottish Enlightenment in another published sermon, "The Probable Sources of Our Savior's Tears at the Tomb of His Friend Lazarus" (1765). The Lord's true humanity involved sympathy with other men, and He "entered into those sentiments of humanity" when He wept (24). In his *Discourses on the Truth of Revealed Religion* (1768) he wrote, "Our duty is written, as it were, with sun beams" in human nature (2.243). Young Hamilton, given the run of Knox's St. Croix library, remembered that phrase in *The Farmer Refuted:*

> The sacred rights of mankind are not to be rummaged for, among old parchments, or musty records. They are written, as with a sun beam, in the whole *volume* of human nature, by the hand of the divinity itself; and can never be erased or obscured by mortal power (*AH*, 1.122).

When Knox transferred his ministry from Saba to the nearby island of St. Croix, the fourteen-year-old Hamilton was working in Nicholas Kruger's store; running that store when, as often happened, Kruger himself was off the island. (I take Hamilton to be fourteen since, as James Flexner puts it, "There is no compelling reason to deny that Alexander, the second of the illicit couple's two sons, was born on the date he himself gave when in the United States: January 11, 1757." The document that gives his age as thirteen in 1768, when his mother died, was more likely to be based on hearsay or approximation than was Hamilton's memory).

Hamilton heard Knox's carefully prepared sermons, and imitated their poetic language in his description of the 1772 hurricane. He traveled to America in 1773 with Knox's letters of introduction, which introduced him to the circle of wealthy Presbyterians at Elizabethtown, New Jersey, to such patrons as William Livingston and Elias Boudinot, who were trustees of the College of New Jersey at Princeton. Livingston, a Yale graduate, was a Presbyterian convert who brilliantly opposed the founding of King's College (later Columbia). He did not want learning in America to be linked with England's established church (Bridenbaugh, *Mitre,* 138–61). These men were colleagues of Knox's own first patrons in America—John Rodgers of Princeton and Francis Alison of Glasgow. Alison, who was vice-provost of the College of Pennsylvania when Hamilton arrived in New Jersey, would be granted an honorary degree from Princeton as one of the continent's leading educators.

Hamilton's first task, in this world of Enlightenment clergymen, was to supplement his precocious knowledge of mathematics with intense coaching in Latin and Greek. For this an Elizabethtown academy, founded by Tapping Reeve, was conveniently at hand. Reeve, a Princeton graduate, had moved on to Connecticut, where his new academy would become the outstanding preparatory school in America. His role in New Jersey had been assumed by Francis Barber, who became Hamilton's tutor three years after taking his master's degree from Princeton. Later Barber would follow his former student (now his superior officer) into the stormed redoubt at Yorktown.

Why, in this group of men whose lives were so closely tied to Nassau Hall, did Hamilton not go there himself? The only reason mentioned in records of his life comes from a friend, Hercules Mulligan of New York, who claims he took Hamilton to an interview with Dr. Witherspoon in 1774. Hamilton asked for permission to advance from the lowest class, at his own rate of progress. According to Mulligan, Witherspoon was unable to grant this request without approval of the board of trustees—which rejected the proposal, despite the fact that Hamilton's own patrons, Livingston and Boudinot, were on the board.

There is something fishy about this story, told over a third of a century after the incident it describes. For one thing, Dr. Witherspoon was far from servile to his board. For another, the college president was at this very moment trying to recruit boys from the West Indies—he had written a famous address to them just two years before. Furthermore, it was customary, not exceptional, to abbreviate the college course—James Madison had completed his undergraduate work at Princeton in just two years.

It is almost certain that Hamilton would have been admitted to Princeton if he truly wanted that (as Mulligan claims). In his favored position, aided by his own wit and charm, he was likely to get his way in this matter. It looks as if, for some reason, he did not want to go to Princeton. Perhaps restlessness and independence made him feel a bit smothered in the pious and learned surroundings of his first year in America. Edward Stevens, his best friend from St. Croix days, had gone to King's College in New York, toward whose opportunities Hamilton had yearned when, as a twelve-year-old, he wrote Stevens about his hopes for preferment. (This letter contains the well-known sentence, "I wish there was a War," *AH*, 1.4). At Livingston's house Hamilton met an elegant young gentleman, John Jay, who had attended King's College. Despite Livingston's earlier opposition to King's, his daughter Sarah was engaged to Jay, a bright lawyer with political ambitions. Jay probably shone in the bookish and clerical company Hamilton was keeping in Elizabethtown. Whatever the reason, he went to King's, where he must have wanted to go.

Not that the content of Hamilton's education would differ much in New York from that available in New Jersey. There, too, the moral system of Hutcheson was taught (*Inventing*, 177). Indeed, Hamilton's tutor there, Robert Harpur, had attended Hutcheson's and Adam Smith's college, Glasgow, before coming to America. It is not surprising, then, that Hamilton was soon quoting Hume as the "celebrated author" of the essay "Of the Independency of Parliament" (*AH*, 1.94–5). The passage he quotes includes Hume's famous maxim that *politically* men must be treated as knaves, though *individually* this is not the case. Taking men singly, "Honour is a great check upon mankind" (1.6.119). This is teaching we shall find Hamilton using in later years, especially in The Federalist.

The appeal to Hume appears in 1775, when Hamilton was still studying with Harpur. The year before, when he had just matriculated at King's, Hamilton wrote his first pamphlet for fellow New Yorkers, the *Full Vindication*, which quoted Hume's doctrine on the cruelty with which free states govern their provinces (*AH*, 1.53). One might presume that Hamilton was taking this unusual line of thought from the essay "That Politics May be Reduced to a Science" (Hume, 1.3.102). But there is no need for inference here. The very next year, Hamilton repeats that argument in *The Farmer Refuted;* and this time he gives the source, quotes it, and notes that Mr. Hume was "enumerating those political maxims, which will be eternally true" (*AH*, 1.100). (This essay, by the way, is the one that Adair found so influential on Madison.) There is ample evidence for Hamilton's early and continued study of Hume, from the time of these first political writings. It is Hamilton's endeavor to work with maxims "drawn from the experience of all ages" (ibid., 126; cf. *Fame*, 108–12 on the Humean basis of this thought). He was already appropriating Hume's characteristic assertion that "utility is the prime end of all laws" (*AH*, 1.126). Thus, in the war, Colonel Hamilton wrote from Washington's camp that men's reputations are based, according to Hume, on their utility to society (*AH*, 2.532).

Separated from Robert Harpur's library, the young soldier Hamilton sent to a friend for Hume's *Essays* (ibid., 595, 604), since he meant to use the economic studies in an ambitious letter to financier Robert Morris—Hamilton's first major treatise on national revenue and credit (ibid., 604–35). An earlier attempt had sketched similar ideas; but Hamilton did not send that letter to its unnamed addressee (ibid., 234–51). In the Morris letter Hamilton quotes Hume's "Of the Balance of Trade" (608)—the very essay Madison had been studying six months before this letter was written. Madison argues for fewer paper emissions, each to expire after a short term. Hamilton, too, wants to fight the "excess of emissions" (239) with short-term notes of three months' duration (245), but he would give them sounder backing (620) provided by a national bank (617). His approach is methodical: He tries to set up "a general principle drawn from the example of other nations" (607) and then "examine how far this rule agrees with experience" (612). The method and conclusions are closer to Hume than were Madison's remarks in his essay on money.

A year after the Morris letter, Hamilton was writing his *Continentalist* papers in favor of congressional power to regulate national trade, and he had to show that his proposals were not at odds with Hume's free-trade essay "On the Jealousy of Trade." Hume is presented as "a very ingenious and sensible writer" (*AH*, 3.77). In his self-education as an economist, Hamilton turned for facts and figures to Malachy Postlethwayt's respected *Universal Dictionary of Trade and Commerce* (two volumes,

1751), drawn from the work of the French economist Savary. It is typical of Hamilton that his military paybook as an artillery officer should alternate citations from Postlethwayt with excerpts from Plutarch, the technician and the romantic jostling each other on the pages of this exact soldier's records (*AH*, 1.373–411).

But Hamilton's larger concepts, his procedure as an economist, came from the writings of Hume—before 1776, when Adam Smith's great work appeared, the best source of Scottish thinking on the matter. The Scots in general opposed the tradition of "agrarian virtue," which treated cities as corrupted and corrupting. Since Scottish thought based society, not on the contract between individuals, but on man's natural sociability, it treated commerce as what Hume calls an "intercourse of kind offices," making the merchant "a common benefactor" (2.4.324–5). Thomas Jefferson shared with Chastellux and others the classical distrust of urban complexity (*Inventing*, 160–1). But Hume, defying the sweeping condemnation of *luxuria*, said that man's refinement and perfection depend on a certain prosperity:

> The more these refined arts advance, the more sociable men become: nor is it possible, that, when enriched with science, and possessed of a fund of conversation, they should be contented to remain in solitude, or live with their fellow-citizens in that distant manner, which is peculiar to ignorant and barbarous nations. They flock into cities; love to receive and communicate knowledge; to show their wit or their breeding; their taste in conversation or living, in clothes or furniture. Curiosity allures the wise; vanity the foolish; and pleasure both. Particular clubs and societies are everywhere formed: Both sexes meet in an easy and sociable manner; and the tempers of men, as well as their behaviour, refine apace. So that, beside the improvements which they receive from knowledge and the liberal arts, it is impossible but they must feel an increase of humanity, from the very habit of conversing together, and contribute to each other's pleasure and entertainment. Thus *industry, knowledge* and *humanity*, are linked together by an indissoluble chain, and are found, from experience as well as reason, to be peculiar to the more polished, and, what are commonly denominated, the more luxurious ages (2.2.302; cf. Giarrizzo, 55–6).

We must distinguish this praise (within proper limits) of *le luxe* from the treatment of it in Mandeville's *Fable of the Bees* (see Schatz, 155–60; Rotwein, xciii). Mandeville, with his dark view of human nature, was a particular target of the more optimistic Scots—Hutcheson had directed his first and most influential book against him in 1725. Hume has Mandeville in mind when he writes that "men of libertine principles bestow praises even on vicious luxury, and represent it as highly advantageous to society" (2.2.300). It is not uncommon for historians to call Hamilton's praise of commerce, which puts avarice to work, a form of Hobbesian thought—though Hamilton thinks it enough to refute "the Farmer" that he can accuse him of Hobbesian beliefs (*AH*, 1.86). Praising "avarice" and condemning Hobbes were not inconsistent positions for one grounded in Hume, who did both these things himself (on avarice, see 2.2.295, 300, and Rotwein, xxxvi; for opposition to "the selfish system" of Hobbes, see *Enquiry*, 267).

In Hume Hamilton discovered an optimistic realism (see Chapter Twenty-two), a union of benevolence with "the encouragement of trade and manufacture" (2.3.319). The frugality of commerce was not treated as stinginess, according to the landed gentry's code. We tend to consider Jefferson "democratic" because of his agrarian ideals, and Hamilton "aristocratic" because he promoted trade and manufacture. But Hume reversed that mode of thought. For him, trade both saves and diffuses wealth; so that

> among merchants, there is the same overplus of misers above prodigals, as, among the possessors of land, there is the contrary. Commerce encreases industry, by conveying it readily from one member of the state to another, and allowing none of it to perish or become useless. It encreases frugality by giving occupation to men, and employing them in the arts of gain . . . (2.4.325).

This was a school of benevolence that took a hard look at anything "chimerical" (2.1.290; cf. *AH*, 2.238, 619). For Hume and Hamilton, as for Adam Smith, there is a "happy concurrence" (Hume, 2.3.310) between private gain and public good (ibid., 2.1.292–3).

While accepting Hume's general framework of economic thought, Hamilton did not follow him slavishly on all points.

Both men thought a moderate tax could spur industry (Hume, 2.8.356; *AH*, 2.635). Both held a qualified labor theory of value (Schatz, 263; cf. 2.1.293–5, 2.3.315). Both attacked extreme mercantilists who equated money with wealth (Rotwein, xiv):

> It is indeed evident, that money is nothing but the representation of labour and commodities, and serves only as a method of rating or estimating them (Hume, 2.3.312; cf. 328).

> The relative value of money being determined by the greater or lesser portion of labor and commodities which it will purchase, whatever these gained in price, that of course lost in value (*AH*, 2.237).

But for his most characteristic contributions—the arguments for a national bank and national debt—Hamilton had to oppose Hume, whom he no doubt had in mind when he wrote: "I am aware of all the objections that have been made to public banks and that they are not without enlightened and respectable opponents. But all that has been said against them only tends to prove that like all other good things they are subject to abuse and when abused become pernicious" (2.617). He claims to follow the spirit of Hume's work even when objecting to its letter.

Actually, Hume later softened his criticism of banks (Schatz, 200–2; Hume, 2.5.338–9, n. 1). But he always opposed a national debt. Hamilton's support of the debt has been read anachronistically by Beard and his followers to show his centralizing tendencies. But for Hume public debt was a *democratic* excess:

> The source of degeneracy, which may be remarked in free governments, consists in the practice of contracting debt, and mortgaging the public revenues, by which taxes may, in time, become altogether intolerable, and all the property of the state be brought into the hands of the public. This practice is of modern date. The ATHENIANS, though governed by a republic, paid near two hundred *per Cent.* for those sums of money, which any emergency made it necessary for them to borrow; as we learn from XENOPHON. Among the moderns, the DUTCH first introduced the practice of borrowing great sums at low interest, and have well nigh ruined themselves by it. Absolute princes have also contracted debt; but as an absolute prince may make a bankruptcy when he pleases, his people can never be oppressed by his debts. In popular governments, the people, and chiefly those who have the highest

offices, being commonly the public creditors, it is difficult for the state to make use of this remedy, which however it may sometimes be necessary, is always cruel and barbarous. This, therefore, seems to be an inconvenience, which nearly threatens all free governments; especially our own, at the present juncture of affairs. And what a strong motive is this, to encrease our frugality of public money; lest for want of it, we be reduced, by the multiplicity of taxes, or what is worse, by our public impotence and inability for defence, to curse our very liberty, and wish ourselves in the same state of servitude with all the nations that surround us? (1.12.162–3; cf. 2.9.372–4; Giarrizzo, 58, 65).

Against the background of Hume's thought, so familiar to him, Hamilton was expressing confidence in the people's ability to discipline themselves by a moderate public debt. This was the more democratic attitude in his time, supported by men like Voltaire and Richard Price, on the basis of Melon's *Essai politique sur le commerce* (Schatz, 208–9). For these people, a debt that increases public "industry" leads to more self-government and freedom of motion. This is the line of thought that makes Hamilton say, in 1781, that "a national debt if it is not excessive will be to us a national blessing" (*AH*, 2.635).

It has been a fashion of long standing to consider Hamilton somehow "un-American" for his praise of commerce in an agrarian republic. But he learned that trade "enlarges" men's thoughts (Hume, 2.1.288, 4.324) precisely where Madison learned that representation in an extended republic "enlarge[s] the public views" (10.62). And even when Hamilton departs from Hume on the issues of public debt and banks, we misread him if we think that this departure implies a rejection of popular freedom. It is quite the opposite. Of Hamilton it can be said symbolically, as of Madison it was said literally, that he spoke his French with a Scottish accent. As we shall see, Douglass Adair came to regret the oversimple contrast of Madison-cum-Hume with Hamilton-cum-Montesquieu in his 1943 dissertation.

EIGHT

Commerce

> Nor can anything restrain or regulate the love of
> money, but a sense of honour and virtue; which, if it
> be not nearly equal at all times, will naturally abound
> most in ages of knowledge and refinement.
>
> —Hume, 2.2.305

In 1943 Douglass Adair defended his Yale dissertation on "The
Intellectual Origins of Jeffersonian Democracy: Republicanism,
the Class Struggle, and the Virtuous Farmer." This broad-rang-
ing and brilliant work has been called the most famous un-
published dissertation in the field of American history, and many
have wondered why Adair never published it.

Actually, he did publish one part of it almost verbatim—the
section on Hume's influence in No. 10 (diss., 248–69 = *Fame*,
98–106). Some minor points were picked up in later articles and
repeated or expanded: Hamilton's use of classical pseudonyms
(diss., 56–7 = *Fame*, 272–85); Hume's use of "experience" (diss.,
27, 34 = *Fame*, 111); John Adams's use of a boudoir metaphor
(diss., 96 = *Fame*, 108). But no other long argument was repro-
duced in its entirety since Adair had come to disagree with his
own thesis.

For one thing, Adair was later an outspoken critic of what he
called Charles Beard's plausible but false theories (*Fame*, 77, 83,
84, 86, 297–8). He knew how plausible those theories could be
because he wrote his dissertation under their influence, as one
might suspect from the second item in his subtitle. To Adair,
writing in 1943, "Beard's arguments are impressive, even irrefu-
table as far as they go" (diss., 18). We hear of Beard's "solidly
documented case" (13) as "undoubtedly illuminating" (16). No.
10 is given a generally Beardian first reading (96–112) and ac-

cepted as Madison's "economic interpretation of history" (230). But it is also "Madison's *modified* theory of the class struggle" (239; my italics).

For Adair would like to rescue the Virginian from Beard's claim that Madison, like Hamilton, supported urban-commercial interests. Adair wanted to detach Madison from Hamilton, to unite him with progressives like Beard (and Adair himself). How, indeed, *could* Madison support the traders in "personalties" when he helped Jefferson found the Republican party to defend agrarian values and virtue—a set of values Adair traces back to Aristotle (65–95)? Hamilton is presented as panicking at the popular unrest of Shays's Rebellion (96–151). Adair neglects to mention that Madison had the same reaction (*JM*, 9.154).

One way Adair tries to separate the two men sharing Publius' mask is to trace Madison's thought to Hume but Hamilton's to Montesquieu, whose theory of mixed government is a "flashy system" (167) of mere cliché (148), a "second-hand theory" (149) Hamilton tried to peddle fanatically (147). Adair does not mention that this fallacious theory was also held by Hume, the source for Madison's ideas, whom it would be inconvenient for Adair to present here as a fanatic peddler of clichés. Besides, as we shall see, Madison also drew on Montesquieu's teachings (see Chapter Twenty-one).

How could two men as different as Adair describes ever collaborate on a single argument? Adair, of course, has to deny that there *is* a single argument in The Federalist. He is one of the early proponents of a schizophrenic Publius (*Fame,* 55). Even when Madison accepts the Hamiltonian checks, he does not do it for Hamiltonian reasons—which were Montesquieu's reasons. Madison saw the extended republic as forcing a discipline of virtue on the people, who must choose uninstructed delegates, on the basis of merit alone, to conduct their affairs at some distance from local pressures (diss., 248–69). The machinery used for a "mixed" government by Hamilton is used for a "refined" republic by Madison. Since the majority of Americans were still virtuous farmers in Madison's day, the discipline of virtue would hold off the pressures of commercialization (273–4, 289–97).

The Beardian class analysis is forcibly yoked, in Adair's dissertation, with the Humean discipline of virtue. This leaves us with a Madison especially fearful of the majority at a time when that majority was still agrarian—and so playing rather simple-mindedly into Hamilton's schemes. Only when Adair became disenchanted with Beard would his view of Madison come into clearer focus and his dislike for Hamilton be dissipated. In his paper on the authorship of disputed Federalist Numbers, written the year after his dissertation, Adair repeated the claim that Madison and Hamilton differed entirely in their work as Publius. But Adair's student and editor, Trevor Colburn, rightly says this reflected merely "his early preference for Madison—a disposition he gradually overcame" (*Fame*, 27). Adair's later references to Hamilton are respectful (141–59, 272–85). He even defended Hamilton from Jefferson's accusation of Caesar worship, though he still presumed the incident Jefferson remembered was authentic (13–15; see Chapter Ten).

But Adair in later years was not only changing his views on Hamilton. He realized that Hume affected others besides Madison—even Hamilton himself (115)—and that the influence of the Scots in general was more profound than his dissertation had acknowledged. This was bound to change his views on the role of agrarian virtue in Madison's thought. The Scots, far from limiting virtue to the farmer, thought virtuous sociability was developed in commercial and urban settings—an assumption that helped Scots take the lead in economic thinking. In a sense, the value of the one major portion of his dissertation Adair later published comes from the fact that he saw the ties to Hume even though his general argument worked, in 1943, against that connection. His fine eye for style of argument and use of words made him spot the key passages and work on them in detective fashion. He was able to sense when a word had a distinctive feel or weight in his authors—words like fame (*Fame*, 8–9), glory (9–10), honor (10–11), experience (109–12). He saw the importance of metaphors and odd words (see 102 on "broken" and 104 on "aliment"). His section on Hume's influence was repeated with only two key omissions—criticism of Hamilton's view of the electoral college (diss., 260) and the passage that connects Hume, of all people, with praise of the virtuous farmer (295).

Scattered hints make it clear how Adair would have developed his dissertation's treatment of No. 10. But he did not get the chance to develop, just to repeat it. When he published "The Tenth Federalist Revisited" in his own journal, *WMQ*, in 1951, it was announced as the first of two essays on that Number. But the second one did not follow. He clearly meant to "revisit" not only No. 10 but his own early treatment of No. 10. Apparently he had despaired of doing that when, six years later, he published the Hume section of his dissertation in another journal, adding nothing but some introductory remarks on the widespread influence of Scottish thought.

The way Adair was moving is clear from his abandonment of Beard and his new emphasis on the Scots. He was bound to see, even before Bernard Bailyn and others made people conscious of the Country party ideology, that Hume was odd company for Madison to be keeping. Hume was for active encouragement of commerce. He differed (and Madison followed him here) with Country ideology on *le luxe* and the corruption of the British constitution. Beyond that, Hume supported a hereditary monarch (1.3.101) and an established religion (2.16.485–6; *History*, 3.26.209, 3.31.441). Adair had at first to pick his way selectively through the Hume essays he was citing in order to keep Madison uninfected by nonagrarian values. For instance, Hume's essay on an ideal republic calls for an established church (Presbyterian, of course), something Adair overlooks when, referring to that essay, he says: "All of Hume's specifics on the ideal government are paralleled in Madison's Notes [on Confederations]" (diss., 260). And, as we shall see, that essay of Hume shaped the very speech by Hamilton that Adair singled out for attack in his dissertation (see Chapters Nine and Ten).

Adair had to present No. 10 as *implicitly* agrarian in its values since there is little about the virtuous farmer in The Federalist. In fact, Madison gives, as an argument for a stabilizing Senate the good effect this will have on business:

> The want of confidence in the public councils damps every useful undertaking [i.e., investment; see Glossary]: the success and profit of which may depend on a continuance of existing arrangements (62.421).

It is true that in the next sentence Madison goes on to say that "farmers and manufacturers" will benefit equally from the government's stability; but first he singled out investments, which is going rather far to disguise his putative differences with Hamilton. That is not disguise; it is impersonation.

In fact, people who bring the stereotypical view of Hamilton and Madison to The Federalist could be fairly easily confounded if given isolated passages and asked to identify the author. The only warning against manufacturing interests in The Federalist is aimed at their use of tariffs:

> They [the duties] tend to render other classes of the community tributary in an improper degree to the manufacturing classes to whom they give a premature monopoly of the markets (35.216).

Hamilton wrote that.

Though Hamilton is supposed to be the Anglophile in the Publius project, his three references to English models were less approving than were Madison's (considered in Chapter Four). Hamilton just notes that the impeachment process was copied from England (65.440–1), as was the life tenure of judges (78.530). He argues that the presidency will be held in check by the legislature's power of the purse—as the House of Commons "reduced the prerogatives of the crown and the privileges of the nobility" in England (71.485).

In his discussion of the taxing power, Hamilton uses both the necessary-and-proper clause and the idea of construction to *deny* any loose concept of "implication" to the Constitution. He says they admit only "necessary and *unavoidable* implication" (33.204; my italics). And he reduces the necessary-and-proper clause to "redundancy," since, "If there is any thing exceptionable, it must be sought for in the specific powers, upon which this general declaration is predicated" (33.205).

Hamilton's defense of strict construction comes in the claim that congressional power to tax does not take away state power to tax. Rather, there is a concurrent jurisdiction based on "the division of the sovereign power" (33.203; this is stronger language than Madison will use on the subject of sovereignty). The Constitution does not remove state power to tax—"it will not bear a construction of the kind" (32.202)—since these are Hamilton's rules of construction:

But as the plan of the Convention aims only at a partial Union or consolidation, the State Governments would clearly retain all the rights of sovereignty which they before had and which were not by that act *exclusively* delegated to the United States. This exclusive delegation or rather this alienation of State sovereignty would only exist in three cases; where the Constitution in express terms granted an exclusive authority to the Union; where it granted in one instance an authority to the Union and in another prohibited the States from exercising the like authority; and where it granted an authority to the Union, to which a similar authority in the States would be absolutely and totally *contradictory* and *repugnant* (32.200).

There is symmetry to these odd reversals in the reputed views of Hamilton and Madison. Not only does the latter defend loose construction; the former supports strict construction.

We are told that Hamilton feared the people while Madison trusted them. It is true that Madison is the only author who cites the Declaration of Independence using quotation marks (40.265). Madison refers obliquely to the Declaration at 43.297 ("law of nature and of nature's God") and 63.422 ("sensibility to the opinion of the world"). But Hamilton uses a Jeffersonian phrase, without quotation marks, in his notorious No. 78, where he says the ultimate check against official departure from the Constitution is revolution: "I trust the friends of the proposed constitution will never concur with its enemies in questioning that fundamental principle of republican government, which admits the right of the people to alter or abolish the established constitution whenever they find it inconsistent with their happiness" (78.527). Nor is this Hamilton's only reference to revolution as the right of the people if the government should overpass its bounds. In his discussion of the necessary and proper clause, Hamilton says the final judges of the matter must be the people:

If the Federal Government should overpass the just bounds of its authority, and make a tyrannical use of its powers; the people whose creature it is must appeal to the standard they have formed, and take such measures to redress the injury to the constitution, as the exigency may suggest and prudence justify (33.206).

He is talking about revolution, and he bluntly uses the word later on:

The improbability of the attempt [of the federal government to "fix" elections] may be satisfactorily inferred from this single reflection, that it could never be made without causing an immediate revolt [strong word, see *Inventing*, 51] of the great body of the people—headed and directed by the state governments. It is not difficult to conceive that this characteristic right of freedom may, in certain turbulent and factious seasons, be violated in respect to a particular class of citizens by a victorious and overbearing majority; but that so fundamental a privilege, in a country so situated and so enlightened, should be invaded to the prejudice of the great mass of the people, by the deliberate policy of the government; without occasioning a popular revolution, is altogether inconceivable and incredible (60.404).

Contrast that language with Madison's attempt to quiet any criticism of the government, in No. 49, and it seems as if Madison and Hamilton had not so much compromised their views as interchanged their minds in order to write as "Publius." We are left, not with a schizophrenic Publius, but with two men each separately schizophrenic, giving us *five* Publii—Jay; the Madisonian Madison, and the Hamiltonian one; and the Hamiltonian Hamilton, as well as the Madisonian one.

Some people, including the early Adair, say there is no mystery so far as Hamilton is concerned: He is simply lying throughout The Federalist. He did not like either component of the Philadelphia draft; he had opposed both the Virginia and the New Jersey plans; he thought them separately bad, and not improved by combination. Therefore he had to feign approval of the result, and there is no reason to take his arguments for the Constitution as reflecting his own real views. They are just propaganda.

That line of thought rests on the notorious speech Hamilton gave to the Philadelphia Convention on June 18, where he imprudently *did* reveal his own views. Since Hamilton's words as Publius are constantly read against the background of that speech— and often dismissed because of it—we must read it very carefully if we are to understand his part in The Federalist.

NINE

Passions

Every thing in the world is purchased by labour; and
our passions are the only causes of labour.
                                                    —Hume, 2.1.293

Douglass Adair at first found Nos. 6 through 9 of The Federalist
a marvel of hypocrisy, since they repeat parts of Hamilton's June
18 speech to the Philadelphia Convention: "It should be remembered, however, that in Philadelphia the purpose of his speech
was to prove that no Constitution based on the Virginia plan
would remedy the situation, while in The Federalist he was arguing that such a Constitution would serve" (diss., 138–9).

Hamilton's much-studied speech comes down to us in his own
outline and in four reports by listeners—by Madison, Robert
Yates, John Lansing, and Rufus King (all cited here from volume
four of Hamilton's *Papers*). Considered brilliant but imprudent,
the speech, which went on for five hours, falls into six main
parts:

1. Hamilton argues that the present Confederation, like any
mere league, is inadequate—well-covered ground (*AH*, 4.179).
The reporters omit this part either because it was familiar or because, reflecting on that, Hamilton did not deliver it.

2. Given the necessity for a new government "with complete
sovereignty" (ibid.), Hamilton asks what are "the principles of
civil obedience" (180) and lists five such principles. In the Confederation, all five principles work for obedience to the separate
states, none for the Confederation. The problem is to redirect
obedience from the states to the general government; and for
that one must recruit the passions, soliciting both ambition and
avarice (181).

3. Without such attachment of the passions to a central government, the American confederacy will go the way of the Greek, German, and Swiss leagues. Its weakness will beget fear rather than ambition (182).

4. But opponents of a strong government say it leads to dynastic wars, while the "Genius of republics [is] pacific" (183). Hamilton answers that "jealousy of commerce as well as jealousy of power begets war." He proves this by examples, and by reasoning on the probable future of the Confederation.

5. Hamilton offers his "sentiments of the best form of government—not as a thing attainable by us, but as a model which we ought to approach as near as possible" (184). For modern commentators, the next four words are a showstopper: "British constitution best form."

6. Drawing on classical thought and Montesquieu (to Adair's earlier horror), Hamilton says government must not be entirely in the hands of the few or of the many, but of both; and the branches speaking for the few and the many must be kept separate—mixed-government doctrine (see Chapter Eleven). "And if separated, they will need a mutual check." Here is another showstopper: "This check is a monarch" (185). The monarchy should be hereditary, the aristocracy should have life tenure; only the democratic branch should be elected by the people.

There, minus introduction and recapitulation, is the offending speech. Of its six parts, only two (the first and third, dealing with the Confederation's faults) look acceptable to Hamilton's critics. We need to examine the other four points, beginning with the second in this chapter and dealing with the fourth, fifth, and sixth in the next.

Some will no doubt find it typical that Hamilton poses the question of political philosophy as one of *obedience* to authority. Madison reports that Hamilton said obedience is "the great & essential principle necessary for the support of Government" (188). Yet this was Hume's customary starting point:

Nothing appears more surprizing to those, who consider human affairs with a philosophical eye, than the easiness with which many are governed by the few; and the implicit submission, with which men resign their own sentiments and passions to those of their rulers. When we enquire by what means this wonder is effected, we shall find, that, as FORCE is always on the side of the governed, the governors have nothing to support them but opinion (1.4.109–10; cf. 2.12.445).

We have already encountered this passage, which opens Hume's "Of the First Principles of Government." It is the source of Madison's statement, in No. 49, that government rests on opinion. Hamilton, too, takes that line of thought: The second of his principles of obedience (after interest) is "OPINION of Utility & necessity" (180). Hume, discussing in another place the way obedience is exacted, says it derives from "the apparent [patent] interests and necessities of human society" (2.12.455).

It is clear from the Madison and Yates reports that the first principle, interest, was treated by Hamilton as the "esprit de corps" (Madison, 188) or "active principle" (Yates, 196) binding the whole together, the joint stake all have in the success of government. Here Hamilton was clearly drawing again on Montesquieu, who argued that every government had its proper *esprit*, on whose preservation the whole depends (see Chapter Twenty-one).

Under opinion, the second principle, Hamilton includes the "love of power" (Madison's report, 189) that makes men seek offices they consider eminent. As we shall see when considering ambition, Hamilton agrees with Hume that this love of power is not ignoble.

The third principle of obedience is the "HABITUAL sense of obligation" (180), what Hume describes as the opinion of right, the view that one *ought* to obey. This, says Hume (in the passage Madison followed in No. 49), *habituates* man to respect for government, so that "Antiquity always begets the opinion of right" (1.4.110). Such a habit should not be disturbed by constant questioning of the government—what Madison disliked in Jefferson's proposal of a constitutional review board:

> Habit soon consolidates what other principles of human nature had imperfectly founded; and men, once accustomed to obedience, never think of departing from that path, in which they and their ancestors have constantly trod, and to which they are confined by so many urgent and visible motives (1.5.115).

Madison's report of the way Hamilton developed this third principle, habit, recalls another Humean doctrine—that government engages the affections (see Chapter Four): "3. An habitual attachment of the people. The whole force of this tie is on the side of the state Govt. Its sovereignty is immediately before the eyes of the people; its protection is immediately enjoyed by them. From its hand distributive justice, and all those acts which familiarize & endear Govt. to a people, are dispensed to them" (189; cf. Madison's own argument at Federalist 46.316, 49.342).

The fourth principle for eliciting civil obedience is force. This seems to depart from Hume's dictum that the few can never rule the many by force, since they are outnumbered. But Hume did not deny the partial agency of force in establishing regimes (1.5.116), nor the internal police power in constraining individuals (rather than "the many" as a whole; see 1.12.161). In the Yates report (197), Hamilton divides force into coercion of law and coercion of arms. The latter is useless in the Confederation —the national government cannot subdue whole states forcibly (see Madison's report, 189). The former, police power, is also useless, since it is exercised internally by each state. The Confederation's claim to obedience is seen as external to the states, resembling that of arms instead of law. The only solution is to form a single government where all the police power will be seen as internal.

The fifth and last principle of obedience is "influence," the power of the state to give rewards to obedience. This, of course, was an illicit appeal for holders of the Country ideology. But Hamilton, like Hume, thought it had proper uses short of outright bribery. In fact, his distinction is Hume's exactly. Madison reports Hamilton's argument thus:

> 5. *influence.* he did not mean corruption, but a dispensation of those regular honors & emoluments, which produce an attachment to the Govt. Almost all the weight of these is on the side of the States (189).

Hume had said:

> By that *influence of the crown,* which I would justify, I mean only that arising from the offices and honours which are at the disposal of the crown. As to private *bribery,* it may be considered in the

same light as the practice of employing spies, which is scarce justifiable in a good minister, and is infamous in a bad one (1.6.121; cf. *History*, 6.141).

These are Hamilton's five principles of obedience. They all work from a psychology of power that resembles Hume's study of the way men act in society, the various attractions they feel when obeying civil law—habit, interest, rewards—based on a sense of necessity (men *have to* live together) and utility (this is a *productive* way to live together). The analysis is hardheaded and thorough. For Hamilton and Hume, cutting off a government's power to reward its citizens by "influence" is unrealistic. They want to found their views scientifically on the way men actually behave.

The Humean ambience of Hamilton's discourse is confirmed by the conclusion to this section, which invokes human passions. The outline reads:

AMBITION   AVARICE

To effect any thing PASSIONS must be turned towa[rd] general government? (181).

Madison's report shows how this was connected with the five principles: "All the passions then we see, of avarice, ambition, interest, which govern most individuals, and all public bodies, fall into the current of the States, and do not flow in the stream of the Genl. Govt." (189).

Passions were a major concern for Hume. A third of the *Treatise of Human Nature* is devoted to them, and that long treatment was later summarized in *A Dissertation on the Passions*. According to Hume, the passions are what put man in motion as a moral agent. They are a reflective second stage of motivation after impingement on the senses (*Treatise*, 275-6). Even virtue and vice are passions, since man must *receive* the impulse for both (ibid., 294-6; *Inventing*, 196-7). The basic passions are pride and humility (*Treatise*, 285-94)—satisfaction or dissatisfaction in a basic sense of the self, whether under a pleasing or a displeasing aspect. Since virtue is connected with joyful contemplation of benevolence and vice with displicence, the pains of humility are not virtuous for Hume. Rather, the spurs of pride —love of fame, ambition, industry—make man act in ways he can be proud of. This is Hume's rationale for the noble love of fame, a constant theme of the Enlightenment:

> Another spring of our constitution, that brings a great addition of force to moral sentiment, is the love of fame; which rules, with such uncontrolled authority, in all generous minds, and is often the grand object of all their designs and undertakings. By our continual and earnest pursuit of a character [distinction], a name, a reputation in the world, we bring our own deportment and conduct frequently in review, and consider how they appear in the eyes of those who approach and regard us. This constant habit of surveying ourselves, as it were, in reflection, keeps alive all the sentiments of right and wrong, and begets, in noble natures, a certain reverence for themselves as well as others; which is the surest guardian of every virtue. The animal conveniencies and pleasures sink gradually in their value; while every inward beauty and moral grace is studiously acquired, and the mind is accomplished in every perfection, which can adorn or embellish a rational creature (*Enquiry*, 251).

Since virtue spreads by a kind of *contagion* in Hume's system, it is man's duty not only to *be* virtuous, but to *display* his virtue (*Inventing*, 317). Hume's was an age when men actually lived by the rhetoric of Addison's *Cato*, when the public virtue of George Washington was the foundation of the first great modern republic.

Thus, when Hamilton argues that the passion of ambition should be attached, first, to the federal government—not to the states—he is following Enlightenment thought in general and Hume's doctrine on the passions in particular. Hamilton was not only proud, but proud of his pride, as he had been taught to be. The popular concept of Hamilton as the victim of an evil pride stems from several misunderstandings—and especially from a story that Jefferson told about him, after he was dead. In an 1811 letter to Benjamin Rush, Jefferson related how, in 1791, he received Hamilton at his Philadelphia home (where Jefferson was serving as Secretary of State):

> The room being hung around with a collection of the portraits of remarkable men, among them those of Bacon, Newton, and Locke, Hamilton asked me who they were. I told him they were my trinity of the three greatest men the world had ever produced, naming

them. He paused for some time. "The greatest man," he said, "that ever lived was Julius Caesar" (*TJ*, 18.533).

Adair, after he came to admire Hamilton, claimed that there was nothing shameful in admiring Caesar, since Jefferson's own hero, Lord Bacon, put Caesar in the highest class of great men, the *conditores imperiorum* (*Fame*, 13–19). Bacon praised the legislative "founders of states and commonwealths." Hume, who said no one could boast more good sense than Julius Caesar (1.13.169), had the same view of such "founders":

> Of all men, that distinguish themselves by memorable atchievements, the first place of honour seems due to LEGISLATORS and founders of states, who transmit a system of laws and institutions to secure the peace, happiness, and liberty of future generations (1.8.127).

Adair's defense of Hamilton in this instance, though based on a sound feel for the importance of glory to Enlightenment leaders, misses the point. In fact, Caesar was generally condemned in revolutionary America. For those who knew their Lucan and Sallust and Addison, Caesar was Cato's enemy, the destroyer of the republic. But there was something Adair did not know when he wrote—that Jefferson's story is almost surely false. In 1960 Jacob Cooke destroyed the principal basis for saying Hamilton admired Caesar, the use of Caesar as a pseudonym in public letters supporting the Constitution—now we know the Caesar letters were not written by Hamilton (*WMQ*, 1960). But it was not till fifteen years later that Thomas Govan made a search through all of Hamilton's writings for references to Caesar, and found them all—with one exception, which refers neutrally to Caesar's skill—pejorative. Early and late, his attitude was uniform, and uniformly disapproving (*WMQ*, 1975). He regularly says that a republic must fear "a Caesar or a Cromwell," its "Catalines [*sic*] and its Caesars." That is why he feared a Caesar in Aaron Burr's designs—and even in Thomas Jefferson's. Jefferson's protestations of reluctance to wield power remind him of "Caesar coyly refusing the proffered diadem" (*AH*, 12.504).

Given the entire record of his writings, it is impossible to believe that Hamilton told Jefferson, of all people, that he thought Caesar the greatest man who ever lived. Whether Jefferson misunderstood him, or recalled the conversation with dim memory and active imagination, he was surely wrong in this instance. (It is also unlikely that Hamilton did not recognize any of the great Enlightenment leaders. Did the story arise from something Hamilton said to tease Jefferson? Humor was not Jefferson's strongest point.)

Hamilton had, perhaps, the makings of a Bonaparte in him. But No. 72 is not inordinate in praising "love of fame" as "the ruling passion of the noblest minds" (72.488). On the contrary, Hamilton joined the philosophes in an "advanced" scorn of "monkish" humility. Pride and ambition were civilizing forces to men of the eighteenth century. Recruiting these forces in the public cause was a statesman's proper task—a task Hamilton took on himself at the Convention. He thought, with Hume, that "honour is a great check upon mankind" (1.6.119); and connecting honor with the state creates a high standard of public service, the aim of modern republicanism.

TEN

Monarchy

But though all kinds of government be improved in
modern times, yet monarchical government seems to
have made the greatest advances toward perfection. It
may now be affirmed of civilized monarchies what was
formerly said in praise of republics alone [especially by
Harrington], *that they are a government of Laws, not
of Men.*

—Hume, 2.12.161

The other passion Hamilton would attach to the national government, along with ambition, was avarice. This may seem too
bluntly realistic, too cynical, today. Yet one of the passions that
make men labor (Hume, 2.1.293) is clearly the desire for gain.
Hume defied the Country party scorn of luxury, finding it a spur
to trade and mutual benefit. The frugality of merchants serves
the public more than does the openhandedness of the landed
gentry. "And this is the reason why trade encreases frugality,
and why, among merchants, there is the same overplus of misers
above prodigals, as among the possessors of land, there is the
contrary" (2.4.325). This was the "happy concurrence" Adam
Smith would develop in his own way: "Now according to the
most natural course of things, industry and arts and trade encrease the power of the sovereign as well as the happiness of the
subjects; and that policy is violent, which aggrandizes the public
by the poverty of individuals" (2.1.292–3). Though Hume condemns vicious avarice as he condemns Mandeville's vicious luxury, he finds a proper use for that passion where public virtue is
not shared by all: "But as these principles are too disinterested
and too difficult to support, it is requisite to govern men by other
passions, and animate them with a spirit of *avarice* and industry,

art and luxury" (2.1.295; my italics). This sentence occurs in the first essay of Hume's series on economics, "Of Commerce," and is probably Hamilton's direct source for the June 18 speech.

In the fourth part of his June speech, Hamilton denies the republican commonplace that wars arose in the past because of monarchic pretensions and dynastic rivalries. Hume turned that argument upside down, saying that modern commercial republics breed wars (1.3.101–4). Republics encourage factious division, but "where the king is an absolute sovereign, he has little temptation to commit such enormous tyranny as may justly provoke rebellion" (2.13.463).

Besides, Hamilton adds, republican forms will not outlaw war, since "wars depend on triffling circumstances every where" (*AH*, 4.183). Under this head he lists, among other things, "Distractions set afloat Vicious humours [Hats Caps]" (184; the last two words are crossed out), and "DOMESTIC FACTIONS." This recalls Hume's discussion of faction, the one Madison drew on:

> Men have such a propensity to divide into personal factions, that the smallest appearance of real difference will produce them. What can be imagined more trivial than the difference between one colour of livery and another in horse races? Yet this difference begat two most inveterate factions in the GREEK empire, the PRASINI and VENETI, who never suspended their animosities, till they ruined that unhappy government (1.8.128).

Part five of the June speech offers Hamilton's own scheme of government, but only as a hypothetical model, to be approximated but not realized:

> Here I shall give my sentiments of the best form of government—not as a thing attainable by us, but as a model which we ought to approach as near as possible (184).

Hume, too, had offered his "Idea of a Perfect Commonwealth" without any illusion that it would be adopted. In fact, his own emphasis on "opinion of right," attached to the "ancient fabric," made him oppose radical change. But:

> In all cases it must be advantageous to know what is most perfect in the kind, that we may be able to bring any real constitution or

form of government as near it as possible, by such gentle alterations and innovations as may not give too great disturbance to society (2.16.481).

And then comes the showstopper, which has earned Hamilton so much later enmity: "British constitution best form." Shocking as the phrase sounds to later Americans, or to Anglophobes among the first ones, it just restated one of the Enlightenment's commonplaces. Voltaire and Montesquieu both celebrated the British government as their ideal, the one that had finally mixed the elements of society in proper balance. And Hume, though he replaces the king with an executive senate in his ideal scheme, most often treated the balance of the actual constitution as something to be maintained. Indeed, he thought the tendency to imbalance was now toward an overpowerful House of Commons; he would strengthen the monarch's hand by "influence" (1.6.120; cf. 1.7.122–6).

We have to remember that, up to the very eve of the Revolution, monarchy was popular in America even when the ministry was not. During the Stamp Act controversy, Benjamin Franklin was in England petitioning the king to make Pennsylvania a royal colony. And when that controversy was happily resolved, New Yorkers raised a statue to George III in thanksgiving. Just a year before the Declaration of Independence, Thomas Jefferson told John Randolph that he blamed the ministry for bad relations; if that could be checked, "I am sincerely one of those [i.e., 'who still wish for reunion with their parent country'], and would rather be in dependence on Great Britain, properly limited, than on any nation upon earth, or than on no nation" (TJ, 1.242).

Richard B. Morris says that the rapid dissipation of enthusiasm for monarchy is one of the mysterious aspects of the Revolution. Much of the credit should go to George Washington, who by his resignation created the counter-myth of Cincinnatus, the embodiment of a resolutely nonmonarchical leadership. By the time Hamilton spoke, those who supported the Enlightenment ideal of a limited monarchy made up a dwindling number of Americans—but a number that included men as formidable as John Adams and Gouverneur Morris. And it should be remembered that Hamilton was offering a hypothetical ideal, not a practical plan.

In the sixth and last part of his speech, Hamilton portrayed the hereditary monarch as a disinterested neutral check between the voices of the few (the legislative aristocracy) and of the many (the legislative democracy). Hume had argued that an *elective* monarch would not have a separate and neutral standing. Jockeying for election at each monarch's death would undermine the realm's stability (1.3.101). This was, indeed, the classical attitude toward mixed government—what the young Adair called a worn collection of clichés. But a view that commanded the best attention and support of Hume, Montesquieu, and Voltaire obviously had a good deal of life left in it during the eighteenth century. Adair was wrong, as he later realized, to say that Hamilton displayed a second-rate mind simply by holding to such a view. By the time he published his dissertation's treatment of No. 10, he called the June 18 speech a "five-hour closely argued historical analysis," a scientific effort "to relate the current difficulties of the thirteen American republics to the universal tendencies of *republicanism* in all nations and in all ages" (*Fame*, 97; italics added). There was never a handsomer palinode.

It may have been imprudent for Hamilton to present his entire theory of government in such detail at the Philadelphia meeting. But that plan was not based on any opposition to liberty. And in offering a theoretical model he indulged the scientific thoroughness and precision he had inherited from Hume. Adair saw the importance of Hume's whole program as resting in the title of one essay, "That Politics may be reduced to a Science" (see *Fame*, 93 ff.).

> So great is the force of laws, and of particular forms of government, and so little dependence have they on the humours and tempers of men, that consequences almost as general and certain may sometimes be deduced from them, as any which the mathematical sciences afford us (1.3.99).

This was Hamilton's ideal as well, one he voiced in The Federalist:

> In disquisitions of every kind there are certain primary truths or first principles upon which all subsequent reasonings must depend. These contain an internal evidence, which antecedent to all reflec-

tion or combination commands the assent of the mind. Where it
produces not this effect, it must proceed either from some defect or
disorder in the organs of perception, or from the influence of some
strong interest, or passion, or prejudice. Of this nature are the
maxims in geometry, that "The whole is greater than its part; that
things equal to the same are equal to one another; that two straight
lines cannot inclose a space; and that all right angles are equal to
each other." Of the same nature are these other maxims in ethics
and politics, that there cannot be an effect without a cause; that the
means ought to be proportioned to the end; that every power ought
to be commensurate with its object; that there ought to be no limitation of a power destined to effect a purpose, which is itself incapable of limitation. And there are other truths in the two latter sciences, which if they cannot pretend to rank in the class of axioms,
are yet such direct inferences from them, and so obvious in themselves, and so agreeable to the natural and unsophisticated dictates
of common sense, that they challenge the assent of a sound and unbiassed mind, with a degree of force and conviction almost equally
irresistable (31.193-4).

Hamilton is aspiring to the Enlightenment's supreme goal, the
construction of a science of man to rank with the Newtonian science of inanimate nature (*Inventing*, 93 ff.). In 1943 Adair wrote,
"Hamilton's research consisted in superficially extracting bits of
a speech of Demosthenes and a hasty reading of Plutarch"
(*Fame*, 62). He knew better later. Hamilton shows a theoretical
approach that came from deep study of Hume as well as Montesquieu. It should be remembered that Hume thought political
science had made its "greatest advances towards perfection" in
showing the way for "civilized monarchies" (2.12.161). Hamilton
must have remembered that when, in The Federalist, he had to
list the other scientific advances without mentioning monarchy:

The science of politics, however, like most other sciences, has received great improvement. The efficacy of various principles is now
well understood, which were either not known at all, or imperfectly
known to the ancients. The regular distribution of power into distinct departments—the introduction of legislative ballances and
checks—the institution of courts composed of judges holding their
offices during good behaviour—the representation of the people in
the legislature by deputies of their own election—these are either

wholly new discoveries or have made their principal progress towards perfection in modern times (9.51).

As Adair himself noted, that Federalist paper was taken from the material Hamilton had worked up for his June 18 speech (diss., 138–9). But at the Convention he called the new *monarchy* a product of advances in political science, while in No. 9 he must end his list with the new science of *representation*—which had failed to convince him when Madison presented it on the floor of the Convention (Farrand, 1.141–7).

This returns us to the problem of Hamilton's "hypocrisy." Can we take seriously anything he says in The Federalist after studying his earlier views (from the June 18 speech), where he rejected Madison's principal point from No. 10? Admittedly, Hamilton will himself repeat and endorse the Madisonian argument. But was this for mere propaganda purposes?

There are a number of things to be considered before we dismiss Hamilton's claim to "candour" in The Federalist.

First, he offered his June 18 plan specifically as "not attainable by us." Some people argue that *that* statement is mere sugarcoating, that the plan was offered for actual adoption. They will not let Hamilton be sincere in *either* place, not in The Federalist nor even in his June 18 speech. But the parallel with Hume's offer of an "idea" to be approximated only gradually, if at all, indicates that Hamilton meant it when he said that his model was unattainable. The very thoroughness, the exhaustive nature, of his long analysis suggests that he was living up to the Humean ideal of impartial and scientific inquiry. The speech was offered as a theoretical prelude to practical action, not as a practical plan itself. If that is the case, then there is no contradiction between offering the model and arguing for the best approximation available.

Second, Hamilton thought Madison's scheme of representation useful, as far as it went, but insufficient for reaching disinterested legislation (see Chapter Thirty-one). Once again, he could support the partial measure once the "perfect" was, almost by definition, excluded from his range of options.

Third, the Philadelphia draft did not exist when Hamilton argued against both the Virginia and the New Jersey plans. Nor had Hamilton experienced the opposition to even this mild constitution (mild by his standards) in New York and other places. His view of what was realizable was bound to be more thoroughly informed by the time he wrote with Madison as Publius.

Fourth, there is no way to exclude absolutely the possibility of real changes of mind between his speech and the composition of The Federalist. He states the argument of No. 10 very forcibly himself. There is always the possibility that he convinced himself, or came to be convinced; especially since Madison's argument came from Hamilton's own favorite source, Hume's *Essays*.

Fifth, the argument about Hamilton's intention or sincerity tends to skew from the outset the way we read what he actually wrote. Adair's dissertation was a perfect example of this, as he came to realize; and a growing respect made him take more seriously what Hamilton wrote in both places, in his June 18 outline *and* in The Federalist. Adair offers us an example of a way to read adequately by shedding prior assumptions.

Sixth, the very stereotypes of Hamilton and Madison are misleading, as I have tried to indicate in the opening parts of this book. Unless we confront these stereotypes at the outset, we are liable to misread, to build on false impressions, as has so often happened with commentary on The Federalist. So, having undergone the preliminary discipline of examining the stock views of Madison and Hamilton, I suggest we turn to the papers written by Publius with the "candour" called for in the essays themselves. What is the constitutional doctrine enunciated there, apart from later writings of Madison and Hamilton, apart from our prior views on them, apart from "interest" or "bias"? Essays that issue a call for the disinterested statesman should be approached, as far as that is possible, by disinterested readers.

PART THREE

CHECKS AND BALANCES (No. 51)

ELEVEN

Mixed Government

> All reasonable men agree in general to preserve our
> mixed government.
>
> —Hume, 1.9.134

The framers of the Constitution were heirs to two centuries of
intense debate over the nature of constitutional government.
That debate had become, by their time, almost equally creative
and confusing. Men had borrowed their enemies' arguments,
added new ones, conflated old ones. They creatively misunderstood or mistakenly expounded each other. Much of the modern scholarship in this area has been a labor of disentanglement.
It is a labor we cannot avoid; avoiding it has scrambled even the
best criticisms of The Federalist (e.g., that of Robert Dahl).

In the eighteenth century, constitutional doctrines came in
clusters. Ideas bunched or overlapped, so close as to be misunderstood for one another. The main cluster we must deal with
had three components: mixed government, separation of powers,
and balanced government. When we have sorted these out, we
must study their relationship with three other ideas that sometimes formed a cluster: sovereignty, legislative supremacy, and
direct democracy.

I begin with mixed government—which, though the oldest of
these constitutional concepts, was the one least important to
Publius. It must be looked at, mainly, to keep it distinct from
ideas that matter more. The framers were bound to use the language of this doctrine; it was the most widespread constitutional
theory in antiquity (see F. W. Walbank, A Historical Commentary on Polybius, 639–41). Its broad appeal came from the fact
that it combined so many concerns of the ancient philosophers,
including these three:

1. The Platonic interest in mathematics as a discipline for thought and life. Government was looked at as a variation on the problem of the one and the many. How does a society achieve unity in multiplicity? The two must communicate with each other through an intermediary—the few. In political typology, the one became monarchy, the few aristocracy, and the many democracy.

2. The Aristotelian interest in virtue as a stable median or mean (*mesotēs*). While, on either side of a seesaw, extremes widely fluctuate, the point of leverage is still. In social terms, stability comes from the meeting of the three types, each in its moderate form, through a further compromise that becomes a "mean of means," a *medium mediorum* (*Politics*, 1293–6—where, however, Aristotle is dealing with the blend of only *two* moderate forms, aristocracy and democracy).

3. The Pythagorean interest in harmony. The "blend" in the few cannot exclude either the one or the many. It must be what Thucydides calls, in his description of the mixed constitution, a "blend with degrees" (*metria xungkrasis*, 8.97.2), a chemical *mixture* which does not become a uniform *solution*. The model for this was the mathematics of harmony, bringing union out of all the strings, highest and lowest—what Cicero would call social *concordia* (cf. Aristotle, *Politics*, 1290.19–29).

The briefest, most influential combination of these themes in the surviving literature comes from the second century B.C.—from Book Six of the *Histories* of Polybius. In Polybius, the three simple forms are unstable—even the middle form, by far the best of the three—because they move with an inherent bias from one extreme (the pure principle) to its opposing caricature: kingship (*basileia*) moves to single dominion (*monarchia*), as control becomes mere willfulness; aristocracy moves to oligarchy, as the few become exclusive rather than intermediary; democracy moves to ochlocracy, as multiple needs become mere endless demands (6.4). The degenerations of each form are inevitable singly, and they make each form cycle inevitably into another, in fixed sequence.

But a partial arrest of the cycle, a shorter or longer escape from its pressures, can be achieved by combining the three, making each less pure (one extreme) by an inoculation against that very purity's tendency to go *beyond* itself *against* itself. Since the degenerating forms slide off in different directions, their innate biases can become mutually correcting. If kingship is opposed to democracy, single dominion is even more opposed to ochlocracy. Opposite willfulnesses may pull each other back (*antispan* in Polybius) from their respective abysses. Virtues compromise themselves, so that vice may counter vice within each system. Polybius "internalizes" in the state the idea that peril can be constructive. Compare Aristotle, *Politics*, 1308a25: "Some states are kept safe, not by distance from what might destroy them, but by proximity—apprehension makes all support the state." For Polybius' transition from external peril to constitutive internal threats, see *Histories*, 6.18.

Polybius puts this self-correcting process in terms of the constant adjustment of weights on a scale's arms. The constitution of Lycurgus is praised for arranging its constituent forms

> so that none, exceeding its own norm, might veer toward its own perversion; but each power, pulling the other back, might keep the balance from sinking much to either side; and the state might for a long time maintain equilibrium precisely by antipathies (*Histories*, 6.10.7—"precisely by antipathies" translates Reiske's reading, *kata ton tēs antipathias logon;* see Walbank, *Commentary*, 661).

In the later course of Western thought, this would prove the most influential early statement of the ideal of *balanced* government. We should isolate its characteristics from the outset.

The mixed theory does not, of itself, look to the ideal state, the best one, but to the best *possible*. Polybius expressly says that only the few are capable of grasping the meaning of Justice (6.10.9); but they must compromise with the one and the many, lest they be overruled by the former or overpowered by the latter. The goal is stability, through placation of contending interests.

A corollary of this first point is that the mixed state has no institutions peculiar to it. Its structure will vary from state to state as the particular society's interests dictate. All that the theory demands is that each of the three main interests have a voice in the government. In Polybius' idealized version of the Roman constitution (6.11–18), the voice of the one is the double consulate; that of the few is the senate; and that of the many is the populace. But this is not a necessary arrangement; different societies could channel the influence in different ways, so long as they are all present and properly vigorous. Indeed, Polybius notes that the Roman constitution assembled itself, without plan, to meet particular crises (*Histories*, 6.10.14); and it will be noted that its "one" is actually two—the consuls.

If the three interests have no institutions proper to them, still less do they have specific governmental functions to call their own. Aristotle had described the main functions of government as legislative, executive, and judicial (*Politics*, 1297b37–1298a3), but he did not correlate these three *functions* with the three *interests*. The one, for instance, does not specialize in legislating, executing, or judging. Neither does the few, nor the many. In Polybius' account of the Roman government, each of the three interests, acting through its own organ, performs acts we would call legislative *and* executive *and* judicial (*Histories*, 6.12–14).

Thus mixed government is not only different from the later concept of separated powers; it is at odds with it. The ideal of mixed government is harmonic fusion, not division. One distinct function does not "check" another equally distinct function. Rather, all the interests should "have a say" on all the issues.

Without such functional checks, how does the counterbalancing take place, the very thing that gives mixed government its equilibrium? Polybius has a rich language for the process of hindering (*blaptein*), preventing (*kōluein*), opposing (*antiprattein*), tripping up (*parapodizein*). There is a similar range of *cooperative* actions available to each interest—taking into account (*stochazesthai*), helping (*ophelein*), advising (*noun prosechein*), agreeing (*symphronein*), so as to add weight to another interest on the scale (by a *rhopē* or *prosklisis*). The range of actions runs from nonsupport, through passive resistance, to active resistance, producing in each component a generalized fear (*phobos*) of what the other interests might do. Since the interests are not limited to specific functions in the government, the spectrum of penalties embraces not merely constitutional or court remedies, but every form of social pressure that shames, ostracizes, isolates, criticizes or penalizes in general. Indeed, in the Lycurgan constitution, the king is considered the *weakest* member since he is most bound to formal *procedures* (6.10.10). But, since all the interests must concur on all measures, all are vulnerable on measures that matter to them most.

The very thing that distinguishes mixed government from a scheme of separated powers makes some modern scholars consider separation unnecessary. The "real" inhibitions on action do not arise from paper divisions in the scheme of government but from the entire arsenal of social pressures that affect human action. We see this in Dahl's criticism of Federalist 10. Granted a conflict of interests, the interests will mobilize themselves. They do not wait to be sorted out in terms of constitutional functions. Thus, having mobilized class interest, Madison brings in separated powers too late, too irrelevantly to control these interests. In Dahl's eyes, as in Polybius', the interests must be made to control each other.

Thus, for some people, the oldest constitutional concept is still the most adequate. Later additions, like separation of powers, are a mere distraction at best. With Polybius on his side, who needs Montesquieu? In 1942 E. E. Schattschneider voiced this criticism in his *Party Government:* "If the multiplicity of interests in a large republic makes tyrannical majorities impossible, the principal theoretical prop of the separation of powers has been demolished" (9). This was the critique James MacGregor Burns would make in 1963: "If, as Madison said, the first great protection against naked majority rule was the broader diversity of interests in a larger republic and hence the greater difficulty of concerting their 'plans of oppression,' why was this not enough?" (*Deadlock,* 21).

These criticisms from recent decades explain the resurgence, at the same time, of Calhoun's constitutional theory of "concurrent majorities." That was a mixed-government scheme in the Polybian sense; and it, too, made the separation of powers irrelevant. For Calhoun, the real divisions in society were geographic and economic, not procedural. For him, as for Polybius, all the major interests should have a mutual veto, so that every measure passed will have the support of every interest. The stress on *economic* stakes made some call Calhoun "the Marx of the propertied class." He offered the modern world an economic reading of the Constitution—one that seemed less tendentious than Beard's because divorced, now, from the occasion of its invention (the defense of slavery). The description of a government by multiple contending pressures seemed not only truer to the Polybian scheme but also to observed reality and the American experience. But Calhoun needed updating and a modern empirical base—whence Dahl's own theory of "polyarchy," the latest variation on Polybius.

It is not surprising that the best use of a contending-pressures analysis to criticize Madison is Dahl's, in the *Preface to Democratic Theory*. This passage is important enough to quote at length:

> Why is the separation of powers necessary to prevent tyranny? Because it provides an external check on the tyrannical impulses of officials. Why does it provide an external check? Because it guarantees that the ambitions of individuals in one department will counteract those in another. Why will these countervailing ambitions be effective? Presumably because individuals in one department can invoke the threat of rewards and penalties against tyrannical individuals in another department. What then are those rewards and penalties?
>
> Here we come to the core of the question. Presumably they are not such things as loss of status, respect, prestige and friendship—unless it be argued that the mere fact of constitutional prescription will itself convey legitimacy and illegitimacy to certain actions; that officials who undertake illegitimate actions will suffer loss of status, respect, prestige, and friendship; and that these penalties are sufficient to prevent tyranny. But certainly this is not Madison's argument. [And, we might add, the *automatic* loss of prestige, etc., would make unnecessary any balancing force to *inflict* the loss.] Nor can the rewards and penalties depend on money, for the Constitution was contrived to restrict this means of control, lest the legislature become all-powerful.
>
> Do the rewards and penalties then involve the threat of physical coercion? In this category might be impeachment and conviction, and use of the armed forces. But in this case, a republic must always be on the verge of violence and civil war; for if physical coercion is the central restraint on tyranny, and if tyranny is the basic danger the argument assumes it to be, then the threat of physical coercion and therefore of violence can never be far removed from the operation of politics. Furthermore, if the main restraint is the

threat of physical coercion, why would the leaders of a majority ever refrain from tyrannizing over a minority—at least if the majority were thought to be physically more powerful than the minority? Taking a more modern look at the way in which coercive control is distributed, why would a minority with control over the instruments of violence and coercion refrain from tyrannizing over a majority?

The fact is that in some nations powerful minorities have not refrained and tyranny has resulted; yet in other nations they have refrained. And whether or not powerful minorities or mass-based dictatorial leaders have refrained from establishing tyranny is clearly not related to the presence or absence of constitutional separation of powers. Many variables are involved in such a situation, but the constitutional separation of powers cannot be established as one of them.

Thus the Madisonian style of argument provides no satisfactory answer to the fundamental questions it raises. Madison evidently had in mind a basic concept, namely, that of reciprocal control among leaders. But in several ways, the Madisonian argument is inadequate:

1. It does not show, and I think cannot be used to show, that reciprocal control among leaders, sufficient to prevent tyranny, requires constitutionally prescribed separation of powers, as in the American Constitution.

2. Either the significance of constitutional prescription as an external check is exaggerated or the argument misunderstands the psychological realities implied by the concept of a check on, or control over, behavior. And the inferences from either type of incorrect premise to propositions about political behavior or the requisites of a non-tyrannical democracy are false.

3. The Madisonian argument exaggerates the importance, in preventing tyranny, of specified checks to governmental officials by other specified officials; it underestimates the importance of the inherent social checks and balances existing in every pluralistic society. Without these social checks and balances, it is doubtful that the intragovernmental checks on officials would in fact operate to prevent tyranny; with them, it is doubtful that all of the intragovernmental checks of the Madisonian system as it operates in the United States are necessary to prevent tyranny (20–2).

I said earlier that Dahl is unanswerable if you accept his assumptions. The key assumption here is that Madison is working, at least in part, from a theory of mixed government. That, we are to suppose, explains his emphasis on checks in the first place, despite the fact that such an emphasis fits ill (or not at all) with the separated-powers theory.

But Dahl's assumption, understandable in itself and widespread among his colleagues, is erroneous. Madison does not work from a theory of mixed government in The Federalist—which means that he does not appeal to "external checks" in the way Dahl supposes. One might have guessed this simply from the wording of one famous sentence in No. 10: "In the extent and proper structure of the Union, therefore, we behold a Republican remedy for the diseases most incident to Republican Government" (65). According to mixed-government theory, republican diseases are countered by the action of *other* principles (kingly or aristocratic). Polybius expressly says that the interplay of *different* interests, each corrected *by the others*, enables the "government as a whole to provide its own remedy for its own diseases" (6.18.5–7).

I admit, at the outset, that my own claim is not only unusual but unlikely on the face of it. How could Madison, in a century that rang with mixed-government arguments, have escaped that theory entirely? Didn't Hume say, in effect, that "we are all mixed-governmenters now"? Hamilton himself had used the theory in his speech before the Philadelphia Convention. Besides, we have been taught by recent scholars that the Constitution finds its proper background in the Country ideology of opposition in England; and mixed government was a vital part of that ideology—the ministry was accused of upsetting tripartite balance in the British constitution.

Yet Polybian theory, in anything like its original form, was denied both Madison and Hamilton if they were going to make their campaign for the *Philadelphia* draft persuasive. Both men constantly refer their argument to the "republican genius" of the American people. Monarchical and aristocratic principles were not to be introduced in the American scheme, even as partial or balancing factors. Thus, when Madison says the governmental functions should not be concentrated in the same hands "whether of one, a few or many" (47.324), he is not saying that the American Constitution took any steps to keep these interests

apart. His "definition" in this place is traditional and exhaustive
—he includes other things not applicable to America ("whether
hereditary, self-appointed, or elective") to cover all conditions.
There *were* no constitutional organs for the one or the few in
America, no legal power all their own to be checked.

The Senate, for instance, was not to speak for a separate interest in the class or economic sense. In England, the House of
Lords was supposed to speak for the few, but Hamilton denies
that the American Senate has any aristocratic "countenance" at
all (66.446). Admittedly, representation in the Senate was by
state; but the state interest is not separable from that of its people, represented proportionally in the House of Representatives.
(In fact, Madison wanted representation in the Senate to be proportional as well—equal representation was a compromise not
based on theory but on the practical difficulty of forming the
union: 62.416–17). Senators are given longer tenure and a higher
age requirement, not to express an interest different from that of
the citizens represented in the House, but to impart a different
quality to the government—stability and continuity of policy
(62.420–2), especially in foreign affairs (63.422–4), where nations might fear engagement with a government of ephemeral
commitments.

Madison therefore contrasts the American Senate with those of
antiquity. The latter, meant to blend different interests, are "repugnant to the genius of America" (63.426), while the former
enables Congress as a whole to "blend stability with liberty"
(ibid.). The interest of the Senate is exactly the same as that of
the House—the welfare of the people. Madison even says that the
Senate protects the people *from* "the enterprising and the mon-
eyed few" (62.421), who could take advantage of instability to
speculate and accumulate (as Madison had tried to do himself in
1786; cf. *JM*, 9.98, 106, 138–41). In America, difference of function is not a difference of interest, as in the mixed theory of the
British constitution.

Madison takes no part in the papers devoted to the executive
branch; but he could not have been more emphatic than Hamilton in denying any kingly interest in the office (67.452–3;
69.462–70). For Hamilton, too, the American branches of government give us no blend of *different* interests but "a government

wholly and purely republican" (73.497). Hamilton certainly meant this when describing the Philadelphia draft; it was precisely his *criticism* of the Virginia Plan at Philadelphia that it did not have the elements for mixed government: "A democratic assembly is to be checked by a democratic senate, and both these by a democratic chief magistrate" (*AH*, 4.186). In fact, without a hereditary royalty and peerage, it is hard to imagine how America could have invented a mixed government, even had people been willing to. This problem beset not only Hamilton and John Adams but the Jefferson of 1781, who criticized the Virginia constitution for providing a separate chamber of the legislature without any separate interest to voice (*Notes on Virginia*, Query XIII).

It might seem that mixed theory was bound to "sneak" into America's Constitution insofar as King-Lords-Commons (thought to represent the one, few, and many) became the model for President-Senate-House. But Madison and Hamilton never use the British model to indicate different social or economic *interests* in the American scheme. In fact, they rarely use that scheme at all, despite the great authority of Montesquieu, who made it his ideal (47.324–5). Madison, in fact, argues that the House of Lords no longer voiced a strong and different interest, even in England (63.430). He means to allay the fear that an American Senate, more republican in its makeup, would speak for interest. Hamilton admits that the Constitution's impeachment scheme is taken from the British example of indictment by the lower house, conviction by the upper house (65.440–1). But, whatever his own feelings about the British constitution, he does not offer this procedure as ideal, or as based on any constitutional theory at all. He concedes that an entirely independent tribunal might be better in itself, apart from expense and cumbrousness (65.443–4). The use of Congress is just a matter of convenience, not of theoretical propriety. In The Federalist, Hamilton no more than Madison tried to approximate the American executive and legislative branches to the British plan. This reticence is not observed merely for propaganda reasons. As Vile notes (126–9), the British model corresponded with American colonial governments by governor-council-assembly. That was a professedly "mixed-government" scheme—a point the young Hamilton made *against* "the Farmer" in 1775 (*AH*, 1.101). The Constitution, by contrast, forswore Polybius.

Of course, it is not enough to say that The Federalist is not based on a Polybian scheme in the strict sense, where the clash of interests must include *kingship,* so repugnant to post-Revolutionary America. What about contending interests in the broader sense—Calhoun's sense, for instance, or Dahl's? It is the criticism of Schattschneider and Burns that Madison first recognized the broad clash of interests in an extended republic, then *superadded* a check of "separated powers." After contending interests have reached equilibrium, separated powers are brought in to produce deadlock.

Dahl thinks Madison believed, for some odd reason, that the "real" social checks would mesh with or reinforce the theoretical divisions of government. That is why Dahl assumes that "mixed-government" checks still played some role in Madison's thought. Before we can challenge that assumption head on, it is necessary to see what "separated powers" meant to Madison.

TWELVE

Separated Powers

Of all men, that distinguish themselves by memorable atchievements, the first place of honour seems due to LEGISLATORS and founders of states, who transmit a system of laws and institutions to secure the peace, happiness, and liberty of future generations.

—Hume, 1.8.127

The two revolutions in seventeenth-century England led to intense speculation on constitutional matters. The inherited and threefold scheme of differing *interests* (King-Lords-Commons) was made, however imperfectly, to mesh with a newer and twofold doctrine of separate governmental *functions* (executive and legislative). Aristotle's judicial function had to be left out at first, for several reasons. According to ancient theory, the whole government had a judicial function, as applying natural law to society, adjusting man's law to God's (Vile, 30, 59). Besides, King and Parliament both had judicial functions. And, finally, the English jury system was left outside the government proper, the sovereignty of "King in Parliament."

Still, the meshing effort went on, continually baffled by the fact that "three into two won't go." One attempt at balance came from Locke's *Second Treatise* (145-8). While Parliament has two branches with one function, Locke argued, the King has two functions in one branch: He holds the treaty power (federative) for dealing with other nations, and the executive power for enforcing laws at home. Montesquieu adapted this pattern to Aristotle's three functions by calling the federative power *executive* and the internal application of the laws *judicial* (*Esprit*, 11.6.1–2). Both French and English theorists had difficulty separating *functions* in a neat scheme because their inherited structures had, for so long, been explained in terms of mixed government's different *interests*. Only the Americans, given a comparatively clean slate, could make the triple division of functions a clean and inclusive one (Gwyn, 125).

Most of the scholarly work done on separated powers has traced the intricate development of the concept, a development just hinted at in the last few paragraphs. But there has been a general assumption that the doctrine struggling toward full articulation was *one* doctrine. That is why M. J. C. Vile begins his book, *Constitutionalism and the Separation of Powers* (1967), with a statement of "the" doctrine in its pure form, then judges all examples of it by their approximation to this ideal (14–18). This approach has its taxonomic conveniences; but it tends to reinforce the general view that there is only one legitimate doctrine of separated powers.

W. B. Gwyn offers us the beginning of wisdom in this matter when he argues that what comes before us with a single name is actually a *multiplicity* of theories. That is: Not only does separation cluster with other things like mixed government and checks-balances. It is *itself* a cluster of concepts that have to be distinguished. Thinkers cannot be ranked by their approximation to Vile's pure norm, since different men had different concepts in mind when they talked of separated powers.

The two most easily distinguishable forms of separation theory are probably the most distant from each other in time as well as meaning. Gwyn argues that the efficiency theory arose first and the checking theory last. The argument from efficiency could be made without hindrance because it did not have to adjust itself to mixed-government theory. It was simply an administrative judgment, leading to division of labor—how should the functions of government be divided up by ministers in order to get things done? This was a view congenial to Hamilton's managerial approach.

Yet Madison was no less firm in holding to an efficiency justification for separated powers (see Louis Fisher, *Am. Stud.* 2.127–9). After all, Madison's long labor to strengthen the Articles, to draft and pass the Constitution was fueled by apprehensions over the *in*efficiency of the Confederation. The Continental Congress had monopolized the few federal powers granted by the Articles, making an energetic executive impossible. So the efficiency argument for separated powers has a certain priority in America as well as England.

It is true that fear of concentrated power made Madison and others stress a complementary aspect of separation: If division of labor makes for swifter performance of the subdivided task, it also guarantees that all power shall not be concentrated in the same hands. Madison and Hamilton both dwell on this latter consideration when making their "pitch" for the Constitution. But both were willing to depart from the pure doctrine of separated powers when efficiency or convenience demanded (see Madison at 51.348; Hamilton at 65.443–4).

Ideally, division of labor and separation of control should complement each other, both using the same means (distinction of governmental functions in divided agencies with different personnel) for their different ends. But however different the ends, they must at times compete for disposition of some shared means. In the efficiency theory, each department looks primarily outward, to the task assigned it. In the checking theory, each looks around at the others in a kind of monitoring role. The fact that the two concepts are potentially at odds is readily established: In order to stress the one, Supreme Court justices have denied the other. In 1926 Justice Louis Brandeis wrote (*Meyers* v. *United States*): "The doctrine of the separation of powers was adopted by the Convention of 1787, not to promote efficiency, but to preclude the exercise of arbitrary power." Chief Justice Earl Warren repeated this view in 1965 (*United States* v. *Brown*), declaring that separation of powers was "obviously not instituted with the idea that it would promote governmental efficiency."

Where did the justices get this view? Not from the Constitution itself, which does not even mention the theory of separated powers, much less spell out the particular form of that theory being endorsed. (A number of states tried, unsuccessfully, to include separation doctrine in the Bill of Rights). Did the judges find their argument in the constitutional debates or The Federalist? Yet both of these use the efficiency argument (see, e.g., Farrand, 1.70, 138; Federalist 70, 471–80). Did the judges look to other writings of the framers or the founders? Yet

Louis Fisher has shown that those writings are filled with the efficiency argument (113-31). We see, then, the consequence of assuming that separation of powers is a single doctrine. By thinking it can have only one authentic form, the justices in question ruled out another form for which there is abundant evidence in every relevant authority.

An error similar to that of the justices can be observed in Dahl's treatment of Madison's "definition" of tyranny in No. 47. Dahl thinks Madison is discussing one form of separation theory while he is actually discussing another. Here are Madison's words:

> The accumulation of all power legislative, executive and judiciary in the same hands, whether of one, a few or many and whether hereditary, self appointed, or elective, may justly be pronounced the very definition of tyranny (47.324).

Dahl says: "As it stands, Madison's explicit definition is unnecessarily arbitrary and argumentative" (*Preface*, 6). It is not empirically verifiable. In fact, it is not even a definition. It states one condition for the realization of tyranny, but that condition is neither necessary nor sufficient. In order to make even minimal sense of Madison before criticizing him, Dahl feels he must recast what is "savable" from Madison's definition as a probability statement:

> The probability that any given individual or group will tyrannize over others if unrestrained by external checks is sufficiently high so that if tyranny is to be avoided over a long period, the constitutionally prescribed machinery of any government must maintain some external checks on all officials (ibid., 19).

It is clear from the language Dahl puts in Madison's mouth that he thinks his author was using the checks-and-balances theory of separation. But was he? If he was not, then Dahl's strictures may be as misguided as Justice Brandeis's statement on *the* doctrine of separation as excluding efficiency.

In order to "save" Madison, at least in part, Dahl recasts his sentence in terms of a testable modern hypothesis. A better way to save him would be to understand him in the context of his own time. In those terms, there are many authors needing rescue, not just Madison. For he was repeating a maxim widely quoted and adhered to in the period of constitutional theorizing. Gwyn studies some of these statements, and we might add others. Early forms of the maxim precede the time when the judiciary was treated as a separate function of government—for example, Marchamont Nedham's statement of 1656: "A fifth Errour in Policy hath been this, *viz.* a permitting of the Legislative and Executive Powers of a State, to rest in one and the same hands and persons" (Gwyn, 131). Or they come from the time when the executive power was treated as judicial—for example, Charles Dallison writing in 1648: "Whilst the Supremacy, the Power to Judge the Law, and the Authority to make new Lawes, are kept in severall hands, the known Law is preserved, but united it is vanished, instantly thereupon, and Arbitrary and Tyrannicall power is introduced" (*The Royalists Defence*).

The main source of separation theory for Americans was, as Madison tells us, the celebrated Montesquieu, "the oracle who is always consulted and cited on this subject" (47.324). And Montesquieu, that Anglophile, drew some of his inspiration from Locke's *Second Treatise*, where we read: "If the three powers are united, the government will be absolute, whether these powers are in the hands of one or a large number" (par. 201). Madison quotes (47.325) Montesquieu's versions of the maxim from *Esprit* (11.6.4–5). He also quotes Jefferson's statement of it in the *Notes on Virginia:* "The concentrating these [powers] in the same hands is precisely the definition of despotic government" (48.335). Finally, there is Madison's fellow author of The Federalist, joining his voice to the chorus by citing Montesquieu: "For I agree that 'there is no liberty, if the power of judging be not separated from the legislative and executive powers'" (78.523).

There we have the *definition* again. If, as Dahl says, Madison's definition is "unnecessarily arbitrary and argumentative," the malady seems to have been catching in his time. Madison's words had a long and honorable ancestry, and Gwyn shows us that they did not arise in the context of checks and balances, but in what Gwyn calls the "rule of law" context. The doctrine Madison repeats was not meant to address the practical problem of keeping powers limited and separate but to see why, in theory, the very legitimacy of a regime depends on their separation. It does not speak to matters of fact but moves in the order of right.

We can see this in the brief statement already quoted from Dallison, who says that union of legislative and judicial powers means that the known law is "vanished, instantly thereupon, and Arbitrary and Tyrannicall power is introduced." He is obviously not claiming that all nontyrannical *acts* vanish instantly. It is the *right* to command that disappears. How the ruler acts thenceforth, whether clemently or cruelly, is irrelevant to the question being addressed in this part of constitutional theory, which inquires after the right to issue any kind of legal command.

Theorists of the seventeenth and eighteenth centuries could not escape Harrington's challenge to erect a government of laws and not of men. Most pointedly, they had to reconcile the "modern" theory of sovereignty with the task of limiting—in England, even of deposing, of beheading—the sovereign. Jean Bodin himself, who taught Europe to consider sovereignty indivisible and unalienable, had said the king must be subject to divine and fundamental law; but he left no human machinery for holding the king accountable.

The seventeenth century found the means of making the sovereign accountable by separating his sovereign power of general legislation from his power to apply the law in judicial particulars, especially the particulars that touched his person and performance. Gwyn shows that both Locke (70) and Montesquieu (104–5) were primarily concerned with this question of the *right* to rule rather than the practical problem of maintaining the separation on which this right is based.

So Madison's statement does define a condition of *legitimacy*. It is not a hypothesis to be verified empirically. He says himself that mere constitutional separation (as in Pennsylvania's constitution) is not sufficient to maintain separation in practice; for that, other measures must be taken (48.336–8). All he claims in his general definition—so general as to touch matters irrelevant to America, like hereditary office, self-appointment, the one and the few—is that legitimacy of reign depends on accountability of the ruler. This was an ancient constitutional teaching already acquired by Hamilton in his twentieth year: "When any people are ruled by laws, in framing which, they have no part, that are to bind them, to all intents and purposes, without, in the same manner, binding the legislators themselves, they are in the strictest sense slaves, and the government with respect to them, is despotic" (*AH*, 1.100).

A frequent way of putting the doctrine of accountability is to say, as Madison does in No. 10, that "no man is allowed to be a judge in his own cause"; no people (not even kings) are fit "to be both judges and parties, at the same time" (10.59; cf. *JM*, 10.213). Jefferson invoked this doctrine in his address to George III: "You are surrounded by British counsellors, but remember that they are parties [to the dispute]" (*TJ*, 1.134). This maxim against judging in one's own case derives from long theorizing on legitimacy of rule (Gwyn, 6-7). Thus, Dahl reduces Madison to absurdity by mistaking the very subject of his discussion. In No. 47 Madison is discussing the Constitution's doctrine of legitimacy, a matter of great concern to legal theorists in the various ratifying conventions. He is defending the Philadelphia draft from objections raised in terms of a pure theory, supposedly derived from Montesquieu (47.324-5). Only in Nos. 48-51 does he take up the practical problem of *maintaining* constitutional separation—and there he says one must go *beyond* theoretical divisions to auxiliary considerations. So he is not quibbling when, in No. 47, he says that the doctrine of legitimacy does not depend on total separation of departments (impossible in any case), but on the minimum needed for accountability of men to the law. He is talking of the essentials of legitimacy, not of practical arrangements, when he writes: "Where the *whole* power of one department is exercized by the same hands which possess the whole power of another department, the fundamental principles of a free constitution, are subverted" (47.325-6; contrast this with the discussion of practical reasons for breaching separation at 51.348).

Gwyn finds three separate strands of thought in "legitimacy" arguments for separation—the rule of law (giving avenues of appeal to the subject), the impartiality argument (not allowing the legislator to be party in his own cause), and the consideration of a common interest (not letting a single interest speak for the whole). These are useful for considering the subtleties of seven-

teenth-century debate; but they can all be treated, for our purposes, as corollaries of the argument over *right* to rule. As such,
they are clearly distinguishable from the *efficiency* argument for
separation of powers. More important, because less recognized,
they are also distinct from the *balancing* argument for separation.

Not only do the legitimacy and the efficiency doctrines look to
different spheres—the order of right and the order of fact, of
theory and of practice; they can be, and have been, held in isola-
tion from each other. Vile agrees with Gwyn on this point; he
considers checks and balances an addendum to, or modification
of, his pure theory (18–19). One can profess the rule-of-law separation without adopting checks and balances; Madison attacks
the Pennsylvania constitution for doing just that (48.336–8). One
can, as well, hold to a scheme of checks and balances without
admitting the theory of separated powers; Polybian mixed government did that, as we have seen. To read one in place of the
other leads to confusion, to charges like Dahl's against Madison,
and to ineffectual attempts to answer Dahl—see, for instance,
Vile, 303–13; and George Carey, *Am. Pol. Sci. Rev.* 1978, 152–6.
Both Vile and Carey argue with Dahl, yet fail to challenge his
assumption that Madison was offering an empirical hypothesis
for verification. They urge that the statement might be partially
verified (in conjunction with other things according to Vile, by
distinguishing government from society according to Carey); but
this merely continues the first confusion. Dahl argues too well
from his assumptions to make him vulnerable anywhere but on
those assumptions.

Nowhere is this more evident than in the way Dahl assumed
that Madison's legitimacy doctrine was, in fact, a doctrine of balancing by "checks." It is time to proceed to this latter subject.
But first let me restate Madison's legitimacy doctrine as advanced throughout No. 47. If men are to be accountable to law,
rather than vice versa, there must be a distinction between the
power of general legislation and the power of particular application (especially in adjudication). Without that distinction, men
may be governed ill or well, but they will not be governed legiti-
mately, by officers who have a *right* to compel others with the

powers of the state. Now, one can agree or not with this legitimacy theory of separated powers; argue with it or not. But to do that one must first take the time to understand it; and Dahl did not.

*

THIRTEEN

Checks

Honour is a great check upon mankind.
                                    —Hume, 1.6.119

We have distinguished, so far, three forms of separated-power theory—the efficiency, the legitimacy, and the balancing arguments for separation. Even if one admits that the last two are separable, their juncture still might seem natural, if not inevitable. How preserve the theoretical separation without practical checks? It is understandable that, in discussion of the Constitution, people tend to conflate the two doctrines. Indeed, as interest in constitutional theory has cooled over the years, we now subsume the theoretical argument in the practical one, leading some to claim that a system of "checks and balances" is the whole secret of our government.

It may surprise some that Madison did not see things that way. For him the characteristic and original thing about the Constitution was not its use of checks and balances—an old concept borrowed from mixed-government theory—but its new concept of representation (see Chapter Twenty-six). It may also be surprising that the conjunction of the very terms "check" and "balance" occurs only once in The Federalist, and there it is *distinguished* from the separation of powers. In No. 9 Hamilton gives us a list of modern innovations in government, beginning with these two: "The regular distribution of power into distinct departments—the introduction of legislative ballances and checks" (9.51). The *legislative* balances are *within* one of the separated powers—Hamilton is referring to bicameralism.

Nor are the terms, taken separately, used very often in The Federalist. Madison, so far as I remember, never used the term "balance" to describe a constitutional principle in The Federalist. When Hamilton uses balance, he is sometimes referring to the balance of power between nations (11.68; see Hume's essay on that subject [2.7]), or of trade (11.72; Hume's subject at 2.5), or of taxes (21.134). He does use it for the general balance of government (the language of mixed government), expressly citing Hume (85.594) from "The Rise of the Arts and Sciences":

> To balance a large state or society, whether monarchical or republican, on general laws, is a work of so great difficulty, that no human genius, however comprehensive, is able, by the mere dint of reason and reflection, to effect it. The judgments of many must unite in this work: Experience must guide their labour: Time must bring it to perfection: And the feeling of inconveniencies must correct the mistakes, which they inevitably fall into, in their first trials and experiments (1.14.185; cf. Federalist 71.484).

The term "check" is used a little more frequently, but hardly more technically than is "balance." It was a popular word in many contexts—Hume's "honour is a check," for instance. Hamilton talks of general checks on violence at 21.131. Madison says periodic reviews might check misconduct (53.365). In the famous No. 10, Madison uses check only once—to say that in a pure democracy nothing can check a majority (10.61). In the second most famous paper used to discuss checks and balances, Madison again uses the former term just once—to describe the general way office can check office (51.349) as a preface to his argument that such a mutual check will not work for the Constitution's separated powers, since they are not equally powerful (51.350). He only uses check to describe a specific constitutional operation twice, and neither reference is to the separated powers; like Hamilton at 9.51, he uses it of the bicameral check *within* the legislative department (62.418, 63.425).

Hamilton's use of the word "check" is only slightly more extensive than Madison's. Once he uses it *pejoratively*, to speak of the states "deadlocking" each other under the Articles (11.68), a situation that could be remedied by federal power to check *them* (28.179). Unlike Madison, who is popularly considered the father of checks and balances, Hamilton applies the term "check" directly to the separation of powers; but in each situation he

treats the check not as *arising from* separation, but as excusing a
partial or apparent *violation* of it—that is, Congress's judicial
function in impeachments (66.446, 81.546); its participation in
the executive's appointment power (76.513); and the Supreme
Court's intervention in the legislature's actions by judicial review
(78.528).

Since these are the only uses of *either* term (check *or* balance)
to describe the action of separated powers, the insight of Vile
and Gwyn is validated: Checks and balances do not arise from
separation theory, but are at odds with it. Checks and balances
have to do with corrective *invasion* of the separated powers—and
no wonder: The checks had their first and most congenial home
in mixed-government theory, where all interests were to have a
say in all matters. Thus Hamilton, who believed in the "mixed"
ideal, uses the language more freely than Madison, who did not.
Madison saw that there was a necessary conflict between separation from other powers and control over them. Effective *"controul* over the acts of each other" entails *"partial agency* in" each
other (47.325). As we shall see, this offered no problem for
Madison, since he thought the key to control was *within* one
branch, not *between* any branches.

Before we consider Federalist doctrine on the checking and
balancing of separated powers, it is best to remind ourselves of
the most common use of balance in Madison's time. It was used
by both Court and Country ideologues in England, each of them
working from a mixed-government analysis of the British constitution. Perhaps the most effective use on the Country side was
made by Bolingbroke, who argued that Walpole's ministry,
by corrupt appointment of men in Parliament to government
"places," had made balance impossible. This jumbled and confused the voices that contend their way toward equilibrium. The
ministry itself had supplanted the voice of the one, the king who
should stand apart, a patriot. And the placemen in the House of
Commons did not speak for a separate interest of the many—
they were spokesmen for the few, infiltrating the ranks of the
many's spokesmen.

Hume, starting from the same Polybian ideal as Bolingbroke,
arrived at a *defense* of the ministry and its use of placemen. For
him, the balance of government had been upset ever since Crom-

well's time: "The pretensions of the parliament, if yielded to, broke the balance of the constitution, by rendering the government almost entirely republican" (1.9.136). The Restoration could offer only apparent remedy, as the revolution proved in 1688. After that, the king's part in the mixed constitution was so drastically reduced that he had to recruit aid in the parliament itself through "the offices and honours that are at the disposal of the crown." What Bolingbroke called corruption, Hume called a rebalancing of the constitution:

> The crown has so many offices at its disposal that, when assisted by the honest and disinterested part of the house, it will always command the resolutions of the whole so far, at least, as to preserve the antient constitution from danger. We may, therefore, give to this influence what name we please; we may call it by the invidious appellations of corruption and dependence; but some degree and some kind of it are inseparable from the very nature of the constitution, and necessary to the preservation of our mixed government (1.6.120–1).

This defense of "corruption" so infuriated Jefferson, who deeply admired Bolingbroke, that he did not want Hume's history (in unexpurgated form) to be read at the University of Virginia (see *Inventing*, 201–2, and Levy, *Jefferson and Civil Liberties*, 143–7).

Some radicals in America wanted nothing to do with either side of this mixed-government controversy, which just made kings respectable. They forswore not only the Polybian ideal (as the Constitution does), but the whole Polybian tactic of balance through checks (see Vile, 136–48). Madison criticized this extreme rejection of checks in No. 47.

But it was not easy to see how checks could belong to the American scheme. Madison did not reject in principle the idea of having the separated powers check each other (48.332, 51.349); he just thought the idea unrealizable. Because the three powers did not represent separate interests, of one and few and many, the social sanctions of Polybius were irrelevant. In fact, because all three departments represent the people (through different channels), the most direct representative of the people— Congress, and especially its popular chamber—would find it easy to overpower either of the other branches. On what principle could *they* ever oppose the *people?* (In fact, why should they ever want to?) Add to this the fact that legislation has a certain priority in the separation scheme (how apply laws until they are made?) and you have a formula for legislative domination bound to destroy the separation of powers.

We have two problems here. One of them, the more difficult, must be postponed to Part Four—namely: Why should a republic ever oppose the people or their representatives? But, once that puzzling goal is assumed, separated powers seem to be the means. Still—here is the second question, more easily answered straight from Madison's text—How is the separation to be maintained in a system where the legislature far outweighs, in Madison's view, the executive and the judiciary, either singly or together? (When Madison proposed a joint legislative-executive veto on legislation, he did not think the two could actually keep the legislature in check, just that they would make the disparity less ominous—Farrand, 2.77).

Montesquieu, the source of separation doctrine for legitimacy, was little help on the practical matter of keeping the separated powers in balance. (According to Gwyn, remember, Montesquieu was not directly concerned with that problem.) It is true that Montesquieu said power should check power (11.4.2). But, in the first place, Montesquieu was discussing a constitutional monarchy; he shifted back and forth between separation theory and mixed government—saying, for instance, that the nobles would play a mediating role between the people and their king (11.6.32). He did not have to face Madison's problem of three powers all expressing a single interest (the people's), a situation in which Madison says power *can't* check power, since "it is not possible to give to each department an equal power of self defence" (51.350; cf. 48.333).

In the second place, Montesquieu was not very clear about *how* power was to check power. The separate judicial branch was, in power terms, a nonentity (11.6.32). The king's judicial power was united in his person with the executive, so they could not check each other (11.6.2). The King and Parliament check each other, but through the intermediation of the nobles (11.6.32, 11.6.55), a resource denied to Madison.

On this matter we should look back at Dahl's hardheaded objections to Madison's scheme (*Preface*, 236–40). What type of leverage, exactly, is necessary to constitute a check? Violence? Accusation? Shame? Social stigma? Mandatory adjudication? Dahl's questions were out of place where he first raised them, to impugn Madison's statement of legitimacy theory. But they are properly raised here. How would a constitutional check—as opposed to the broadly social check of Polybian schemes—have power to bind?

Madison could find only one point of leverage in this whole scheme—not from mere separation of powers (No. 47), nor from action of one branch on another (the legislative is too powerful to be checked by the others—51.350). Nor by supervision from outside the governmental machinery, whether by periodic review (No. 48) or special panel (No. 49). Madison seems, in the course of Nos. 47 through 50, to have painted himself into a corner. There can be no check from other parts of government, and none from outside government. What is left?

The check can only come from the potentially erring member itself—an internal check:

> The remedy for this inconveniency is, to divide the legislature into different branches; and to render them by different modes of election, and different principles of action, as little connected with each other, as the nature of their common functions, and their common dependence on the society, will admit (51.350).

It is somewhat misleading to apply the plural "checks and balances" to Madison's separation theory. For him there is only one powerful check in the three powers, and that is *within* the legislature. If it restrains itself, the other two will be safe. If it does not restrain itself, they are helpless against it. Admittedly, Madison says that two other things are necessary to keep the three functions separate—distinct personnel and assured independence of income (51.35–51); but these are not checks, merely definitions of separation. Even the Pennsylvania constitution, which forswore checks, had these distinctions. It is only when Madison comes to "the great security" against encroachment (51.349) that he talks of the power to check, and his only use of check in a technical sense applies to the *bicameral* division of the government's most powerful department (62.418, 63.425).

I cannot state too emphatically how Madison's whole theory of separation turns on the power of the legislature. He describes it as almost irresistible in Nos. 47 through 50. And even when he finds the key check in No. 51, he fears that this is barely adequate, and offers his single suggestion for revision of the Philadelphia draft: "It may even be necessary to guard against dangerous encroachments by still further precautions" (51.350). It is an extraordinary step Madison takes here. He disagreed with various things in the Philadelphia draft. We know, for instance, that he wanted a veto of state laws by the federal authority; but he no longer argues for that in The Federalist. He wanted representation in the Senate to be proportional, and he gives only weakhearted defense to the equal votes given each state (51.416–17); but he *does* defend it—he does not advance his own proposal in opposition.

Yet in No. 51 Madison does, for the first and last time in The Federalist, revive one of his own proposals (in an even stronger form), to deal with his intense fear of legislative self-aggrandizement. Madison had argued long and hard at the Convention for an absolute veto on the Congress, not a relative veto with provisions for an override. This was far more important to him than the veto on state legislatures, since the federal legislature would be far more powerful. In his original scheme he thought the judiciary would have to participate in the veto to make it "stick." That proposal had been rejected by the Convention. Yet in No. 51 Madison, who did not propose any *other* changes in the draft while urging states to ratify—not even a Bill of Rights, the most popular call for a change—does propose an amendment. Instead of having the judiciary join with the executive in an absolute veto, Madison proposes a joint veto of President *and Senate* to control the popular branch of Congress:

As the weight of the legislative authority requires that it should be thus divided, the weakness of the executive may require, on the other hand, that it should be fortified. An absolute negative, on the legislature, appears at first view to be the natural defence with which the executive magistrate should be armed. But perhaps it would be neither altogether safe, nor alone sufficient. On ordinary occasions, it might not be exerted with the requisite firmness; and on extraordinary occasions, it might be perfidiously abused. May not this defect of an absolute negative be supplied, by some qualified connection between this weaker department, and the weaker branch of the stronger department, by which the latter may be led to support the constitutional rights of the former, without being too much detached from the rights of its own department? (51.350).

We have here another confirmation that checks are not the necessary *consequence* of divided powers but a partial *denial* of their division. In order to form a check, Madison is willing to pit Senate and President against House, forming an executive-legislative union against the popular aspect of the legislature.

So, in strict terms, Madison argues for *two* checks at the level of separated powers; but one was not in the draft he was defending, and was never to be put there. Of things actually in the Constitution, he defended only the one check, bicameralism.

But we still have not done with Dahl's pointed question. Once we have located the key check *within* the legislature, how is it to operate? What force has one house on another? Madison thinks this too obvious to spell out—Montesquieu had spelled it out when he mentioned bicameralism (11.6.55). Since each must concur on any measure, each has the power to block ("faculté mutuelle d'empêcher") any law brought up by the other. What would motivate them to do so? Addressing himself to "the necessary constitutional means, and personal motives" for resisting encroachment, Madison writes one of his most famous sentences: "Ambition must be made to counteract ambition" (51.349). He is not talking about personal ambition in the sense of merely private advantage, for he goes on in the very next sentence: "The interest of the man must be connected with the constitutional rights of the place." It is the ambition expressed in *office* that Madison calls a combination of personal motive and constitutional means. Those in office identify their own reputation with that of the institution, and do not like to see it diminished. The motive is, as Madison says, less than angelic; but it performs a useful service. (Nor was ambition despised in the eighteenth century, as we saw in Chapter Nine.)

But if we take this *general* doctrine of checking and apply it to the *actual* check Madison relies on—bicameralism—a serious problem at once suggests itself. Pride of office may keep senators from letting House members trample on their dignity as a legislative body, and vice versa. But what if the two should join to attack the executive or the judiciary? What if the ambition stirred up in their separate chambers should take the form of a *joint* ambition of the whole legislative branch? What is left to check their *joint* ambitions? The other two branches? But Madison has declared them hopeless in an open contest with Congress. Not only does Madison's basic check fail to work in this case; he has further weakened the two departments whose weakness he was trying to remedy. By mobilizing ambition in the legislative chambers, to blunt each other's aggressions, he has added weight to their joint aggression against any other department. They now attack with a double prestige of office, with the weight of their concurrence.

This objection seems so obvious, and so fatal to Madison's scheme, that it is hard to imagine that he failed to see it; and hard to believe, having seen it, that he was not forced to abandon or alter his argument. Some have foisted a different view on Madison—this one seems too simpleminded to be held by so sensible a statesman. But there the doctrine is, plain as can be, in No. 51; and nothing Madison says elsewhere in The Federalist alters it—indeed, he reasserts it in the sections on Congress (62.418, 63.425). No wonder the critics, like Noah's sons, have averted their eyes, have thrown what cover they can on their father's nakedness. This problem alone is enough to justify Dahl's opprobrium. But if we carefully take off all the protective cloaks thrown over the Constitution's father, we may find he is not naked after all.

FOURTEEN

Legislative Supremacy: Hamilton

> The executive power in every government is altogether
> subordinate to the legislative.
>
> —Hume, 1.6.120

We should not leave Madison's treatment of the legislative check
without questioning him on legislative supremacy. Though he
claims that the executive and judiciary branches are powerless
against the legislature in themselves, he uses an internal check
on the legislature to keep it within bounds. Does that reduce it
to a level of equality with the other two branches? That is a popular reading of his theory, one adopted by "pluralists" of various
persuasions, and one supported by the common view that separated-powers theory precludes single sovereignty (see Chapter
Seventeen).

During the Watergate period, President Nixon tried to protect
his tapes by executive privilege, arguing that the Constitution
forbids any one branch of government to prevail upon another.
His lawyer, James St. Clair, made that argument before the Supreme Court:

> Of these doctrines, none is more fundamental to our governmental
> structure itself than the separation of powers—with all its inherent
> tensions, with all of its necessary inability to satisfy all people or all
> institutions all of the time, and yet with the relentless and saving
> force that it generates toward essential compromise and accommo-
> dation over the longer term even if not always in the shorter term.
> Often a price has to be paid in the short term in order to preserve
> the principle of separation of powers and thereby to preserve the
> basic constitutional balances in the longer term. The preservation of
> this principle, the maintenance of these balances, are at stake in the
> case now before this Court.

Though the Court ordered President Nixon to surrender his tapes, it did not address the issue of coequal branches.

Yet we are not studying the Constitution itself, at the moment, just Madison's theory of its operation, and he says: "In republican government the legislative authority, necessarily, predominates" (51.350). Is he speaking only in the order of fact—that it *can* overpower the other two? Or in the order of right as well—that it *should* prevail? His specification of republican government might suggest the former, which also fits the context better. Doctrines of legislative supremacy were more often stated in terms of *all* legitimate governments (see Hume's quote at the head of this chapter).

But to say the legislature *can* prevail in a republic is not to deny that it *should* prevail in any government; and Madison implies as much, in No. 43, when he says a legislature should control the site of its meetings as an expression of "its general supremacy" (43.289). Why, then, if the legislature should prevail, did Madison take steps to insure that it would not? The effort seems contradictory. Thus Gottfried Dietze can flatly refer to Publius' "rejection of legislative supremacy" (*The Federalist*, 1960, 326).

Yet there was no conflict between identifying the supreme power and putting it under limits. That was, in fact, the task attempted by most constitutional theorists of the seventeenth and eighteenth centuries. They labored to make sure that supremacy did not mean unaccountability. So Bolingbroke could say, in his *Dissertation Upon Parties* (1754): "The legislator is a supreme, and can be called, in one sense, an absolute, but in none an arbitrary power."

As we saw in Chapter Twelve, *all* supremacy had to be limited in order to be legitimate, and it was limited so long as *application* of the law was in separate hands. While holding to that doctrine, all the major schools that influenced American thought believed in legislative supremacy—the schools of Locke and Blackstone and Montesquieu, of Hume and Hutcheson and Burlamaqui. The arguments at the Constitutional Convention assumed the doctrine of legislative supremacy when they did not assert it (e.g., Farrand, 1.101). And Hamilton, answering Robert Yates's attack on the Philadelphia draft as denying legislative supremacy, recognized the gravity of the charge—it would put the federal Constitution at odds with all the state constitutions: "As this doctrine is of great importance in all the American constitutions, a brief discussion of the grounds on which it rests cannot be unacceptable" (78.524).

The Constitution itself does not, as we saw, even mention separation of powers; it could hardly mention equality of the separated powers. But it does mention supremacy, calling the duly passed measures of Congress "the supreme Law of the Land" (Article VI). It might be argued that the legislature is only given legislative supremacy—that there may be a matching executive supremacy and judicial supremacy (raising the classical sovereignty question: What can be supremer than supremacy?). Besides, as we shall later find, there is a problem over *duly passed* measures.

Still, the Constitution's measures fit the presumed background of legislative supremacy. Congress is given what might be called "shoot-out" power, the weapons for final showdown with both other branches. Suppose a President refuses to execute the laws passed by Congress. Congress has a resort: It can impeach the President. The President, unlike even limited or constitutional monarchs, cannot dissolve his parliament. He can veto; but if the Congress overrides, he has no further resort.

The Supreme Court is in the same situation. It can declare a law passed by Congress unconstitutional. But Congress has a further resort in the law: It can amend the Constitution on the contested point. Then the Court has no further say in the matter. Actually, Congress has a variety of weapons—it can impeach the justices; it can refuse to levy funds for enforcing the Court's decision; it can pass constitutional laws on related matters that make the Court's original declaration of unconstitutionality nugatory; it can change the makeup of the Court; it can amend the Constitution to deny judicial review. In all these cases, the Court will have no further say in the matter.

Hamilton, after denying that the Court should have any power of loose construction, said that the inhibition on this would be precisely the kind of "shoot-out" power the Philadelphia scheme gives to Congress:

It may in the last place be observed that the supposed danger of judiciary encroachments on the legislative authority, which has been upon many occasions reiterated, is in reality a phantom. Particular misconstructions and contraventions of the will of the legislature may now and then happen; but they can never be so extensive as to amount to an inconvenience, or in any sensible degree to affect the order of the political system. This may be inferred with certainty from the general nature of the judicial power; from the objects to which it relates; from the manner in which it is exercised; from its comparative weakness, and from its total incapacity to support its usurpations by force. And the inference is greatly fortified by the consideration of the important constitutional check, which the power of instituting impeachments, in one part of the legislative body, and of determining them in the other, would give to that body upon the members of the judicial department. This is alone a complete security. There never can be danger that the judges, by a series of deliberate usurpations on the authority of the legislature, would hazard the united resentment of the body entrusted with it, while this body was possessed of the means of punishing their presumption by degrading them from their stations. While this ought to remove all apprehensions on the subject, it affords at the same time a cogent argument for constituting the senate a court for the trial of impeachments (81.545–6).

The very structure of the Constitution, as a document, indicates the order of the branches, both in logic and in scope. The first three Articles treat the legislature (beginning with "the first house," the popular chamber), the executive, and the judiciary— in that sequence, reflecting a natural hierarchy in men's minds: Without prior passage of laws, no laws can be executed; and until laws are executed, there can be no appeals from their execution. This was the order Madison observed in the Virginia Plan; it was the general order the Convention tried to follow in its debates; and it is the order The Federalist itself follows. After preliminary discussion of the Confederation's flaws and of confederacies in general (1–37) and of the Constitution's powers in general (38–51), the separate powers are considered in a sequence and at a length that indicate their relative importance— fifteen numbers for the legislature (52–66, with ten devoted to the House, five to the Senate), eleven for the executive (67–77), and six for the judiciary (78–83).

Of those who question the doctrine of legislative supremacy, few until our own day thought the executive might be supreme— not even Hamilton wanted that, and he was accused of leaning too far toward monarchy. But some thought (or feared) the judicial branch would be supreme in fact if not in theory. According to the famous statement of Bishop Hoadley in 1717: "Whoever hath an absolute authority to interpret any written or spoken laws, it is he who is truly the lawgiver, to all intents and purposes, and not the person who first wrote or spoke them."

People continue to deny that the Constitution implied judicial review, since that would amount to judicial supremacy, and the framers clearly believed in legislative supremacy. These critics start from the premise of Robert Yates, voiced in his "Letters of Brutus," that judicial *review* would amount to judicial *supremacy* (a thing Yates feared as a danger to the states' courts). But Yates developed his argument in a way not left open to those who shared his premise after ratification of the Constitution. These later critics said that review equals supremacy, therefore it could not be in the Constitution. Yates said it would amount to supremacy, *and it was in the Constitution;* therefore New York should not ratify.

The Yates position undermines extreme claims that Hamilton, in effect, "invented" judicial review in No. 78. Hamilton was answering Yates, who *already* discerned judicial review in the Philadelphia draft. But Leonard Levy tries to use this Yates-Hamilton sequence to suggest that No. 78 is a mere tour de force of special pleading:

> Federalist #78, in other words, was an attempt to quiet the fears stimulated by Yates; turning the latter's argument against him, Hamilton tried to convince his readers that the Court's power was intended to hold Congress in check, thereby safeguarding the states against national aggrandizement. A few other advocates of the Constitution, like Oliver Ellsworth and John Marshall, sought in the same manner to allay popular apprehensions that Congress might exceed its power, especially in the absence of a Bill of Rights to protect the people. Their remarks, like Hamilton's in #78, are evidence of shrewd political tactics, not of the framers' intention to vest judicial review in the Supreme Court over acts of Congress (*Judicial Review and the Supreme Court,* 1967, 6).

I agree with Professor Levy that Hamilton did not write No. 78 to establish the doctrine of judicial review—it is the mistake of most commentators to think that was its purpose. But Levy makes an even greater mistake when he says the "real" purpose of Hamilton was to show that the Court would check legislative usurpations. Hamilton could not have stated his aim more clearly, nor argued more strictly in accordance with that aim:

> Some perplexity respecting the right of the courts to pronounce legislative acts void, because contrary to the constitution, has arisen from an imagination that the doctrine would imply a superiority of the judiciary to the legislative power. It is urged that the authority which can declare the acts of another void, must necessarily be superior to the one whose acts may be declared void (78.254).

Hamilton is not, in the first place, arguing *for* judicial review or *against* congressional encroachments. He is attacking the Hoadley argument as Yates had advanced it. He is saying that judicial review (which both he and Yates find in the Constitution—there is no argument there) *is not equivalent to judicial supremacy.* "Nor does this conclusion by any means suppose a superiority of the judicial to the legislative power" (78.525). A failure to recognize that this is the point of the paper has confused almost all later comment on No. 78. Quotes from the framers and founders have been adduced to show they did not believe in judicial *review* because they did not believe in judicial *supremacy* (see Levy, *Judicial Review,* 5–8). This does not recognize the force of Hamilton's argument that the two are very different things, an argument Madison fully endorsed.

The will of the people, expressed through their representatives, is the source of law in a republic. Since periodically elected legislators represent the people more directly than do judges appointed for life, judicial review would thwart the will of the people, the very source of law. Henry Steele Commager and others therefore conclude that judicial review is "undemocratic." Hamilton does not counter this argument directly—as some force him to do in paraphrase—by saying the United States is not a pure democracy, that sometimes the will of the people should be checked. That argument shows up in The Federalist; but it is more often voiced by Madison than by Hamilton.

No, Hamilton distinguishes two acts of the people, both performed through representatives, but one more direct and "participatory" (to use a modern term) than the other. The more direct mode is that of the ratification procedure that establishes fundamental law. This is a "solemn and authoritative act" (78.528), not to be put aside but by an equally solemn act. The ratification process—going foward in the very debate Yates and Hamilton were conducting—is more democratic in procedure than ordinary acts of legislation.

Congress makes law by concurrent *majorities*. Ratification, as Madison points out (39.254), must be by *unanimous* consent of those entering the compact. Those who sit in Congress are elected for generalized acts, accomplished at some distance from the people, over a set period of time. The ratification congresses were called for one specific act, performed close to the people, with no other mandate. It was a case of direct "instruction" by the electorate. This justifies Hamilton's claim that the people themselves spoke in ratification, while the people's agents perform duties for them in Congress. Madison holds the same view:

> [Ratification] must result from the unanimous assent of the several States that are parties to it, differing no other wise from their ordinary assent [at the state level] than in its being expressed, not by the legislative authority, but by that of the people themselves (39.254).

Constitution must judge statute, not vice versa: "The constitution ought to be preferred to the statute, the intention of the people to the intention of their agents" (78.525). All Hamilton's argument turns on the distinction between the more direct action of the people and the indirect action. He cannot repeat this point too often:

> There is no position which depends on clearer principles, than that every act of a delegated authority, contrary to the tenor of the commission under which it is exercised, is void. No legislative act therefore contrary to the constitution can be valid. To deny this would be to affirm that the deputy is greater than his principal; that the servant is above his master; that the representatives of the people are superior to the people themselves; that men acting by virtue of powers may do not only what their powers do not authorize, but what they forbid (78.524).

Until the people have by some solemn and authoritative act annulled or changed the established form, it is binding upon themselves collectively, as well as individually; and no presumption, or even knowledge of their sentiments, can warrant their representatives in a departure from it, prior to such an act (528).

Hamilton does not argue for a *judicial* check on the legislature, as Levy claims. He is describing the more democratic law as superior to the less direct statement of the people's will. The Constitution came about by the people's *legislative* act.

All this is fine in theory, some objectors say—but in fact the Court, by applying the Constitution, determines what it shall henceforth be. That is true only in the sense that *all* applications of the law are distinguishable from the act of legislation itself—they *have* to be for reasons of accountability. This was the whole basis of legitimacy according to separated-powers theory (see Chapter Eleven). When a legislator is party to a cause, he cannot be judge as well. If applying the law were an act of judicial supremacy, we would not have to recognize judicial review at the *federal* level to establish such supremacy; every judgment on the applicability of statutes would be an act of supremacy so defined. That is Hamilton's argument at 78.526:

> It can be of no weight to say, that the courts on the pretence [claim] of a repugnancy [between statute and Constitution], may substitute their own pleasure to the constitutional intentions of the legislature. This might as well happen in the case of two contradictory statutes; or it might as well happen in every adjudication upon any single statute. The courts must declare the sense of the law; and if they should be disposed to exercise WILL instead of JUDGMENT, the consequence would equally be the substitution of their pleasure to that of the legislative body. The observation, if it proved any thing, would prove that there ought to be no judges distinct from that body [i.e., it would undermine the whole argument for separation of powers].

But it is often urged that a review of acts in Congress does more than apply law to one particular case; by precedent, it makes law for future cases of a similar sort. That, too, is true of judgments based on statutes. What differs in Supreme Court judgments is less the higher dignity of the Court than the higher claim of the law it is interpreting. The Supreme Court ministers to Congress when it applies *its* laws to the citizenry. But in up-holding the Constitution, even against Congress, the Court is ministering to the ratification conventions, whose "solemn and authoritative act" was a more direct expression of the people's legislative will than any majority-passed statute of Congress.

If anyone argues that Congress gives a more *immediate* be-cause a more *recent* expression of the people's will, one can an-swer that Congress was not elected to voice its opinion on just one subject, with direct instruction from the people. Hamilton says we should not judge by mere temporal succession, but by the purity of the democratic *procedure*. The issue is not whether the people spoke yesterday or the day before, but whether they spoke directly or indirectly. Admittedly, with laws passed by the same authority, later acts are to be preferred to earlier:

> But in regard to the interfering [self-crippling—see Glossary] acts of a superior and subordinate authority, of an original and derivative power, the nature and reason of the thing indicate the converse of that rule as proper to be followed. They teach us that the prior act of a superior ought to be preferred to the subsequent act of an infe-rior and subordinate authority; and that, accordingly, whenever a particular statute contravenes the constitution, it will be the duty of the judicial tribunals to adhere to the latter, and disregard the for-mer (78.526).

Over and over in this paper Hamilton is stressing one thing—legislative supremacy, the supremacy of the more democratic rat-ifying conventions over indirect representation by majority vote in the Congress.

But what if the Court should misinterpret the people's will as expressed in their direct and most formal legislative act, the Constitution? In that case, the question returns to the people, for them to rectify the misrepresentation of their will. This can occur in one of two ways. If the constitutional process has not been corrupted, the people will speak through their repre-sentatives, amending the Constitution, making their intention clear to the misinterpreters of it on the bench. If the process is corrupted, the people retain their right to revolution—their will is the source of law; the corrupt process is the thing at odds with law. Here, as we have seen, Hamilton quotes Blackstone's doctrine of the Glorious Revolution from Jefferson's Declaration of Independence (*Inventing*, 54-5, 89-90): "I trust the friends of the proposed constitution will never concur with its enemies in questioning that fundamental principle of republican government, which admits the right of the people to alter or abolish the established constitution whenever they find it inconsistent with their happiness" (78.527). He goes on to say that this will not be necessary where the people can peacefully change the Constitution by another "solemn and authoritative act"; but he situates all law in the legislative will of the people.

Thus, in theory, judicial review does not supersede the legislative will of the people; and in practice the Constitution does not give the Supreme Court "shoot-out" powers. When the Court declares an act of Congress unconstitutional, the Congress has resorts—amendment, nonfunding, change of the Court's makeup, impeachment of the judges. Probably Congress will "get away with" such measures only if it has popular support; but that is the whole point—its legislative authority has force only so far as it represents the people.

No. 78 is not a defense of judicial review—much less an "invention" of it. Review was assumed; it was the common ground Hamilton had with Yates. The real subject of No. 78 is legislative supremacy, the thing Yates thought incompatible with judicial review. Hamilton argues that the two are not only compatible but that judicial review *demands* a theory of legislative supremacy—in the constitution-making act—as its necessary justification. Judicial review is not at odds with legislative supremacy, but depends on it. Without it, judicial review would make no sense at all:

> Nor does this conclusion by any means suppose a superiority of the judicial to the legislative power. It only supposes that the power of the people is superior to both; and that where the will of the legislature declared in its statutes, stands in opposition to that of the people declared in the constitution, the judges ought to be governed by the latter, rather than the former. They ought to regulate their decisions by the fundamental laws, rather than by those which are not fundamental (78.525).

That is what Hamilton said throughout No. 78; yet few have listened because they were looking, here, for his defense of judicial review. They were looking in the wrong place. They should have read three papers further.

FIFTEEN

Judicial Review: Hamilton

Not to mention that the legislative power being always
superior to the executive, the magistrates or representatives may interpose whenever they think proper.
—Hume, 2.16.489

The misreading of No. 78 comes, in part, from the habit of quoting "proof texts" from The Federalist without regard for context,
for the larger strategies of argument or the march of interrelated
Numbers. People too often quote Madison on the hasty nature of
Publius' enterprise (TJ, 13.498–9) and dwell too little on the
scientific aim and method of the book. Hamilton's six Numbers
on the judiciary have the structure one should expect after reading prior Numbers. Madison's concern in taking up the discussion
of any power is to justify its republican genius (see Chapter
Twenty-one). That is true of the Constitution's general powers
(No. 39), and of those powers lodged in the House (No. 52) or
the Senate (Nos. 62 and 63). Hamilton showed a similar concern
when introducing the topic of executive power (No. 67).

So, with the judiciary, Hamilton asks first if its jurisdiction fits
the republican character of the American people. That question
can only be given a positive answer if the legislature remains
supreme; No. 78 is devoted to proofs of that supremacy. Hamilton does not mean, by endorsing the judiciary's maximum claims
at the outset, to scare away supporters of the Constitution. He
rightly traces the *limits* on judicial power. The "manner of constituting" this department (78.521) guarantees that it "will always be the least dangerous" branch (522), "beyond comparison
the weakest of the three" (523). It is only in this context that
Hamilton takes up the *false* claim of Robert Yates that judicial
review involves an inordinate supremacy over the legislature.

Hamilton grants the existence of review power to demonstrate that even this claim does not—in a republic, cannot—run counter to the people's sovereignty as exercised in the legislating power.

John Hart Ely has recently called Hamilton's a "fake argument" so far as the real "democratic" effect of judicial review is concerned. That may or not be the case as review has actually been exercised. My aim, here, is not to discuss the problem in general but to establish Hamilton's position on review. This is less obvious than it has seemed to people who pounce on No. 78 as the extreme statement of the reviewing power. The assumption that judicial review is the subject of No. 78 has been so constant and casual that Edward Corwin, in the first of his two influential books on that subject, supposed "this doctrine" in the following sentence must be the doctrine of review:

> As this doctrine is of great importance in all the American constitutions, a brief discussion of the grounds on which it rests cannot be unacceptable (78.524; cf. *The Doctrine of Judicial Review*, 1914, 44).

But Hamilton was not certain that judicial review was a doctrine important in all the American constitutions. He tells us himself that four of the thirteen states did not even have a separate judicial department (81.544–5). What *was* recognized in all the constitutions was legislative supremacy (545). It is true that Hamilton referred, earlier in the paragraph at 78.544, to the reviewing power as a "doctrine." But that power is presented as troubling only because it seems to override an even more basic doctrine—the one implied in the sentence immediately preceding Corwin's excerpt from the paragraph and expounded in the passage immediately following. The republican demand for legislative supremacy was so firm that Hamilton simply assumes it is the first order of business. This very assumption makes him a bit careless of the antecedent for "this" in the reference to "this doctrine."

After describing the limits on this weakest branch, Hamilton argues for a compensatory independence in No. 79, for a status protected by assured pay and by tenure during good behavior (as opposed to shorter terms or mandatory retirement). Only in No. 80 does Hamilton come to the question of the judiciary power's extent, defined from the department's objects (80.534–8) and from its enabling clause in the Constitution (538–41). No. 81 defines the relationship between various federal courts, and No. 82 the relationship of federal to state courts. No. 83 considers a final objection to the Philadelphia draft, that it would preclude jury trials in civil cases. Juries are not precluded, Hamilton says —just not required.

Given this shape to the argument, we should expect Hamilton to put judicial review among the powers defended in No. 80. In No. 78, he had just assumed the existence of this power, in order to put limits around it. It may be said, then, that he still assumes the power's existence in No. 80, where it is nowhere mentioned. But why would he do that? He defends the existence of more obvious powers; indeed, he purports to give us an exhaustive division of all the judicial powers—six of them grounded in the very objects of the department, then all six individually related to the seven enumerated grants of the judiciary clause. Which leaves us with a mystery—not only is judicial review neglected in this list of powers; the argument accompanying the list seems to exclude the possibility of a power to review legislation. So true is this that if No. 78 had somehow perished from historical memory, No. 80 could be used with great confidence to prove that Hamilton did not believe in the doctrine of judicial review. How can a power taken for granted in No. 78 be not only forgotten but implicitly denied in No. 80?

The depth of this problem has been underestimated—partly, no doubt, because Hamilton's implicit argument against judicial review does not mesh with modern attacks on the concept. Most of the debate for and against review has centered on two phrases in the Constitution, and Hamilton does not give these the narrow reading favored by most opponents of review. The two phrases are "arising under" from Section 2 of Article III and "in Pursuance" from Article VI (the second paragraph).

In the judiciary grant it is said that "the judicial Power shall extend to all Cases, in Law and Equity, arising under this Constitution, the Laws of the United States, and Treaties made, or which shall be made, under their Authority . . ." Friends of judicial review argue that the Supreme Court cannot enforce law in cases "arising under this Constitution" unless it first identifies what laws and principles actually *do* arise under it. Others would restrict "arising under" to mean laws passed by the government set up under the Constitution. Congress, established "under" the Constitution, makes laws; the Court just enforces those laws, whatever they may be.

Corwin tries to recruit Hamilton to this narrow reading of "arising under" (*Court Over Constitution,* 1938, 36–8). His evidence comes from Hamilton's words at 80.539:

> It has been asked what is meant by "cases arising under the constitution," in contradistinction from those "arising under the laws of the United States." The difference has been already explained. All the restrictions upon the authority of the state legislatures, furnish examples of it. They are not, for instance, to emit paper money; but the interdiction results from the constitution, and will have no connection with any law of the United States.

Corwin breaks off the quote here, and concludes from it that Hamilton "confines cases 'arising under this Constitution' to cases arising in consequence of direct transgressions of specific prohibitions of the Constitution" (37–8). But Hamilton is simply giving one example of the distinction between constitutional and nonconstitutional cases. He does not limit himself to the one sample offered *exempli gratia.* He goes on, immediately, to say:

> Should paper money, notwithstanding, be emitted, the controversies concerning it would be cases arising upon the constitution, and not upon the laws of the United States, in the ordinary signification of the terms. This may serve as a sample of the whole.

Hamilton is distinguishing the two kinds of cases to show such a distinction can exist. He is not describing the extent of the judiciary's power in each case.

In fact, the gloss Hamilton gives to "arising under" in this last passage suggests that he reads it broadly. For "arising under" has become at 80.539 "arising upon the constitution," where "upon" clearly means "on the basis of." Elsewhere he uses "arise out of" to gloss "arising under" (80.534, 81.547). Even more loosely he refers to "cases which may grow out of" the Constitution (82.554). This certainly frees him of the narrow view that "arising under" means, simply, decreed by the government set up under the Constitution. He sees questions growing out of the Constitution itself. And it frees him, *a fortiori,* from Corwin's even narrower construction of the phrase. Corwin rightly sensed that an argument against judicial review could be fashioned from materials supplied in Hamilton's No. 80. But he was wrong in trying to attach it to the phrase "arising under." Just as he assumed that the primary subject of No. 78 had to be judicial review, so he assumes that Hamilton must ground his argument on one of the two canonical sources for modern debate.

Corwin has no better luck when he turns to the other phrase at the center of disputes on judicial review. The supremacy clause of the Constitution reads, in the part relevant here: "This Constitution, and the Laws of the United States which shall be made in Pursuance thereof . . . shall be the supreme Law of the Land." Who is to decide what is "in Pursuance of" (in accord with) the Constitution, ask the friends of review, but *judicial* interpreters? Corwin, however, turns back to No. 33, where Hamilton expressly asked "Who is to judge of the necessity and propriety of the laws to be passed for executing the powers of the Union?" (33.206; misquoted by Corwin at *Court Over Constitution,* 44). Since Hamilton does not expressly answer his own question, and since he uses "pursuant to the Constitution" three times on the very next page, Corwin concludes that Hamilton did not pin review to the phrase "in Pursuance thereof." A strange and not very convincing argument. If Hamilton did not answer his question at all, he did not *exclude* arguing from "in Pursuance" any more than he demanded it.

Can No. 80 be cited to back Alexander Bickel's claim that "in Pursuance" means only laws enacted "in accordance with the constitutional forms"—that is, "by the concurrence of both Houses and with the signature of the President"? (*The Least Dangerous Branch,* 1962, 9). Not if we look to Hamilton's gloss at 80.534, where he says the judiciary power reaches to cases "which arise out of the laws of the United States, passed in pursuance of their just and constitutional powers of legislation." The observance of forms is not at issue in this passage. The antecedent of "their" is the United States. (Here, as elsewhere, the federal government under that title is a plural noun.) Their laws are to be enforced only as they accord with the *just and constitutional* powers delegated to them. This formulation raises the broadest judicial questions. The same is true of Hamilton's language in No. 33, where the issue is, once again, an accord with substantial powers granted, not with mere forms:

> If a number of political societies enter into a larger political society, the laws which the latter may enact, pursuant to the powers entrusted to it by its constitution, must necessarily be supreme over those societies . . . But it will not follow from this doctrine that acts of the larger society which are *not pursuant* to its constitutional powers but which are invasions of the residuary authorities of the smaller societies will become the supreme law of the land . . . [The supremacy clause] *expressly* confines this supremacy to laws made *pursuant to the Constitution* . . . (33.207).

By eighteenth-century usage, pursuance or pursuit of a thing is prosecution of it—or persecution. The word is intensive and inclusive (see *Inventing*, 245). Dr. Johnson not only gave as his first definition of "pursue" to "persecute"; he often spelled "persue" in a way that brought out this etymology (e.g., at *Rambler* 4.23; 7.36; 8.41, 42, 44 in the Yale edition). Hamilton, along with most men of his time, would favor a broad sense for "pursuance." Jefferson was not talking about adherence to the mere forms of felicity when he made "the pursuit of happiness" a basic right.

Why all the fuss, then, if Hamilton gives a broad construction to "arising under" and "in Pursuance thereof"? Isn't that what we expect? After all, we know from No. 78 where Hamilton is going to come out on the question. Why should we expect him to differ from other supporters of review on the two phrases that seem to favor it? Well, for one thing, the others use those phrases to claim that judicial review is present in the very language of the Constitution; but Hamilton says it is not in those phrases—and not in any other particular terminology of the Constitution (81.543).

In terms of most modern debate, Hamilton "blows his chance" to use the key phrases to anchor judicial review in the Constitution. When he lists six powers arising from the very objects of the judiciary, the first power is defined with the help of both phrases (80.534)—yet he explains this power solely in terms of the Court's relationship to state laws, not federal law (80.535). If he is not going to argue for review in this place, and from these phrases, where else can he hope to?

Throughout No. 80 Hamilton is thinking of the judiciary's

power as exercised over the states. He thinks here of the federal branches as allies against the pretension of any state or set of states, referring to "the national tribunals" as supreme in "controversies between the nation and its members or citizens" (80.535). He speaks of "the judicial power of a government being coextensive with its legislature" (ibid.)—that is, qualified to enforce all the laws of the Congress, but not (apparently) to pass judgment on them.

In No. 81, Hamilton seems to be moving toward a statement of the reviewing power when he writes: "That there ought to be one court of supreme and final jurisdiction is a proposition which has not been, and is not likely to be contested. The reasons for it have been assigned in another place . . ." (81.542). A footnote is appended to those last words—referring back, not to No. 78 (as we might expect), but to No. 22, where the issue was supremacy of the federal court over state courts: "If there is in each State, a court of final jurisdiction, there may be as many different final determinations on the same point, as there are courts" (22.144). Hamilton appeals to universal history in concluding that "all nations have found it necessary to establish one court paramount to the rest [of the courts]" (81.143-4).

Hamilton's most famous defense of judicial review prior to The Federalist was also a matter of reviewing state laws in the light of Confederate legislation. In *Rutgers* v. *Waddington* (1784), he argued: "The judges of each state must of necessity be judges of the United States [under the Articles]—And they must take notice of the law of Congress as a part of the law of the land" (Goebel, *Law Practice of Hamilton*, 1964, 1.380).

The significant omissions of No. 80 are followed by some significant assertions in later Numbers. In No. 81, Hamilton describes a kind of judicial review by the legislature. Congress can set limits on an express constitutional grant to the judiciary: "To avoid all inconveniencies, it will be safest to declare generally, that the supreme court shall possess appellate jurisdiction, both as to law and *fact*, and that this jurisdiction shall be subject to such *exceptions* and regulations as the national legislature may prescribe" (81.552). Hamilton seems to assume a kind of constant regulation of the courts by Congress. Speaking of the federal courts inferior to the Supreme Court, he writes:

"Whether their authority shall be original or appellate or both is not declared. All this seems to be left to the discretion of the legislature" (82.557). The lack of any requirement for juries in civil cases can also be left to the discretion of Congress: "The pretence therefore, that the national legislature would not be at full liberty to submit all the civil causes of federal cognizance to the determination of juries, is a pretence destitute of all just foundation" (83.560). Madison had claimed that the legislative powers of the Constitution could not be enumerated (44.303-5); but Hamilton says the judicial powers are strictly enumerated—seven of them specified, embracing all six powers needed for the departmental objects (80.534-41). The Supreme Court has only two areas of original jurisdiction (81.548-9). Federal courts are limited by a concurrent jurisdiction of state courts "where it was not expressly prohibited" (82.555). The whole federal court apparatus is confined to "certain cases particularly specified" (83.560).

We can imagine how all this material would be used by critics of judicial review if only No. 78 could be spirited away. Everywhere else, it would be argued, Hamilton speaks not only as if judicial review *did* not exist but as if it *could* not. Corwin—followed, we have seen, by Leonard Levy—tries to solve this puzzle by assuming that No. 78 was a narrowly conceived answer to the "Brutus" letters of Robert Yates. We are to think of Hamilton's views as fixed, originally, on mere predominance of the federal courts over state laws. He does not, from his general theory of government, envisage a power to review. After all, he did not mention any such power in his long speech of June 18 to the Constitutional Convention, where his whole system of government seems to be expounded.

But why, if No. 78 were meant to stand apart from the general argument, was it made to open Hamilton's treatment of the federal courts? The judiciary section initiates those late Numbers printed first in a body between hard covers. When Hamilton sent them to press, they were not dispatched singly to meet a newspaper deadline, as with the earlier Numbers. He had the final essays laid out before him. Moreover, when he had more leisure, he helped revise The Federalist for its second edition of 1802 (Cooke text, xv–xvi). It would have taken little effort to insert a recognition of the reviewing power at the expected place in No. 80 (on the general powers) or in No. 81 (on the Supreme Court). If judicial review was an odd and last-minute insertion into Hamilton's scheme of thought, that very intrusive character should have put Hamilton on alert. The more alien this review looked in its setting, the more obviously would it call for harmonization with the other essays. Yet Hamilton let the judiciary section stand essentially as written, all apparent discrepancies unresolved. Why?

SIXTEEN

Celebrated Maxim

> Men must, therefore, endeavour to palliate what they
> cannot cure. They must institute some persons, under
> the appellation of magistrates, whose peculiar office it
> is, to point out the decrees of equity, to punish trans-
> gressors, to correct fraud and violence, and to oblige
> men, however reluctant, to consult their own real and
> permanent interests.
>
> —Hume, 1.5.114

If Hamilton gave a broad meaning to the phrases "arising
under" and "in Pursuance thereof," why did he say that judicial
review is not particularly called for by the Constitution itself?
Chief Justice John Marshall used both these phrases (along with
three others) to anchor his doctrine of review in the Constitution. Raoul Berger, in the most thorough modern defense of review, said that everything rides on the phrase "arising under." If
judicial review "does not 'arise under' that clause, it 'arises' nowhere" (*Congress* v. *the Supreme Court*, 1969, 200). Hamilton,
by contrast, wrote:

> I admit however, that the constitution ought to be the standard of
> construction for the laws, and that wherever there is an evident op-
> position, the laws ought to give place to the constitution. But this
> doctrine is not deducible from any circumstance peculiar to the
> plan of the convention . . . (81.543).

Ironically, if the Bill of Rights Hamilton argued against in No.
84 had existed as he wrote No. 81, he would have possessed a
phrase in which to anchor the concept of judicial review. He had
appealed to the New York State constitution's bill of rights when

demanding, early in 1787, judicial reversal of a law that excluded some from political office:

> We had in a former debate, travelled largely over the ground of the constitution, as applied to legislative disqualifications; He would not repeat what he had said, but he hoped to be indulged by the house in explaining a sentence in the constitution, which seems not well understood by some gentlemen. In one article of it, it is said no man shall be disfranchised or deprived of any right he enjoys under the constitution, but by the *law of the land*, or the judgment of his peers. Some gentlemen hold that the law of the land will include an act of the legislature. But Lord Coke, that great luminary of the law, in his comment upon a similar clause, in Magna Charta, interprets the law of the land to mean presentment and indictment, and process of outlawry, as contradistinguished from trial by jury. But if there were any doubt upon the constitution, the bill of rights enacted in this very session removes it. It is there declared that, no man shall be disfranchised or deprived of any right, but by *due process of law*, or the judgment of his peers. The words *"due process"* have a precise technical import, and are only applicable to the process and proceedings of the courts of justice; they can never be referred to an act of legislature (*AH*, 4.35).

If the Fifth Amendment had existed when Hamilton wrote The Federalist, he could have used the "due process" provision in support of judicial review. But I doubt that he would have been eager to use it. He cited a particular article of the New York constitution, as well as its bill of rights, to argue the limited issue of electoral exclusions; but the passages cited would not vindicate judicial review where the Supreme Court has original jurisdiction. Hamilton shies repeatedly from pinning review to positive enactment or particular articles of law. Even in the New York case he relied on "due process" only as a secondary and confirming argument. He does not think review should arise from the Constitution's enactment but from its very nature. It is a principle that precedes any constitutional provision in a republic with separated powers:

> But this doctrine is not deducible from any circumstance peculiar to the plan of the convention; *but from the general theory of a limited constitution* . . . (81.543; italics added).

In No. 81, Hamilton has returned to the Yates claim that a Supreme Court's very existence undermines legislative supremacy (81.542). He responds that the absence of a supreme court would violate "the celebrated maxim [rule—see Glossary] requiring a separation of the departments of power" (81.543). As in No. 78, he is arguing from the legitimacy theory of separated powers. No one, not even a sovereign, can be judge and party in his own case. This is true under every constitution that establishes a limited government—even a constitutional monarchy. It must be especially true, *a fortiori*, under a republic.

> There can be no objection therefore, on this account, to the federal judicature, which will not lie against the local judicatures in general, and which will not serve to condemn every constitution that attempts to set bounds to the legislative discretion (81.543).

Some had argued that the British constitution let Parliament review its own laws. But Hamilton answers that the House of Lords in its judicial role is not acting as part of the sovereign (King in Parliament) nor as one branch of the legislative process. It has reassembled itself into a special court (as congresses resolved themselves into committees of the whole).

> The theory neither of the British, nor the [American] state constitutions, authorises the revisal of a judicial sentence, by a legislative act. Nor is there any thing in the proposed constitution more than in either of them, by which it is forbidden. In the former as well as in the latter, the impropriety of the thing, on the general principles of law and reason, is the sole obstacle. A legislature without exceeding its province cannot reverse a determination once made, in a particular case; though it may prescribe a new rule for future cases. This is the principle; and it applies in all its consequences, exactly in the same manner and extent, to the state governments, as to the national government, now under consideration. Not the least difference can be pointed out in any view of the subject (81.545).

Corwin asked why Hamilton raised the question of review in No. 33 if he did not mean to answer it. But for Hamilton, merely alluding to the "celebrated maxim" is an answer—and he alludes to it when he says that the "Pursuance" clause implies a limitation that "would have been to be understood though it had not been expressed" (33.207).

Hamilton comes close in that passage to resting the case for review on "Pursuance" in the Constitution. But there is another place in that document, not often cited in the debates over review, that better fits his argument. In fact, if the issue of review had been "up" at the time when Hamilton wrote—up, that is, in any important form except Yates's charge that it violated legislative supremacy—Hamilton would have given it a more thorough treatment, as he did the "hot" subject of judicial supremacy over state courts. In that case, the constitutional citation he all but makes in Nos. 80 and 81 would have been brought to greater prominence.

In No. 80, we are told that the federal judiciary must have powers extending "to all those (cases) in which the United States are a party" (80.534)—by which, Hamilton says, he means all "controversies between the nation and its members [states] or citizens" (535). The "nation," here, means the (legislative) sovereign power; but a Court is brought in because the sovereign has become a party to an action where, by definition, it cannot also be a judge. In the same way, the Court must be called in to adjudicate treaty laws that "relate to the intercourse between the United States and foreign nations" (534).

As the federal government must submit to judicial decision where it is a party, so must the states, in disputes where "the state tribunals cannot be supposed to be impartial and unbiassed" (ibid.). We shall see, in Madison's treatment of "party," how the very term is considered legally disqualifying for any judicial (or even judicious) role. Hamilton puts it this way:

> The reasonableness of the agency of the national courts in cases in which the state tribunals cannot be supposed to be impartial, speaks for itself. No man ought certainly to be a judge in his own cause, or in any cause in respect to which he has the least interest or bias (80.538).

No man ought to be judge in his own case—that is the corollary and cause of the "celebrated maxim" on separation of powers. Legitimacy theory grounds separation of powers on the need to keep judge and party from becoming identical. That is what the great authority on separation—Montesquieu—had taught the framers. Hamilton had already quoted him in No. 78: "For I agree that 'there is no liberty, if the power of judging be not separated from the legislative and executive powers'" (78.523).

So, in describing the fourth grant of the judiciary clause, Hamilton quotes the Constitution as bestowing jurisdiction in "Controversies to which the United States shall be a Party" (Article III, Section 2), and expressly links this with the third power given to the judiciary from the very nature of its objects—cases "in which the United States are a party" (80.540; cf. 534). In calling the federal sovereign a *party*, the Constitution has necessarily denied it jurisdiction over the controversy *to which* it is a party.

Hamilton also quotes the Constitution as giving original (not merely appellate) jurisdiction in cases "in which A STATE shall be a party" (81.548). It is more than likely that the federal government will be the opposing party in some of these cases—so it cannot be the judge as well. As Charles Pinckney said at the Philadelphia Convention, while arguing for high standards in the judiciary: "They will be the Umpires between the U. States and individual States as well as between one State & another" (Farrand, 2.248).

So it is consonant with all parts of Hamilton's argument—with his constant reliance on the "celebrated maxim" of separation in order to prevent a party from acting as judge—to say that the Constitution does inescapably imply a power of judicial review; but not in the two phrases where that power has most frequently been sought. It is inescapably implied in Article III, Section 2, giving the Court jurisdiction when "the United States shall be a Party" to legal challenge. In envisioning that possibility, the Constitution allows for only one outcome—judgment by a *non*-party. By the Court.

SEVENTEEN

Judicial Review: Madison

We are, therefore, to look upon all the vast apparatus
of our government, as having ultimately no other object
or purpose but the distribution of justice, or, in other
words, the support of the twelve judges.

—Hume, 1.5.113–14

The same people who think Hamilton's topic in No. 78 was judicial review (where his real subject was legislative supremacy)
often think Madison had nothing to say about judicial review in
The Federalist, and had only confused things to say in his other
writings. They are justified when they point to some of his later
statements, made in the heat of the Jeffersonians' battle with the
courts. But, up through the ratification of the Constitution, the
only confusion is that of men who read his denial of judicial supremacy as a denial of judicial review.

We cannot expect to hear much from Madison on judicial review, in the modern sense, at the Constitutional Convention. He
was earnestly promoting a much stronger role for the Supreme
Court at that time. He wanted it to join with the executive in vetoing congressional legislation (Farrand, 1.108, 110, 138–9, 144;
2.73–4, 77, 80–2). The term used for this joint body with the
power to negative was "revisionary council." Review and revision are etymologically the same word, and were used inter-
changeably. Thus Hamilton criticizes the idea of preferring a
final review by legislators to one by judges:

And there is a still greater absurdity in subjecting the decisions of
men selected for their knowledge of the laws, acquired by long and
laborious study, to the *revision* and control of men, who for want
of the same advantage cannot but be deficient in that knowledge
(81.544; italics added).

In the same essay he uses other forms of the same root:

> The theory neither of the British, nor the state constitutions, author-
> ises the *revisal* of a judicial sentence, by a legislative act (81.545;
> italics added).

> The expression taken in the abstract, denotes nothing more than the
> power of one tribunal to *review* the proceedings of another, either
> as to the law or fact, or both (81.550; italics added).

The term "revision" is properly used of Madison's proposal,
since the inclusion of the judiciary on the board makes it clear
that a law's constitutionality would be considered in this veto
power. The fact that the law had not gone into effect would not
preclude review (or revision) of the proposed law's constitutionality. As we shall see, Madison wanted even the executive
singly to have a veto on grounds of constitutionality.

This scheme was a stronger limit on the Congress than either
the executive veto or judicial review; that is why Madison was
still trying to insert something like his original proposal when he
came to write No. 51. The fact that the Convention expressly
rejected the revisionary council, but did not exclude the weaker
scheme of judicial review, seems to indicate that the framers
took the latter as given in the draft already on the table. Indeed,
Elbridge Gerry used this very fact as the basis of his opposition
to Madison's review council:

> Mr. Gerry doubts whether the Judiciary ought to form a part of it,
> as they will have a sufficient check agst. encroachments on their
> own department by their exposition of the laws, which involved a
> power of deciding on their constitutionality (ibid., 1.97).

He was already assuming judicial review, even in conjunction
with an executive veto. The other framers shared Madison's fear
of the legislature precisely because they knew the Constitution
had to give it supremacy. That is just the situation that calls for
limits.

Madison did not give up his hopes for a stronger negative on
the legislature, even after the draft excluded it. He retreated
from his executive-judiciary council to a proposed executive-
Senate role (51.350). But he still thought the original proposal
was best, and he raised it again, in 1788, when making sugges-

tions for a new constitution in Kentucky. His plan had become unworkably complex, an indication of his "diehard" desire to save it. He envisaged five possible steps (*TJ*, 6.315):

1. All proposed legislation will be submitted separately to both the executive and the judiciary for possible veto.

2. If either branch vetoes the bill on nonconstitutional grounds, Congress can override by a two-thirds vote in each house. But if both veto it on nonconstitutional grounds, it will take a three-fourths vote in each house.

3. If either (or both) reject the bill on constitutional grounds, there is to be no override. The bill can be proposed again, but only after a new election of the lower house.

4. After such an election, the proposed bill must pass by a two-thirds majority if there was only one veto on constitutional grounds, but by three fourths of each house if both the executive and the judiciary vetoed on a constitutional point. It will be seen that this is, in effect, a recourse to the people—parallel to the passage of an amendment after judicial review declares a modern bill unconstitutional.

5. Any bill that has run this elaborate gauntlet and been repassed by overwhelming majority becomes, at last, untouchable by either of the vetoing powers: "It should not be allowed the judges or the Executive to pronounce a law thus enacted unconstitutional and invalid."

Madison's Kentucky plan gives the Court a much more active and constant role in legislation, even in nonconstitutional matters, than the modern Court has had at its most aggressive moments. And it would pose a constant temptation to "up the ante" on a veto by moving from nonconstitutional grounds (overridable) to constitutional grounds (killing the original bill). In describing this extraordinarily strong role for the judiciary, Madison put the Philadelphia draft in its worst light, as giving the Court *more* power—though Madison knew it did not; that is why he kept arguing for such a major check on the legislature he feared. (It should also be noted that Madison assumes here that judicial review exists in the state constitutions.)

In the State Constitutions and indeed in the Federal one also, no provision is made for the case of a disagreement in expounding them [the laws]: as the Courts are generally the last in making their decisions, it results [reverts—see Glossary] to them by refusing or not refusing to execute a law, to stamp it with its final character. This makes the Judiciary Dept. paramount in fact to the Legislature, which was never intended and can never be proper.

This passage is obviously a bit of special pleading, putting the plan Virginia had just ratified in the worst possible light, to show that Madison's own scheme was still necessary. That strategy emerges from three points:

1. When Madison says the Constitution took *no* provision for disagreement over the laws, he clearly means that it did not make *his* provision for settling matters. The Convention considered his revisionary council at length, and deliberately rejected it. Since Madison thought this plan the only adequate one, rejection of it meant for him rejection of any meaningful way to settle constitutional disputes.

2. He presents the system actually to be used—judicial review in the modern sense—as a mere "result" (reversion) to the only procedure left when Madison's was excluded. Opponents of judicial review have used this passage to say it does not exist in our constitutional scheme; but Madison is saying that it *does* exist there, and *lamenting* that fact, because it cannot in practice check the Congress as well as his plan would (his point at 51.350).

3. Thus he represents judicial review as a "result" *faute de mieux*—the only way the Constitution could operate once its framers forswore his plan. The Court is bound to get the final say "in fact," which makes the judiciary "paramount, which was never intended and can never be proper" (294). By allowing judicial review, Madison says, the framers ironically scrapped his own practical role for the judiciary and ended up with de facto judicial supremacy.

But we have seen that the Court does not really have the final say, in theory or in practice. It is easier for the present Congress to amend the Constitution, impeach a justice, pack the Court (a power Madison deplored, at *TJ*, 6.313), refuse funding, or have other recourse to popular opinion, than it would have been to defeat "suspension" of a bill by Madison's double-veto scheme.

In Madison's plan, Congress not only has to wait for a new election; it has to pass a constitutionally challenged bill by a three-quarters majority in each house—more than is needed presently for a constitutional amendment. Admittedly, under the present scheme, three quarters of the states must agree—but popular support *at least* that great would be needed to create the electoral majority needed as a *first* step toward resubmission of the challenged bill under Madison's Kentucky plan. And even with that kind of majority, a recalcitrant Senate could *still* block the suspended bill if that house had not enough changed its makeup or its mind to reach the three-quarters majority Madison calls for.

Madison's plan would make the Court far more intrusive in the passage of legislation than the existing Court has ever been or pretended to be. By ignoring the "shoot-out" weapons given Congress under the present system, Madison tries to make *his* Court look less than "paramount," though it would be far more powerful. This 1788 proposal reflects Madison's dogged, almost obsessive attempt to limit what he saw as the vast power of the legislature's more popular house. (The Senate would be given joint veto power in his suggested addition to the Constitution at 51.350.) It cannot be said that the Madison of The Federalist opposed judicial activism, though some have taken certain words out of context to maintain this. His own plan would have been the greatest nightmare possible for those who have twisted his words in that fashion.

Critics of judicial review like Henry Commager claim that it is antidemocratic in its treatment of the popular legislature. But Madison wanted to go *beyond* the Court's present power of review *precisely* to inhibit that part of the government. And remember that his Court would have, for its canon of interpretation, Madison's own defense of loose construction (Chapter Five). If Madison, speaking as Publius, ever opposed judicial review, it was because it did not go far enough. As we shall see in the next chapter, he never doubted that some power of review had to exist under the Constitution and would "result" to the Court of necessity if his council were not adopted.

EIGHTEEN

Legislative Supremacy: Madison

> The share of power, allotted by our constitution to the
> house of commons, is so great, that it absolutely com-
> mands all the other parts of the government.
> —Hume, 1.6.120

Some claim that Hamilton retroactively inserted judicial review
into the Constitution. Logically they have to assume that
Madison did not, independently, create it too. The assumption or
assertion is that Madison, if not actually opposed to review, was
silent on the subject. But, apart even from his efforts to create a
revisionary council and to encourage loose construction, Madison
argues in The Federalist for a view of fundamental law that entails judicial review of necessity. He does this in No. 53.

At the end of No. 52, Madison makes a surprising remark—
surprising because it seems to take away supremacy with one
hand while bestowing it with the other:

> . . . the Foederal Legislature will possess a part only of that
> supreme legislative authority which is vested completely in the
> British parliament (52.358).

This not only raises the classical sovereignty question—how can
supremacy be partial? It might also cause one—since the legislature and the legislative power are at times used synonymously in
The Federalist—to look for some partial *sharing* of supremacy on
the part of the executive or the judiciary.

But the beginning of the next paper establishes Madison's
meaning. The legislative power is supreme, but the legislature
does not possess it all because there is another organ of legislative power—the ratifying conventions that passed fundamental
law:

The important distinction so well understood in America between a constitution established by the people, and unalterable by the government, seems to have been little understood and less observed in any other country (53.360).

The British Parliament, in particular, has "actually changed, by legislative acts, some of the most fundamental articles of the government," because that system has "no constitution paramount to the government."

This would not be the case under the American plan, with "a government limited as the federal government will be, by the authority of a paramount constitution" (53.361). Fundamental law is superior in its claims to mere statute. Yet there will be no way of asserting that paramountcy if the Court does not decide between new laws and the fundamental law. Who else is to judge? Congress? But it is a party to the case—it has just passed the new law. It cannot be both party and judge. By making the same argument that Hamilton did in No. 78, Madison is implying the same logical outcome. For conflict to be resolved, a judicial act is needed. That act cannot be the legislature's, since Madison has offered this as a reflection *limiting* the legislature, making it less absolute than the British Parliament. The ratifying conventions cannot speak for themselves, since they have been dissolved after performing their instructed task. The only way the fundamental law can be spoken for is through the Court, which was created to expound it. Thus Madison, like Hamilton, does not grant any natural supremacy to the *Court;* rather, he grants a supremacy to the legislative bodies whose acts have been entrusted to the Court for careful retention. The legislature shares its supremacy not with the Court but with those other legislating bodies, the state conventions that enacted the Constitution.

Madison is at one with Hamilton in stressing the supremacy of fundamental law—which means stressing the dignity of the bodies that enacted it, the instructed delegations of the people at their ratifying conventions. These instructed representatives performed the "solemn and authoritative act" (78.528) that must be binding until it is undone by an equally solemn operation.

Only by taking this matter as seriously as Madison did can we make sense of one argument in No. 39. Madison maintains, there, that the states' sovereignty was respected in drawing up the

Constitution. Not only was a residual sovereignty left to the states; the same states exercised *full* sovereignty in the ratifying act. One wonders at first why Madison thought this a persuasive argument. He is trying to assure the states that they will not go out of existence, and he does this by saying that they made a surrender of sovereignty (or at least part of it)—which act, however voluntary, is nonetheless a surrender. He says the resulting union can be called federal because:

> Each State in ratifying the Constitution, is considered as a sovereign body independent of all others, and only to be bound by its own voluntary act (39.254).

It might look as if Madison is quibbling here. Surrendering sovereignty may be a sovereign's act—how can you give what you do not have?—but it still leaves you without that sovereignty after the bestowal. Yet Madison's stress on the special nature of fundamental law, and therefore on the status of the ratifying conventions, leaves the states with a kind of *potential* sovereignty under Article V. Three quarters of the states can order Congress to call a new constitutional convention "for proposing amendments." This call would qualify as the "solemn and authoritative act" that can change fundamental law. We have seen how broadly Madison construed the call of the Continental Congress to the first Constitutional Convention (40.259–60). Such a convention, demanded by the states, could decide to redraft the *whole* Constitution, as the Philadelphia body reworked the Articles. But an entirely new fundamental law would have to be ratified by the states *in their original capacity as sovereigns*.

Admittedly, this hypothesis sounds absurd. The states were *already* sovereign under the Articles of Confederation. They *had* to act as sovereigns in *surrendering* their sovereignty to the federal government constituted by that very act. In the same way, new states have been sovereign, or at least freed of all foreign sovereignty, when they were later admitted to the Union. But the states addressed by any new constitutional convention exist within the federal government now. They would go from one government directly into another one formed by the new plan.

The old Constitution would not cease to bind until ratifiers had substituted a new one.

Yet, the states would *have* to resume their sovereignty, to meet Madison's ratifying test at 39.254, if the new convention offered in effect a new constitution. According to Article V—which looks in its normal operation to mere amendment (whether by the states responding to Congress or to a convention)—approval by three quarters of the states would make this new plan the fundamental law. But such a plan would not be mere alteration under the *old* Constitution if, for instance, it dissolved the states in favor of other (regional) administrative units. We have an exact parallel to this in the ratification of the Constitution. That document did not become, what was at first planned, an amendment to the Articles; it supplanted them. If the modern states voted to dissolve themselves, they would do no more than the original states had in dissolving the Articles that guaranteed their sovereignty.

In that situation, a three-quarters vote would obviously not bind the remaining quarter of the states, *or any one state,* that refused consent to the new arrangement. Fifty states cannot impose a government from outside on one state. We have returned to the situation Madison described in No. 39. Adoption of a radically new constitution

> must result from the unanimous assent of the several States that are parties to it, differing no other wise from their ordinary assent than in its being expressed, not by the legislative authority, but by that of the people themselves . . . Each state in ratifying the Constitution, is considered as a sovereign body independent of all other, and only to be bound by its own voluntary act (39.254).

So Madison's paradoxical assurance to the states *was* meant to comfort them. He was saying that the making of fundamental law in its entirety is a sovereign's act, and the scheme cannot be completely remade without being submitted again for unanimous vote of the sovereigns. The failure of any state to ratify this new scheme would be a peaceful act of secession, the only one conceivable under the provisions of the Constitution.

This is, admittedly, the statement of an unlikely hypothesis; but it is also the only fair statement of what ratifying the Constitution meant. The states, sovereign at the moment of their decision to ratify, committed themselves to *one* basic scheme, not to any other. They provided for amendment, certainly; but not for entire remaking—any more than the Articles bound states to the remaking involved in the Constitution. It makes no sense in legal theory or plain fairness to say that the states' original submission was to any entirely new plan three quarters of the states might come up with in the future.

And wild as the hypothesis may seem, others have recognized it as a logical corollary of The Federalist's doctrine on the ratifying act. In order to oppose Justice Marshall's concept of judicial review, Edward Corwin said that the Court could not speak for the ratifying conventions, but that new conventions could—and that this would constitute a second revolution, allowing the people to speak directly for themselves (*Michigan Law Review*, 9.108; cf. *Doctrine*, 34–5).

Nor would this have seemed an unlikely development to Madison himself. He was adamantly opposed to further constitutional conventions, and even to review panels on constitutional performance (No. 49). These would be unsettling, in his view, because he had experienced the way conventions construe their mandate widely (No. 40). He feared them because he knew their power—just as he feared the legislative branch because it *had* to be supreme. He tells us himself that the Philadelphia Convention was but the latest in a series of attempts at refashioning the Confederation. Antifederalists thought another convention was needed before ratification. Madison knew that their proposal, if adopted, would spell the end of the Philadelphia draft. There would be no way of binding the new convention, and enemies of the draft would come prepared this time. The idea of getting together again and starting from scratch was not unthinkable to men who had just done that. There could be no authority superior to the states meeting in order to ratify a new body of fundamental law. This is just the complement of Madison's (and Hamilton's) teaching on fundamental law as opposed to statute.

Thus, in The Federalist's scheme of constitutional law, there is a natural hierarchy of legislative acts performed by the people, who can act through various channels:

1. The people can, as members of sovereign states acting through their ratifying conventions, adopt the fundamental law itself.

2. After adopting such a body of law, the people can reassemble in their conventions to substitute a new constitution, presented to them by a constitutional convention.

3. The people, by unanimous ratification of the states, can adopt a new constitution presented to them by the Congress.

4. The people's intent, in adopting the fundamental law, can be reasserted by the Supreme Court when statute contravenes that intent.

5. Three fourths of the states, acting through their legislatures, can adopt a constitutional amendment within the basic scheme of the original government (whether the amendment is proposed by Congress or by a specially summoned convention).

6. Most common of all, the people can, through their representatives in Congress, enact the legislative program of the United States.

As Hamilton argued in No. 78, the law is more binding insofar as it reflects a more direct participation of the people in its enactment. The people remain sovereign, acting through all the various legislative channels. This is true in the order of fact as well as of right: "In republican government the legislative authority, necessarily, predominates" (51.350). For both Madison and Hamilton, legislative supremacy and judicial review are not contradictory, not things at odds, but natural corollaries. Each asserts, in its own way, the primacy of fundamental law.

NINETEEN

Sovereignty

Every county-law may be annulled either by the senate or another county; because that shows an opposition of interest: In which case no part ought to decide
for itself. The matter must be referred to the whole,
which will best determine what agrees with general interest.

—Hume, 2.16.490

In the main argument of No. 51, Madison relied on one governmental check loosely related to separation of powers—the bicameral check *within* the most powerful department. He proposed
another check—the joint executive-Senate veto on the House of
Representatives—that was not adopted; but it was related to separation theory only as a blatant violation of it.

Yet, at the end of No. 51 Madison added two other checks—
one related to federalism (expounded in Nos. 37 and 46) and the
other to representation (expounded in Nos. 10, 56, and 58). Here
is the passage on a check arising from federalism:

In a single republic, all the power surrendered by the people, is
sumitted to the administration of a single government; and usurpations are guarded against by a division of the government into
distinct and separate departments [the check resulting from separation theory]. In the compound republic of America, the power surrendered by the people, is first divided between two distinct governments, and then the portion allotted to each, subdivided among
distinct and separate departments. Hence a double security arises
to the rights of the people. The different governments will controul
each other; at the same time that each will be controuled by itself
(51.350–1).

That seems clear enough; the scheme parcels out sovereignty to the several members, preventing concentration of power in one place. The classically undivided sovereignty was said to be incompatible with separated powers (Vile, 13, 40-2, 84). If that is true of separation doctrine taken by itself, it should be doubly true of a compound republic where *both* state and federal governments have separated powers. We seem, almost, to have an Aristotelian blend of mild regimes, a *medium mediorum*. No wonder Madison calls the result a "double security" for the rights of the people.

Besides, in practice, state governments have both reason and means to resist federal encroachment—the local legislature's power (in Madison's day) to appoint senators, the ties of local affection (46.316), the immediacy of local impact (17.107), the power to join with other states resisting federal infringement. In extreme cases, this would become the right to revolution. There is, indeed, an eerie anticipation of Madison's own part in later resistance to the Alien and Sedition Acts at No. 46. Madison says the federal government is bound to recognize not only its common stake and ties with the localities but its inability to impose schemes of aggression by military force.

So in practice (Madison thought) the states do not need to fear encroachment. Does that mean that in theory they retain their sovereignty, or part of it? We saw in the last chapter that they retained a potential sovereignty, to be exercised in case of return to the ratifying situation of 1787. But we should remember that such a return would, as Professor Corwin said, be a kind of revolution in government; and the right to revolution under any form of government, if abused, is a tenet Madison shared with all theorists of limited constitutions. So this potential sovereignty offers less than it seemed to. If the checks of a compound republic are to do what most people expect of them, then sovereignty should be retained state by state, at least in partial form, for preventing abuses—not just held in "the whole body of the people" for potential remedy of extreme grievances.

Madison seemed to provide for such partial sovereignty when he argued, in No. 37, that it was impossible to draw precise boundaries between state and federal powers; that experience would be needed to fix them; that compromise would make men agree in a process of give and take. Since the limits of *both* powers are imprecise, bargaining must take place between them. But in a bargaining process, one party cannot be dependent to begin with, submissive to the other's offer, no matter what. That is not a bargain but mere imposition; not compromise but fiat.

Some find in American history a confirmation of the view that the states keep powers for use as a check on the federal government. They say things have happened as the framers intended. Our government has not worked things out by appeal to some final authority. States and the various federal branches have negotiated, balancing their claims—and balance implies not only difference but rough equality of things poised on the scale. Our system therefore shows an aversion to "showdowns." The power to prevail may rest here at one time, there at another; but it does not rest there by some final right. Power shifts about, following the stresses of our "polyarchy." If this strange entity does not fit the classical view of sovereignty, so much the worse for the classical view. America broke the rules to become a new thing.

That is a very common view of our government, and one that Madison is supposed to have promoted. True, he might have given weapons to the centralizers by his Federalist teaching on implication and construction; but doesn't his *general* teaching resemble that of the "new" federalists, the pluralists who stress *circulation* of authority through our whole system? In short, if America's practice defies the doctrine of undivided sovereignty, is that not because Madison showed the way? The question may seem to answer itself. But not if we look very carefully at The Federalist. The answer to the question, as given there, is a simple no, several times given.

Though Madison says, in No. 37, that the boundaries between state and federal jurisdiction await future "liquidation" after discussion and experience, he also tells us who, after all the discussion, will get the final word:

> It is true that in controversies relating to the boundary between the two jurisdictions, the tribunal which is ultimately to decide, is to be established under the general Government. But this does not change the principle of the case. The decision is to be impartially made, according to the rules of the Constitution; and all the usual and most effectual precautions are taken to secure this impartiality. Some such tribunal is clearly essential to prevent an appeal to the

sword, and a dissolution of the compact; and that it ought to be established under the general, rather than under the local Governments; or to speak more properly, that it could be safely established under the first alone, is a position not likely to be combated (39.256–7).

We shall consider later the precautions for impartiality established within the federal government itself. But Madison leaves no room for evasion of his central point here—that the power *"ultimately* to decide" lies in the federal government, not the states; that it could safely be lodged in it *alone;* that the alternative would be two states in one, resolving conflict by the sword or by breakup of the compact. This is classic sovereignty doctrine, denying the possibility of two supreme decision makers in the same body, an *imperium in imperio.*

Some think Madison departs from classic theory because his sovereign is not absolute, like that voiced in the first thorough statement of the theory, Jean Bodin's. Bodin made sovereignty unlimited as well as undivided. His sovereign was politically "infallible." But even Bodin, if Julian Franklin is right, first conceived of sovereignty as nonabsolute (*Jean Bodin and the Rise of Absolutist Theory,* 1973, pp. 23–40). And others find limits even in his final statement of the theory (see Kenneth McRae's introduction to the *Six Bookes,* 1962, pp. A23, A35, A38). We need not linger over such disputes since seventeenth-century theorists quickly separated the concept of undivided sovereignty from that of unlimited power. The sovereign (supreme) power was legislative in the scheme of constitutional monarchy, but even it could not judge in a case where it was a party. The separation of powers was not, for Grotius or Pufendorf or Locke, a division of sovereignty. That had to remain single if the society was to be *a* society, single, a whole. If there is to be a whole, there must be a final and single "say" for that whole. It does not have to be the first say on all matters, or the entire say on any of them—just the last say.

For Locke, the majority's will (expressed either virtually or actually, tacitly or expressly) was sovereign. He uses the indivisibility of sovereignty to argue that where "one *Body Politick*" exists, "the Majority have a Right to act and conclude the rest" (par. 95)—else there would not be one body. To get the full force of his sentence, we must remember that "act" as a transitive verb meant "activate," even "animate," as in Pope's "Self-love, the strong spring of motion, acts the soul" (*Essay*, 2.39). That is how Locke uses the verb in the very next paragraph, when he says the majority "acts any Community." He implies the normal analogy for sovereign power—the single soul in a multiple body.

The second verb in the phrase "to act and conclude" is also transitive and means "determine" (*OED*, s.v. 11). We find that meaning, too, in the next paragraph, where the minority is bound "to be concluded by the majority." This means that the majority "determines . . . the whole." In paragraph 97, "to submit to the determination of the majority" is "to be concluded by it." And in paragraph 98 we read that the majority not only can "conclude the rest" in general but can "conclude every individual."

The legal sense of "conclude" is still alive in Hamilton's use of "conclusive power" for the right to determine the whole at 68.460 and 78.524. This power to speak for the entire body, when an ultimate decision must be made, is sovereignty; and Madison places that—so far as the Philadelphia draft is concerned—in the federal legislating power. That is the very meaning of legislative supremacy, as of the Constitution's own supremacy clause: The federal law "shall be the supreme Law of the Land . . . *any Thing in the Constitution or Laws of any State to the Contrary notwithstanding.*" That is power to conclude the whole; and it is not shared with the states because it cannot be shared with any other *imperium* without making that *imperium* an alien power, not part of the whole. Madison, in expounding the supremacy clause, says that the Constitution had to situate the final say in the federal government. Otherwise

> the world would have seen for the first time, a system of government founded on an inversion of the fundamental principles of all government; it would have seen the authority of the whole society every where subordinate to the authority of the parts; it would have seen a monster in which the head was under the direction of the members (44.306).

This language of head and members was traditional in descriptions of *sovereign* power.

One wonders why people ever expected Madison to speak against singleness of sovereignty. It was implicit in his and Hamilton's constitutional theory from the outset, in their view of legislative supremacy, of ultimate recourse to the people. The sovereignty in "the whole body of the people" is enunciated by the legislative power, acting through those hierarchical channels I traced at the end of Chapter Seventeen. Madison's whole analysis of confederacies traced their weakness to the retention of sovereignty in their parts (17.108; 18.110; 19.119, 120, 122). "Partial" is always a political "swear word" for him. He draws his argument to its ineluctable conclusion:

> Experience is the oracle of truth; and where its responses are unequivocal, they ought to be conclusive and sacred. The important truth, which it unequivocally pronounces in the present case, is, that a sovereignty over sovereigns, a government over governments, a legislation for communities, as contradistinguished from individuals; as it is a solecism in theory; so in practice, it is subversive of the order and ends of civil polity, by substituting *violence* in place of *law*, or the destructive *coertion* of the *sword*, in place of the mild and salutary *coertion* of the *magistracy* (20.128–9).

There can be no "sovereignty over sovereigns," no *imperium imperiorum*. This is the classic doctrine, expressly cited by Madison when writing to Jefferson (*JM*, 10.209). Sovereignty is single. In the Convention, as well as in his pre-Convention writings, Madison persistently located the weakness of the Confederation in the sovereignty of the states. He can hardly have written The Federalist to maintain that condition.

But the greatest proof of Madison's view is his original plan to give the federal government a veto over state laws, to be enforced by arms (Farrand, 1.21; *JM*, 10.209–14). That proposal was too blunt and radical in its centralizing tendency to be adopted. But it shows that, in this detail as in others, Madison was following Hume's "Idea of a Perfect Commonwealth." Hume wrote there that "no part [of a society] ought to decide for itself." Instead, "the matter must be referred to the whole" (2.16.490). Determination of the whole for the whole is the very meaning of sovereignty.

It is significant that those who look to The Federalist for a concept of divided sovereignty tend to find it only in Madison.

Hamilton wrote as much, and more strikingly, about "residual" or "concurrent" sovereignty. But the people who do not quite believe Madison when he voices the classic doctrine are ready to take Hamilton at his word when he attacks those trying to retain a sovereignty for the states:

> While they admit that the Government of the United States is destitute of energy; they contend against conferring upon it those powers which are requisite to supply that energy: They seem still to aim at things repugnant and irreconcileable—at an augmentation of Foederal authority without a diminution of State authority—at sovereignty in the Union and complete independence in the members. They still in fine seem to cherish with blind devotion the political monster of an *imperium in imperio* (15.93).

Hamilton, like Madison, calls division of sovereignty—any *imperium in imperio*—a political "monster," a body with two or more heads. People also take Jay at his word when he says the Confederation is failing because it retains "independent sovereignties" in the body (5.27; cf. 2.8-9).

Why, given the overwhelming evidence of the Convention debates and The Federalist itself, do some people maintain that Madison thought sovereignty divisible? The fault lies in Madison's own language (also Hamilton's, but fewer scholars look to him for decentralizing arguments). The Federalist was a protreptic exercise; it had to sweeten the pill of sovereignty's surrender. So, even while voicing the classical doctrine when the subject of his discourse left him no room for maneuver (e.g., at 20.128-9, 39.256-7, 44.306), Madison was willing to talk elsewhere about a "kind-of" sovereignty, emphasizing that the states would not be totally absorbed or obliterated, that the union would be distinctly *articulated*, that many areas were outside the purview of the general government. In this whole area, emotion had clouded men's language before Publius took up his three pens. Emotional language had to be countered with persuasive terminology, beginning with the crucial term "federalism."

TWENTY

Federalism

Divide the people into many separate bodies; and then
they may debate with safety, and every inconvenience
seems to be prevented.

—Hume, 2.16.487–8

Federalism has come to mean, in the common discourse of the
present, division of jurisdictions to decentralize government.
Jackson Turner Main reminds us that it started out meaning
much the same thing (*The Antifederalists*, 1961, xi–xii). The
word comes from *foedus*, meaning treaty, and should apply most
readily to those leagues and loose alliances that are criticized by
Hamilton and Madison in the earlier Federalist essays. There is,
in fact, no etymological reason to distinguish a federation from a
confederation.

But precisely because the Articles set up a Confederation of
the sovereign states in America, those wanting to strengthen the
general government began to talk of *federal* power as going
beyond the Confederation's claims upon its member states.
Madison himself was an early and consistent user of "federal" in
this sense, as Main notes (cf. *JM*, 8.335). By a kind of pre-emp-
tive verbal strike, the centralizers seized the word and cast the
original federalists in the role of antifederalists. Some of the ten-
sion involved in this recasting of the word's role remains in the
famous ending of No. 10. The last sentence asserts an apparent
paradox in arguing that centralization can be a vindication of republican values (as opposed to the despotic values feared by
"antifederalists"):

In the extent and proper structure of the Union, therefore we
behold a Republican remedy for the diseases most incident to Re-

publican Government. And according to the degree of pleasure and pride, we feel in being Republicans, ought to be our zeal in cherishing the spirit, and supporting the character [reputation] of Federalists (10.65).

That ringing last word was a kind of *défi*, and may explain why the collected papers were called The Federalist (rather than the expected Letters of Publius).

A touchiness about words surrounded the whole effort to make states surrender their sovereignty. The second Article of Confederation had proclaimed the states' unwillingness to do this—reflecting a concern that had been written into the very instructions on voting for independence (*Inventing*, 31–2). Opponents of the Constitution were sure that a stronger government than the Confederation would obliterate the states as distinct units, and they seized on a word in Gouverneur Morris's covering letter (signed by Washington) that recommended the draft Constitution to ratifying conventions:

> In all our deliberations on this subject we kept steadily in our view, that which appears to us the greatest interest of every true American, the consolidation of our Union, in which is involved our prosperity, felicity, safety, perhaps our national existence.

That penultimate word "national" stuck in some critics' craws; but the one they stormed and fretted over was "consolidation." What better proof that the new plan would dissolve the states and congeal them in an undifferentiated mass? Morris should have known better than to use "consolidation." When Edmund Randolph incautiously voiced it at the Convention, Luther Martin harped on that word to criticize the planned Constitution (Farrand, 1.24, 143). It was clear to Publius that terms for stronger union would have to be carefully chosen. In fact, Hamilton tried to repair the damage done by "consolidation" with a rather grand counter-metaphor:

> To this catalogue of circumstances, that tend to the amelioration of popular systems of civil government, I shall venture, however novel it may appear to some, to add one more on a principle, which has been made the foundation of an objection to the New Constitution, I mean the ENLARGEMENT of the ORBIT within which such systems are to revolve either in respect to the dimensions of a sin-

gle State, or to the consolidation of several smaller States into one great confederacy (9.52; cf. Farrand, 1.169).

The Enlightenment's favorite image of the solar system "loosens up" the idea of consolidation, making it all a matter of *larger* orbit. Hamilton found the same image useful when arguing against sovereignty in the lesser members at 15.97. He asked why anyone would encourage, in a grand system, "a kind of ex-centric tendency in the subordinate or inferior orbs, by the operation of which there will be a perpetual effort in each to fly off from the common center" (15.97). Madison used the figure at 18.112; and the picture of balanced orbs with a "common center" lies behind Hamilton's claim that the states in the new plan would just be more rationally "concentered" (11.70)—a word repeated by Madison at 14.84.

Publius had to convince the states that subordination would not lead to their obliteration. No one had that in mind. Even in his June 18 speech, calling for a sovereignty entire in the central government, Hamilton had provided for retention of the states as administrative units. But clearly he could not use such blunt language while soothing fears that the states would not remain as articulated parts with their own roles to play. So, as a kind of "sweet talk," Hamilton referred to *partial* incorporation or consolidation:

> An intire consolidation of the States into one complete national sovereignty would imply an intire subordination of the parts; and whatever powers might remain in them would be altogether dependent on the general will. But as the plan of the Convention aims only at a partial Union or consolidation . . . (32.199–200).

Hamilton tried to keep the *language* of the confederacies while attacking their rationale. One term was especially useful, since it came from Montesquieu, invoked by antifederalists to prove that no extended republics could exist. James Wilson pointed out, at the Convention, that even Montesquieu had granted the possibility of a "confederated republic" whose extent would lead to comparative independence of the parts (*Esprit*, 9.1.3). Hamilton took down this comment by Wilson in his own notes at the Convention (Farrand, 1.71, 73). He was squirreling away his ammunition. He lost no time in using this valuable term, which the *Independent Journal* set in capital letters:

> An intelligent writer expresses himself on this subject to this effect—
> "NEIGHBOURING NATIONS (says he) are naturally ENEMIES
> of each other, unless their common weakness forces them to league
> in a CONFEDERATE REPUBLIC" (6.35–6; cf. *AH*, 4.276).

Hamilton gives the source here as the Abbé de Mably, since the reference is more to a treaty-union than a single republic. Hamilton uses his big gun, Montesquieu, just three papers later:

> So far are the suggestions of Montesquieu from standing in opposi-
> tion to a general Union of the States, that he explicitly treats of a
> CONFEDERATE REPUBLIC as the expedient for extending the
> sphere of popular government and reconciling the advantages of
> monarchy with those of republicanism. "It is very probable (says
> he) that mankind have been obliged, at length, to live constantly
> under the government of a SINGLE PERSON, had they not con-
> trived a kind of constitution, that has all the internal advantages of
> a republican, together with the external force of a monarchical gov-
> ernment. I mean a CONFEDERATE REPUBLIC" (9.53).

Adair chided Hamilton, in his Yale dissertation, for relying on Montesquieu. But in this case he had to fight fire with fire. And Madison followed suit when he argued for a "confederated republic" (63.425).

Montesquieu's term was useful for calming fears because it kept the familiar note of a confederacy. We see here another example of Hamilton going further to placate the enemy than Madison would. Madison is so convinced of the weakness of confederacies that all his uses of the term (except a neutral one at 15.89) are pejorative. But Hamilton is willing to call the proposed new government a confederacy (9.52, 53, 55; 25.158; 27.173–4; 28.179; 29.181; 69.465).

It is this kind of sweet talk to the states that has led modern readers of The Federalist to think the book argues for decentralization of power rather than centralization. But decentralization existed at the time; that is what Publius was fighting. Still, to reassure people that the "consolidation" would not mean complete homogenization, Hamilton used his strict-construction arguments to show that things outside the Constitution's claims for the federal government would remain as they were in the states' sovereign condition. This amounted, he said, to a kind of residual or concurrent sovereignty. He refers to Montesquieu's confederate republic as granting potential sovereignty to the parts, to be resumed in case of aggression from the central authority (9.54–5). He stresses that, in raising their own taxes, states have "co-equal authority with the Union" (34.209), a "co-ordinate authority," like that which "in the last resort, resided for ages in two different [Roman] political bodies." But, as we have noticed all along, people do not take Hamilton very seriously when he talks of decentralization. It is Madison who is quoted on this subject. Were his mentions of "residuary sovereignty" (62.417) mere sweet talk?

Yes, they were. In No. 39, for instance, Madison says that the states will not be "consolidated into one nation," but will retain authority "within their respective spheres" (39.256). Yet on this very page Madison tells us who will decide how the spheres are bounded, who will have the "last say." We have already considered Madison's statement of the classical sovereignty doctrine. Before he gets to that sentence, though, Madison writes: "In this relation then the proposed Government cannot be deemed a national one; since its jurisdiction extends to certain enumerated objects only . . ." (39.256). That is technically true. But the government's enumerated *objects* are so vague ("promote the general welfare") that the real argument is always over enumerated *powers*—and in No. 44 Madison will tell us that the Constitution did *not* enumerate those, and should not have done so, because it should construe its mandate very broadly (44.303–35). Article X of the Bill of Rights will change this; but in The Federalist Madison is making an argument that leaves all the weapons on the federal government's side.

At 43.296, again feigning ignorance of the Convention's inner workings, Madison says that

> the equality of suffrage in the Senate was probably meant as a palladium to the residuary sovereignty of the States (43.296).

He has done a card trick on us. The Senate is part of the *federal* government. Its powers, no matter how registered, are federal—not a power of the states, far less a sign of their "residuary sovereignty." Madison had not only opposed equal votes in the Senate; he later tells us this was a measure adopted more on practical than theoretical grounds (62.416–17).

In No. 45 Madison says

> as far as the sovereignty of the States cannot be reconciled to the happiness of the people, the voice of every good citizen must be, let the former be sacrificed to the latter. How far the sacrifice is necessary, has been shewn. How far the unsacrificed residue will be endangered, is the question before us (45.309).

He settles this question by taking back some of the things he said in Nos. 18 and 19. He reasons that the ancient leagues did not degenerate into "one consolidated government" (45.310), so neither will the new union. But he had criticized those leagues for *not* having sacrificed their sovereignty. Now, while telling the states to do that, he says they should have no fear because of an example taken from states that did *not* do it. Madison tries to cover the argument's inadequacy by assuming the very thing he is trying to prove—that the states will retain "a very extensive portion of active sovereignty" that makes "inference" from "dissimilar" situations allowable (45.310). An argument of this sort is obviously placatory, not to be taken with the same degree of seriousness as the more precise formulations of the classic view that some single power must "conclude the whole" for there to be one body politic.

Many have dwelt on Madison's sweet talk and disregarded his basic argument for more power to the central government. In this way they steal back the term "federalist," which (as Main says) Madison first stole from the advocates of a looser league for the states. Yet those who argue from "the way America actually works" have a hard time proving that in our history the federal government did not have the final say on disputed matters—on slavery, for instance, or work conditions, voting rights, civil rights, whatever. Some claim the federal power has grown by usurpation, and this is not the place to decide what the Constitution itself intended. But surely the federal power to "conclude the whole" on matters like these would not have surprised Madison in his Publius phase—the Madison who wanted the federal government to have a veto over state laws, enforceable by arms.

If there has been balance and cooperation between the state and federal authorities, that was not because of some mutual power to *compel* forbearance. It arose from the efficiency argument for separation: Administrative division of labor is necessary in a republic extended far beyond that which the framers first envisioned. There is also lingering respect for the "amity" referred to in Morris's covering letter signed by Washington. There is, as well, a natural reluctance to force things to a "showdown" or shoot-out where ultimate power is in question. The greater the power, the more people hope to hold it in reserve, to find its use unnecessary, since the very use will be a confession that more amicable means have failed. It is to everyone's advantage to keep government flexible, nicely articulated in its parts. But that does not mean that Publius endorsed the view of some modern "federalists," who find a healthy clash between competing sovereignties in state and federal relations. For Publius, pitting *imperium* against *imperium* was a prescription for destruction, not a way to create order. In the solar system of "well constructed" government,* sovereignty—like "cosmic attraction"—is a single force.

* For the interest in a "société bien organisée," see *Inventing*, 115; Federalist, 13.81, 30.189, 65.439; Hume, 2.2.303, 305, 2.16.480; and *History*, 2.14.108.

PART FOUR

REPRESENTATION
(No. 10)

TWENTY-ONE

Genius of the People

Each nation has a peculiar set of manners.
—Hume, 1.21.244

Montesquieu's influence on The Federalist is usually discussed in terms of separated powers—on which, of course, Madison calls him "the oracle" (47.324). But he was less useful on this subject than one might expect, since his separation doctrine was joined, confusingly, with "mixed government" ideas. And his "extent of territory" argument was more a nuisance than a benefit to Publius.

But another aspect of Montesquieu's work was more pervasive in discussions of the American Constitution. Montesquieu's main task was to identify the *esprit général* expressed in different forms of government. The very title of his major work means something like *The Ethos of Legal Systems*. This was a subject that had intrigued Montesquieu since 1717, when he wrote an essay (now lost) *De la différence des génies*. He divided the factors forming a national spirit into the physical and the moral. Of the former, climate was the most important, so much so that Montesquieu has been considered a geographical determinist. But he studied other influences, too—population (Book 23), extent of territory (9.6), nature of the soil (Book 18).

The moral causes shaping national character include religion, legal standards, historical ideals, customs, manners (19.4). The art of the wise legislator is to frame laws that suit the spirit of the particular people (19.14). So true is this that Montesquieu abandons his ideal of government moderated through checks when he talks of "following natural genius" (19.5.3) in giving laws to a people. The French, for instance, are a volatile people

(19.5), somewhat like the ancient Athenians (19.7); it would be wrong to give them laws suited to the graver Spartans. Though one should check power, one should follow genius, since custom is more powerful than law. Law that tries to correct or over-balance custom is bound to lose in the contest (19.14–23). The legislator must say, with Solon, that he gives not the best laws but the best laws possible for his people.

Montesquieu reflects the taxonomic preoccupations of his age, the attempt to create a science of human society and happiness. The labors that began with the demographic and probability studies of the Royal Academy went forward in Scottish eco-nomics and the categorizing impulse of the Encyclopedists and Ideologues (see *Inventing*, Part Two). On all these counts Mon-tesquieu appealed to thinkers of the American Enlightenment. He was the Buffon of human society, and Madison—who studied Buffon with care (*JM*, 9.29–54, 78–81)—was bound to show an equal interest in the various species of the political animal.

Montesquieu was most useful to Americans in his claim that there exist monarchical and republican characters in all countries not cowed by despotism. They are differentiated by the two principles that motivate free societies, as by two drivesprings (3.1). In a monarchy, the drivespring (*ressort*) is honor; in a republic, virtue. (In despotism the motive force is fear.)

Richard B. Morris has remarked on the speed with which re-spect for monarchy disappeared during the Revolution. One force that helped men reject the whole monarchic ethos was Montesquieu's teaching on the *esprit général*. Throughout the constitutional debates we hear that America's government must be tailored to "the genius of the people" (Farrand, 1.101, 113, 153). Madison learned this doctrine from Dr. Witherspoon in Nassau Hall (V. L. Collins, 2.207).

Even when Hamilton proposed an American monarch, he real-ized it must be of a kind that consulted "the republican genius" (Farrand, 1.72). William Paterson, in offering the New Jersey Plan, gave it a rationale straight out of Montesquieu: "The Plan must be accommodated to the public Mind—consult the Genius, the Temper, the Habits, the Prejudices of the People" (1.186). Elbridge Gerry argued that Madison's scheme of separated powers sounded too much like Montesquieu's ideal of a limited monarchy to fit the American genius:

> Mr. Gerry repeated his opinion that it was necessary to consider what the people would approve. This had been the policy of all Legislators. If the reasoning of Mr. M were just, and we supposed a limited Monarchy the best form in itself, we ought to recommend it tho' the genius of the people was decidedly adverse to it, and having no hereditary distinctions among us, we were destitute of the essential materials for such an innovation (1.215).

Throughout The Federalist, Hamilton and Madison both defend the proposed Constitution as attuned to the genius of the American people. Madison says this is the very first test to be applied to the document:

> The first question that offers itself is, whether the general form and aspect of the government be strictly republican? It is evident that no other form would be reconcileable with the genius of the people of America; with the fundamental principles of the revolution; or with that honorable determination, which animates every Votary of freedom, to rest all our political experiments on the capacity of mankind for self-government. If the plan of the Convention therefore be found to depart from the republican character, its advocates must abandon it as no longer defensible (39.250).

In Book 13 of his *Esprit*, Montesquieu works out a sociology of taxation, since nothing calls for greater wisdom than the tailoring of tax demands to the genius of a people (13.1.4). He says that, so long as taxes are gradated roughly proportionate to income, a republic will pay them with confidence, knowing the funds serve the citizenry and are productive (13.13.1). Hamilton repeats that rather hopeful doctrine in Montesquieu's terms:

> There is no part of the administration of government that requires extensive information and a thorough knowledge of the principles of political economy so much as the business of taxation. The man who understands those principles best will be least likely to resort to oppressive expedients, or to sacrifice any particular class of citizens to the procurement of revenue. It might be demonstrated that the most productive system of finance will always be the least burthensome. There can be no doubt that in order to a judicious exercise of the power of taxation it is necessary that the person in

whose hands it is should be acquainted with the general genius, habits and modes of thinking of the people at large and with the resources of the country (36.222).

Madison says that the scheme of representation calls for a populace of republican genius. But aren't representatives bound to betray that populace's trust?

> I must own that I could not give a negative answer to this question, without first obliterating every impression which I have received with regard to the present genius of the people of America, the spirit, which actuates the state legislatures, and the principles which are incorporated with the political character [ethos—see Glossary] of every class of citizens. I am unable to conceive that the people of America in their present temper, or under any circumstances which can speedily happen, will chuse, and every second year repeat the choice of sixty-five or an hundred men, who would be disposed to form and pursue a scheme of tyranny or treachery (55.375–6).

This passage should be kept in mind when we hear that Madison did not trust the people. Both he and Hamilton find the American genius to be republican through and through.

Yet the people's shared character does not prevent local differences that will be useful in preventing overcentralization. In No. 60, Hamilton refers to Montesquieu's two great influences on the national spirit, the physical and moral causes:

> There is sufficient diversity in the state of property, in the genius, manners, and habits of the people of the different parts of the union to occasion a material diversity of disposition in their representatives towards the different ranks and conditions in society. And though an intimate intercourse under the same government will promote a gradual assimilation, of temper and sentiment, yet there are causes as well physical as moral, which may in greater or less degree permanently nourish different propensities and inclination in this particular (60.405).

The genius of the people must be fitted to the genius of the system designed for it. Thus both Hamilton (22.137) and Madison (18.114) study the genius of those confederations that failed. Madison observes that the Senate proposed by the Constitution is not "repugnant to the genius of America" (63.426), and

Hamilton says the same of the proposed executive (70.471).
Hamilton finds the American people pacific (16.101) and amicable in trade (22.137).

Although the most celebrated source of thinking on the *esprit
général* was, for Publius as for most Americans, Montesquieu,
Hamilton and Madison read a good deal about the genius of
peoples in that favorite book of theirs, the essays of Hume. In
criticizing the two revolutions of the seventeenth century, Hume
did not excuse either Charles I or James II for misreading the
nature of the people they governed: "Some of our British sovereigns mistook the nature of the constitution, at least, the genius
of the people; and as they embraced all the favourable precedents left them by their ancestors, they overlooked all those
which were contrary, and which supposed a limitation in our
government" (2.15.472).

Hume treated the art of the orator as similar to that of Montesquieu's legislator:

> An orator addresses himself to a particular audience, and must
> have a regard to their particular genius, interests, opinions, pas-
> sions, and prejudices; otherwise he hopes in vain to govern their
> resolutions, and inflame their affections. Should they even have en-
> tertained some prepossessions against him, however unreasonable,
> he must not overlook this disadvantage; but, before he enters upon
> the subject, must endeavour to conciliate their affection, and ac-
> quire their good graces. A critic of a different age or nation, who
> should peruse this discourse, must have all these circumstances in
> his eye, and must place himself in the same situation as the audi-
> ence, in order to form a true judgment of the oration (1.23.276).

But Hume's most important discussion of the *esprit général* occurs in the essay entitled "Of National Characters." This essay,
which appeared in the same year as Montesquieu's great work,
took a totally different approach to climate as a determinant of
national character. Montesquieu saw it as the principal physical
cause. Hume denied physical influence on national character in
general and that of climate in particular (1.21.246–55). This accords well with Hume's stress on the various forms of sociability
as the main shaping factors in human life:

> The human mind is of a very imitative nature; nor is it possible for

any set of men to converse often together, without acquiring a similitude of manners, and communicating to each other their vices as well as virtues. The propensity to company and society is strong in all rational creatures; and the same disposition, which gives us this propensity, makes us enter deeply into each other's sentiments, and causes like passions and inclinations to run, as it were, by contagion, through the whole club or knot of companions (1.21.248).

So far we have considered the national character in general. Montesquieu has more definite things to say of the republican genius, things we must consider next. But even at this stage we can see how closely Publius thought a government must be tailored to the national genius. This reminds us that Madison is unfairly accused by Dahl of neglecting social pressures and sanctions in setting up his governmental system. Madison knew that the success or failure of his scheme depended on influences shaping what Montesquieu called the national spirit. He did not offer the "mechanics" of his system as working automatically. He expressly said that even his favorite device—representation— depended on the ethos of the people (55.376). And he had a very definite concept of that ethos.

TWENTY-TWO

Virtue

> When a man denies the sincerity of all public spirit or affection to a country and community, I am at a loss what to think of him.
>
> —Hume, 1.11.154

In making virtue the drivespring (*ressort*) of republics, Montesquieu had a specific form of virtue in mind—political or public virtue, defined as preference of the common good to one's private interest. "Virtue in a republic is a very simple matter—it is love of the republic" (5.2.1). This is a *sentiment*, not a rational calculus or the end of a syllogism of conscience (ibid.; see *Inventing*, 279–81). It is an action of the heart, not the head. High and low alike can have it in its purity.

Only when virtue is defined this way can Montesquieu explain the eighteenth-century paradox of the English people—that, even though they enjoy more freedom than other Europeans, they are incapable of democracy. Montesquieu, who met Bolingbroke in England and accepted his Country party analysis, thought corruption and faction showed a lack of the requisite public virtue. Corruption—the bribe system—is related to the classical analysis of decline as the result of *luxuria*. Faction, Aristotle's *stasis*, prefers a part of society to the whole. These are the supreme sins against political virtue.

So when Montesquieu speaks of virtue he is not discussing theological, Christian, private, or ascetical virtue. He means the virtue of a Brutus, sacrificing his own sons to the state. He means the virtue Addison celebrated in Cato. When critics objected that he had excluded virtue from monarchy, even the limited monarchy he praised, he had to explain that virtues can exist in a monarchy, even public virtue, but they are not essential to it, as to a republic. They are not the mainspring. Honor is the driving force of monarchy.

These assurances were not enough to keep *De l'esprit* off the Vatican's index of forbidden books. The secularizing of virtue, the reduction of it to this world, to political goals, was as upsetting to the Holy Office as Beccaria's secularizing of happiness (*Inventing*, 151-2). Montesquieu's excisions and explanatory notes did not placate the religious authorities. He was dangerous. He suggested the possibility of a purely secular state, which America accomplished forty years after Montesquieu's book was published. Authority would come, now, not from religious or regal office but from republican virtue, the disinterested dedication of that modern Cincinnatus, George Washington.

For Madison and Hamilton, the only thing that should recommend a man to his political fellows is the union of public virtue with wisdom. These linked qualities make up a kind of refrain in The Federalist, and are the only grounds for holding republican office. When the pairing is not expressly of virtue with wisdom (2.10, 36.230, 73.495), synonyms are used: "considerate and virtuous citizens" (10.57), "candid and judicious" (36.230), "upright intention and a sound judgment" (53.363), "abilities and virtue" (64.433), "able and honest" (64.434), "talents and virtues" (72.487; cf. 1.3). Madison accepts the distinction between gifts of the head and of the heart, saying that state legislatures in the Confederation showed a deficiency of the head's gifts but not of the heart's (62.419). He defines their different provinces thus: "A good government implies two things; first, fidelity to the object of government, which is the happiness of the people; secondly, a knowledge of the means by which that object can be best attained" (62.419). Devotion to the happiness of the people is public virtue. As Montesquieu puts it, "In a republic, loving democracy means loving the people" (5.3.1).

Hamilton's analysis of the difference between a monarchy and a republic is based directly on Montesquieu. First, honor directs the monarch (*Esprit*, 3.7.2, 5):

An hereditary monarch, though often disposed to sacrifice his subjects to his ambition, has so great a personal interest in the government, and in the external glory of the nation, that it is not easy for a foreign power to give him an equivalent for what he would sacri-

fice by treachery to the State. The world has accordingly been wit-
ness to few examples of this species of royal prostitution, though
there have been abundant specimens of every other kind (22.142).

But corruption can reach the private citizen whose honor is not
identified with the glory of the realm. This makes virtue indis-
pensable as the directing force of a republic (*Esprit*, 3.4.3–8):

> In republics, persons elevated from the mass of the community, by
> the suffrages of their fellow citizens, to stations of great pre-
> eminence and power, may find compensations for betraying their
> trust, which to any but minds animated and guided by superior vir-
> tue, may appear to exceed the proportion of interest they have in
> the common stock, and to over-balance the obligations of duty
> (22.142; the point is repeated at 75.505; it had been made in
> Hamilton's speech at the Convention [*AH*, 4.193]).

Do our authors really mean what they are saying? If so, much
that has been written about The Federalist must be discarded.
Publius claims, with Montesquieu, that public virtue is an absolute necessity for the existence of a republic. Madison said that
the virtue of the people will insure the choice of good representatives (55.375–6). How does this square with the assertion,
so common in the literature, that Publius took a dark view of
human nature, thought of it as needing to be checked, distrusted,
and bound down? Dahl, for instance, says that the Madisonian
system is based on "certain psychological axioms that were
widely accepted in his day—and perhaps are now. These axioms
are Hobbesian in character and run something like this: Men are
instruments of their desires. They pursue these desires to satia-
tion if given the opportunity. One such desire is the desire for
power over other individuals, for not only is power directly satis-
fying but it also has great instrumental value because a wide variety of satisfactions depend on it" (*Preface*, 8). Then Dahl
quotes Madison on the nature of man as always seeking more
power.

If Madison took a Hobbesian view of man, he would have
been forced to abandon Montesquieu's view of republics. Unless
men can transcend private gain for public good, a republic is impossible. An assertion that such virtue is beyond man dooms the
enterprise from the outset, as Madison realized. Answering the

charge that the President will corrupt members of the House with newly created "places," Madison replies:

> The members of the Congress are rendered ineligible to any civil offices that may be created or of which the emoluments may be increased, during the term of their election. No offices therefore can be dealt out to the existing members, but such as may become vacant by ordinary casualties [accidents]; and to suppose that these would be sufficient to purchase the guards of the people, selected by the people themselves, is to renounce every rule by which events ought to be calculated, and to substitute an indiscriminate and unbounded jealousy [suspicion], with which all reasoning must be vain. The sincere friends of liberty who give themselves up to the extravagancies of this passion are not aware of the injury they do their own cause. As there is a degree of depravity in mankind which requires a certain degree of circumspection and distrust: So there are other qualities in human nature, which justify a certain portion of esteem and confidence. Republican government presupposes the existence of these qualities in a higher degree than any other form. Were the pictures which have been drawn by the political jealousy of some among us, faithful likenesses of the human character, the inference would be that there is not sufficient virtue among men for self-government; and that nothing less than the chains of despotism can restrain them from destroying and devouring one another (55.377–8).

That passage does not suggest that the American system is built on distrust of one's fellow citizens. On the contrary, Madison says it is built on qualities that merit esteem and confidence, qualities present "in a higher degree" here than in any other form.

This doctrine is not confined to Madison. Hamilton, too, accepts Montesquieu's norm: "The supposition of universal venality in human nature is little less an error in political reasoning than the supposition of universal rectitude. The institution of delegated power implies that there is a portion of virtue and honor among mankind, which may be a reasonable foundation of confidence" (76.514). There must be sufficient virtue and honor for the republic to be built on that, not on mutual distrust. The Federalist, far from glorifying distrust, or relying on it, attacks foes of the Constitution for their indiscriminate jealousy (suspicion). Madison says these foes reject features of the plan "from a partial [partisan] view of the subject; or from a jealousy which discolours and disfigures every object which is beheld" (58.391; cf. 55.378). Hamilton attributes the same doubts to "the extravagant surmises of a distempered jealousy" (59.399), indulged by men "inclined to consult their jealousy only" (61.411; cf. 1.5).

It is true that the various Publii can describe man's dark side. But sometimes this is done as a foil to brighter hopes offered by the American experience. Madison says the record of great councils is "a history of factions, contentions, and disappointments; and may be classed among the most dark and degrading pictures which display the infirmities and depravities of the human character" (37.238). But he does this to contrast that picture with the surprising amity and mutual concessions of the federal Convention (239). Hamilton writes: "The history of human conduct does not warrant that exalted opinion of human virtue which would make it wise in a nation to commit interests of so delicate and momentous a kind as those which concern its intercourse with the rest of the world to the sole disposal of a magistrate, created and circumstanced, as would be a president of the United States" (75.505–6). But he goes on to say that the President will add his own note of wisdom and integrity to the *joint* consideration of treaties with the Senate: "And whoever has maturely weighed the circumstances, which must concur in the apointment of a president will be satisfied, that the office will always bid fair to be filled by men of such characters as to render their concurrence in the formation of treaties peculiarly desirable, as well on the score of wisdom as on that of integrity" (75.506).

Cumulatively, the quotations considered in this and the last chapter present an "optimistic" view of the American genius, of the republican virtue that will exist in the citizens and lead to a choice of wise and virtuous leaders. Yet all this material is overlooked or de-emphasized by those who fasten on the two or three most famous statements of a "dark view" of man's nature. Certainly Dahl had to read The Federalist very selectively to claim that it presents a Hobbesian view of men as entirely given over to selfish motives.

Yet those few dark passages *do* exist in The Federalist. How are we to reconcile them with the reliance on virtue as preserving the American republic? Madison's most famous statement calls government "the greatest of all reflections on human nature," since men would not need government if they were angels (51.349). Hamilton, too, talks of men's faults as the cause of government:

Why has government been instituted at all? Because the passions of men will not conform to the dictates of reason and justice, without constraint. Has it been found that bodies of men act with more rectitude or greater disinterestedness than individuals? The contrary has been inferred by all accurate observers of the conduct of mankind; and the inference is founded upon obvious reasons. Regard to reputation has a less active influence, when the infamy of a bad action is to be divided among a number, than when it is to fall singly upon one. A spirit of faction which is apt to mingle its poison in the deliberations of all bodies of men will often hurry the persons of whom they are composed into improprieties and excesses, for which they would blush in a private capacity (15.96).

One of those "accurate observers of the conduct of mankind" who had noticed a difference between the behavior of men singly and in groups was David Hume. He began that essay quoted by Hamilton in his teens, "Of the Independency of Parliament," with a famous statement of that difference for the uses of political analysis:

Political writers have established it as a maxim, that, in contriving any system of government, and fixing the several checks and controuls of the constitution, every man ought to be supposed a knave, and to have no other end, in all his actions, than private interest. By this interest we must govern him, and, by means of it, make him, notwithstanding his insatiable avarice and ambition, co-operate to public good. Without this, say they, we shall in vain boast of the advantages of any constitution, and shall find, in the end, that we have no security for our liberties or possessions, except the good-will of our rulers; that is, we shall have no security at all. It is, therefore, a just *political* maxim, *that every man must be supposed a knave:* Though at the same time, it appears somewhat strange, that a maxim should be true in *politics* which is false in *fact*. But to satisfy us on this head, we may consider, that men are generally more honest in their private than in their public capacity, and will go greater lengths to serve a party, than when their own private interest is alone concerned. Honour is a great check upon mankind; But where a considerable body of men act together, this check is, in a great measure, removed; since a man is sure to be approved of by his own party, for what promotes the common interest; and he soon learns to despise the clamours of adversaries. To which we may add, that every court or senate is determined by the greater number of voices; so that, if self-interest influences only the majority, (as it will always do [in the present depraved state of mankind]) the whole senate follows the allurements of this separate interest, and acts as if it contained not one member who had any regard to public interest and liberty (1.6.117–19; Hume deleted the bracketed phrase from later editions).

Hume rejected the theories of "Hobbes and Locke, who maintained the selfish system of morals" (*Enquiry*, 267), but that did not make him sappily optimistic when talking about power relationships: "In the smallest court or office, the stated forms and methods, by which business must be conducted, are found to be a considerable check on the natural depravity of mankind. Why should not the case be the same in public affairs?" (1.3.105). One can collect other passages from Hume, more than there are in The Federalist, on the need to thwart men's selfishness; but Hume will never admit that this is the most basic instinct or political motive in man. He addresses the general problem directly in "Of the Dignity or Meanness of Human Nature," where he makes three arguments, all for the Dignity side of the question.

In the first place, it is more *useful* to think in terms of human loftiness:

> I must, however, be of opinion, that the sentiments of those, who are inclined to think favourably of mankind, are more advantageous to virtue, than the contrary principles, which give us a mean opinion of our nature. When a man is prepossessed with a high notion of his rank and character in the creation, he will naturally endeavour to act up to it, and will scorn to do a base or vicious action, which might sink him below that figure which he makes in his own imagination (1.10.151).

Hume was not one to dismiss an argument as "merely" utilitarian; and, besides, for him the reality of the self *is* self-opinion. In his essay on national character, he says that Caesar's tenth legion, collected promiscuously, "having once entertained a notion, that they were the best troops in the service, this very opinion really made them such" (1.21.255).

But here he is not ready to stop at the pragmatic argument.

After dismissing another view, which he considers a matter of tricks played with perspective, he comes to the only matter that "decides any thing in the present question." In the perspective argument, Hume says that those who would degrade man do not compare him with creatures near to him in the observable universe—animals "blindly conducted by instinct," but with imaginary or unseen beings—angels, or humans in an imagined state of perfection (i.e., the myth of Adam): "Man falls much more short of perfect wisdom, and even of his own ideas of perfect wisdom, than animals do of man; yet the latter difference is so considerable that nothing but a comparison with the former can make it appear of little moment" (1.11.153). Thus man's own gifts of imagination are used to sink him in the scale of being. Also, only the *superlative* of wisdom and virtue is treated as its *positive* degree in most discourse. In all these ways man ingeniously slanders himself.

But the third, and the only important, argument is the actual motive that prevails in human action. That, Hume says, is the moral sense, or social virtue: "Were our selfish and vicious principles so much predominant above our social and virtuous, as is asserted by some philosophers, we ought undoubtedly to entertain a comtemptible notion of human nature" (1.11.154). He says those are wrong who deny "public spirit or affection to a country"—the thing needed to make a republic work at all. But those are even more obviously wrong who doubt that private friendship can exist "if no interest or self-love intermix itself." The fallacy is to think that pleasure in friendship and virtue must be a selfish pleasure (1.11.156)—the very thing the theory of moral sense was elaborated to deny (*Inventing*, 193–5).

In Hume, a politics of checks on self-aggrandizement does not imply a "selfish system" like that of Hobbes or Locke. In the same way, Publius can talk of human nature as needing political guards and safeguards, without precluding the high degree of public virtue needed to create and maintain a republic. This does not, of course, mean that Publius had to hold Hume's theory *in toto*. But it should make us look a little more carefully at the political evils criticized in The Federalist—the principal of which is faction.

TWENTY-THREE

Faction

> Factions subvert government, render laws impotent,
> and beget the fiercest animosities among men of the
> same nation, who ought to give mutual assistance and
> protection to each other.
>
> —Hume, 1.8.127

If the distinguishing note of a republic is public virtue, which
encourages all to participate in decisions for the common good,
the evil to which it is most vulnerable must be faction, which reduces public discourse on the common good to mere squabbling
among private interests. "The friend of popular governments,
never finds himself so much alarmed for their character [reputa-
tion] and fate, as when he contemplates their propensity to this
dangerous vice" (10.56). We get some idea of the concept's importance to Madison when we note that the canonical analysis
traced republics' downfall to *luxuria*, to corruption brought
about by excesses of prosperity or greed (*Esprit*, Book 7).
Madison did not accept the Country party analysis on this point,
which Montesquieu picked up from Bolingbroke. Madison followed Bolingbroke's critic, Hume, whose misgivings about organized opposition led to his key essays on faction.

Yet there is some doubt that Madison's concept of faction can
be very useful. Dahl predictably pushes him hardest on this
term, and concludes that Madison fails because of "the absence
of any definite meaning of the word faction" (*Preface*, 29). If
Madison failed, it was not for lack of trying to define his term:

> By a faction I understand a number of citizens, whether amounting
> to a majority or a minority of the whole, who are united and ac-
> tuated by some common impulse of passion, or of interest, adverse

to the rights of other citizens, or to the permanent and aggregate interests of the community (10.57).

Dahl argues that this definition is useless for what seem the two most obvious purposes of Madison—defining an objective abuse, or deciding who is to declare it an abuse.

In the first place, Madison defines "faction" as an invasion of two unknowns—and if one does not know what is being invaded, one cannot identify the invader. The two things faction invades are "the rights of other citizens" and "the permanent and aggregate interests of the community." The definition, again according to Dahl, assumes that one knows what these two things are. But how? By divine revelation? By prior definition? From some unquestioned authority? For the modern pluralist, government is itself a process not only for protecting rights and the common interest, but for finding out what these are, for reaching a joint decision on such matters. While that deciding process goes on, faction not only cannot be excluded or opposed, it cannot even be identified (*Preface,* 25).

Well, if there is no prior and objective test of faction by declared right or aggregate interest, is there a way *in the process* of identifying these two? If the people themselves are going to define rights and common interests *ambulando,* there seem to be only three possible groups for enunciating these rights. One enunciation might be by unanimous vote—an outcome unlikely in itself and irrelevant to the problem of faction: If the people were unanimous against a faction, the faction would have no spokesmen at all, would not exist. A second way is by majority decision; and that works fine, Madison says, so long as the minority is really factious (really opposed to individual right and the common good). But what if it is not factious? And how does one determine that? Not simply by its failure to muster a majority.

The last remaining group, after we have rejected unanimous decision and majority decision, is the minority. Should it be given the power to decide? Yet being in a minority is no more proof of right than being in a majority; and giving the minority power will satisfy fewer people than would decision by a majority. Does Madison actually give the minority a power to decide? Dahl thinks Madison just ducks the difficulties here and comes up with a nonsolution—instead of decision by minority, non-decision by minority (or minorities). Minorities can make use of dispersed and staggered governmental machinery to clog, delay, slow down, hamper, and obstruct the majority. But these weapons for delay are given to the minority irrespective of its factious or nonfactious character; and they can be used against the majority irrespective of its factious or nonfactious character. What Madison prevents is not faction, but action. What he protects is not the common good but delay as such.

Dahl thinks this is not much of a solution, and I agree. Yet at least three different schools accept this "solution" as Madison's principal contribution to political theory. The first school might be called conservative, and I shall discuss it in this chapter. The other views are, in a broad sense, liberal and polyarchal; they will be treated in the next two chapters.

In the conservative view, delay as such is a good where legislation is concerned. The governmental powers of coercion are so great that they should come into play only after a sincere attempt at persuasion. For Willmoore Kendall, the whole point of Madison's machinery is to guarantee that any decision registered in law should represent "the deliberate sense of the community." He says of The Federalist:

> It treats *deliberation*, that is, dialogue back and forth among members of the assembly and among the "branches" of the government, as the be-all-end-all of the democratic process, and claims for it that it will produce the "sense" (*not* the will) of the people as a whole . . . It postpones actual decisions concerning policy issues until a relatively tardy moment in the process of deliberations (*Willmoore Kendall Contra Mundum*, 1971, 500–1).

In effect, Kendall says the government should offer proof, principally tested in terms of hours spent on the problem, that there was an attempt to reach *unanimous* agreement: "My guess, based on long meditation about the relevant passages, is that they hoped the deliberation would be of such character that the votes would seldom be 'close,' so that the popular majority represented would be overwhelming" (ibid., 216). For Kendall, the nation's law should not only be, but should bear the marks of, "a 'deal' hammered out, in the course of *lengthy* deliberation and negotiation" (ibid., 414; italics added).

Kendall, as usual, refreshes by his absence of cant. He makes no bones about the fact that what is involved is delay for delay's sake. Only that, he thinks, will create the moral credentials for imposing any decision on a minority. A certain "conservative" fear of government tends toward the Kendall analysis—also voiced by men like Martin Diamond and George Carey. What are we to make of this analysis, in terms of the text of The Federalist, of its own logic, and of its applicability to our history?

First, in terms of the text, Kendall constantly quotes the phrase "deliberate sense of the community" without identifying the Number or Numbers he draws it from. He is rather vague about the textual anchoring for what is the "be-all-end-all" of Federalist teaching. I find the phrase used only once by Hamilton and once by Madison. Hamilton's use is at 71.482:

> The republican principle demands, that the deliberate sense of the community should govern the conduct of those to whom they entrust the management of their affairs; but it does not require an unqualified complaisance [compliance] to every sudden breese of passion, or to every transient impulse which the people may receive from the arts of men, who flatter their prejudices to betray their interests.

Madison, like Hamilton, puts the phrase in a concessive first clause, then goes on to say that popular passion should be resisted:

> As the cool and deliberate sense of the community ought in all governments, and actually will in all free governments ultimately prevail over the views of its rulers; so there are particular moments in public affairs, when the people stimulated by some irregular passion, or some illicit advantage, or misled by the artful misrepresentations of interested men, may call for measures which they themselves will afterwards be the most ready to lament and condemn (63.425).

These passages will, indeed, strike most people as "conservative," as opposed to democracy of the direct sort that might voice passion. Their words are in accord with No. 49. Madison adds "cool" to the phrase "deliberate sense." And Hamilton, in the very paragraph I quote, sounds the same note:

When occasions present themselves in which the interests of the people are at variance with their inclinations, it is the duty of the persons whom they have appointed to be the guardians of those interests, to withstand the temporary delusion, in order to give them time and opportunity for more cool and sedate reflection (71.482–3).

"Cool" judgment is praised elsewhere as checking passion (50.346). This reflects Montesquieu's emphasis on *sang froid* in those making governmental decisions. It reflects Hume's thought in passages like this: "A man reads a book or pamphlet alone and coolly. There is none present from whom he can catch the passion by contagion" (1.2.197). And it is true that coolness implies, in both "deliberate sense" passages of The Federalist, a cooling off *period,* a delay. Hamilton opposes a *"sudden* breese" of passion, and Madison describes the deliberate sense as that which "ultimately" prevails in a free society.

There we have the textual evidence for Publius' interest in "deliberate sense of the community." Not only is it rather exiguous for what Kendall calls the "be-all-end-all" of The Federalist; both Hamilton and Madison are describing the same situation, which is not the one Kendall sketches for us. Publius presents us with "rulers" (Madison's word) withstanding the people when their passions are wrought on by the "art" of demagogues. Kendall, by contrast, talks about a reasoning process *among* the rulers. His is an intellectual debate over differing opinions. The note of passion does not enter. He talks of "dialogue back and forth among members of the assembly" (*Contra Mundum,* 500). He writes that

because it [The Federalist] clearly takes a dim view of decision by a bare majority, it puts the [elected] participants (whom it *expects* to arrive at a "consensus") under severe pressure to come to know and understand one another, to "feel each other out" (ibid., 502).

Kendall has, in effect, tacitly corrected Publius to give him what he considers a more defensible position. Publius' two sentences say nothing about internal debate among the rulers, just about the rulers' defiance of the populace.

Kendall's distance from the text of The Federalist appears when he stresses as particularly "Publian" things that Publius never supported—things like committee assignments by party, chairmanship by seniority, or anticloture rules to protect filibusters. These things do prolong what Kendall is interested in— legislative debate within both houses; but they have nothing to do with the passages on "deliberate sense" actually written by Hamilton and Madison. An attempt to understand those passages would take us (as I hope to prove) in a direction different from Kendall's when he airily assures us that his views are there in The Federalist (somewhere).

But what of Kendall's argument considered apart from its textual basis? Does it describe the way the American system should work or does work? Well, it certainly does not describe the way it has worked. Kendall, remember, says there should be no close votes in the legislature, that the delaying process should keep people from acting until the majority is "overwhelming." But on most matters contested at all, legislative votes tend to be rather close. Kendall might reply that these close votes often reflect a bargaining process, "logrolling," not related to merits of the single issue up for vote but to deliberative processes taken as a whole. Here we get even further from Publius, and endanger Kendall's own case for delay—that it will present, on its face, some evidence of unwillingness to foist resisted changes on a minority. If the vote is close, the evidence that the persuasive process has taken place is not (in Kendall's terms) very convincing.

Another problem with Kendall's picture of governmental process is that it calls up a scene of people sitting around a table and thoroughly "thrashing through" a problem before doing anything about it. People are "under severe pressure to come to know and understand one another, to 'feel each other out.'" Kendall seems to have faculty meetings in mind—things with little resemblance to public debate over a protracted period. In the latter case, new people are entering or leaving the electorate, sending new representatives to speak for them while others retire. Even an old question is a new one to many of the late arrivals. For a parallel, we would have to imagine a faculty meeting that discusses one problem all day long, but with members of the meeting (including the chairman and the secretary) constantly coming and going at irregular intervals. Perhaps, by the end of the day, all major points will have been canvassed, but not by all the people involved. For many of them, key points remain undiscussed.

Madison criticized Thomas Jefferson for imposing a static picture on situations still in flux when he said contracts should be canceled every nineteen years (*Inventing*, 123–8). Madison saw that those coming in and out of the scheme at irregular intervals would not observe, each of them, the equitable nineteen years. In the same way, the fluidity of public debate is not properly represented in the static image of a single discussion at a meeting (however prolonged).

The importance of this will be seen if we notice that Kendall presents his argument in some places as explicating No. 10, which nowhere mentions the general sense of the community, but makes a good deal of the protections to be derived from an extended territory. How does that affect Kendall's view of the book's "be-all-end-all"? It is true that the business of sending delegates from distant places may delay decision; but, if anything, it would tend to disrupt discussion (which is the supposed beneficiary of delay in Kendall's scheme). It is equivalent, not to prolonging discussion at the faculty meeting, but to sending new people into it, calling others out, in order to break up the deliberative line of thought.

But the real flaw in Kendall's argument is that it gives us a Publius who forgets what question he was asking himself. His Publius asks how to avoid faction, and then tells us how to avoid precipitancy. This would make sense only if a hastily formed majority were by definition factious—i.e., opposed to right and the common good. But that is obviously not the case. We are returned to the problem Madison labors under in all interpretations that make mere opposition to the majority a virtue. A minority, whether factious or nonfactious, can block a majority, whether factious or nonfactious, for as long as its will, its skill at using the tools of delay, are equal to those of the majority. Granted, the majority can get its way in time—if it is determined enough, can hold itself together, can deploy the right parliamentary or propaganda skills. In effect, it is granted the final say so long as it agrees not to have the first say—or any say, for quite a while. We get eventual decision by majority, but only after a protracted period of nondecision by minority.

This glorification of delay as salvific in itself has no relation to the government we observe in our history. We all know of laws now considered just that were put off for decades by the delaying tactics Kendall praises—civil rights laws filibustered to death, labor laws lobbied against, corporation-control laws buried in committee. Delay just prolonged conditions of injustice; and it is this situation that Kendall bluntly defends. But his defense is marred in three ways. First, as I say, the things that actually killed such laws were not included in the scheme Publius was describing. The committee chairman and staff, the lobbying apparatus, and the cloture rules did not exist in 1787. Before we assume that these devices are Publian, we must look harder at the "deliberate sense" passages than Kendall gives any evidence of having done.

Second, the way the minority was finally worn down had little to do with persuasion, the putative goal in Kendall's system. Few minds were actually changed among the original participants of legislative debate. Some participants were removed electorally, some outmaneuvered in parliamentary terms, others forced to yield for fear of losing on another issue. It became a question of who could outlast the others, a process not unfamiliar to those who have sat on committees or boards.

Third, even if one found a real debate taking place in Kendall's terms—if, that is, we had a faculty meeting up on Capitol Hill every day—theorists of committee decision making, from Condorcet and Lewis Carroll to Duncan Black and Kenneth Arrow, have shown that this kind of deliberation does not guarantee the right (i.e., the nonaccidental) decision. Those who admire mere process are at the mercy of mere process—of things like the order in which resolutions come up, the use of "sophisticated" voting, the reliance on rules to prevent persuasion rather than promote it. Kendall defines a view as factious or nonfactious according to the time it takes one to reach that view—which is like saying that only the dimwitted can be wise, because it takes them so long to make up their minds.

TWENTY-FOUR

Interest

But, besides this difference of *Principle,* those parties
are very much fomented by a difference of INTER-
EST, without which they could scarcely ever be dangerous or violent.

—Hume, 1.9.134

Some liberals have used The Federalist in ways that bear a
superficial resemblance to the conservative argument just considered. They, too, think the deciding process should be sheltered
and prolonged; but not because they consider delay a good thing
in itself—as obviously good as precipitancy is obviously evil.
They are willing to pay the price of delay in legislation to protect their own higher value—the competition of ideas. Interest
should strive with interest, in a "free market" of debate and maneuver; be tested by conflict and prove its worth (or lack of it).

In this scheme, faction will be defined, at last, as failure. By a
survival of the fittest, the latest decision reached must be considered nonfactious, tried in the furnace of conflict and surviving as
the best law—or the best that can be arrived at now—by its mere
passage. If the deliberative approach was too static, this one
hardly fails in that direction; it is entirely dynamic, ongoing,
evolutionary. The interplay of interests leads to an equilibrium
that is best for all concerned in the long run, even if temporarily
favored things must be lost along the way.

Here we have the pluralist reading of Madison, which denies
Beard's claim that Publius rigged the system against majorities.
This Publius is an admirer of democracy in action; he loves the
free interplay of competing interests. What the conservatives
think of as a check on instant majorities the pluralists equate
with antimonopoly laws: No idea or interest should "corner the

market" to the exclusion of competitors who may be weaker at the moment but can contribute to the general striving for excellence.

This Madison has much to say for himself—though others tend to do the saying, and not quite in his words. For one thing, he fits quite handily into the Louis Hartz pattern of a Lockean orthodoxy expressed everywhere in our early history as a nation. Admittedly, this is a Locke looked at backwards by way of Mill and Darwin—a Locke secularized and updated; less apologist for the Glorious Revolution than the spokesman for an ongoing revolutionary process. But no matter. This was *our* Locke, embodied in our history, as Hartz and his followers read that history in the 1950s. And for a while—in the interval, say, between Beard and Dahl—the pluralists' Madison almost became our Madison, the man whose doctrine we did not have to *interpret* because we *lived* it every day.

But surely Burns and Dahl were right in arguing with their liberal colleagues that the Madisonian scheme does not so much act against monopolies in the name of intellectual free trade as impose a general and prior restraint on trade. If this plan draws on John Locke, it is the Locke who did not live to read *The Wealth of Nations*. The result is more Burns's "deadlock" than Adam Smith's "invisible hand." If we look carefully at Madison's text, we do not find the language we would expect if pluralists have read him right. Is it true, for instance, that he encourages the competition of contending interests? He seems more intent on discouraging or inhibiting it: "Interested" is as pejorative a term in his view as "disinterested" is favorable. One does not encourage trade by calling it bad names.

The pluralists do quote Madison in apparent agreement with their interpretation. They even go outside the faction paper (No. 10) to the bicameral one (No. 51):

Ambition must be made to counteract ambition. The interest of the man must be connected with the constitutional rights of the place (51.349).

To make this passage suit the pluralists' view, it has to undergo a series of quick and silent mutations. "Ambition," for one thing, must be drastically expanded in meaning, without regard for

context. At the least it should mean, for the pluralist interpretation, something like Montesquieu's "le pouvoir arrête le
pouvoir" (11.4.2). But Montesquieu is talking of the check
created by mere separation of powers, while Madison brings in a
needed auxiliary to separation—ambitious interest. And then he
writes: "It may be a reflection on human nature, that such devices should be necessary to controul the abuses of government.
But what is government itself but the greatest of all reflections
on human nature?" (51.349).

What is the unworthy thing in the blend of office with interest? Obviously not the office itself (in this case, the Senate); so it
must be the *interest* that Madison joins to "rights of office." As
usually happens when we look at Madison's language describing
personal interest (as opposed to the general interest, the common good), we find he has a low regard for the thing. Interest is
not something to be encouraged in its own right—as it would
have to be in a free-market interplay of interests. In No. 51, the
curse is taken off interest by blending it with office in a particular circumstance—that of the bicameral check, where a specific
quality, ambition, makes men protect the general office (in this
case the Senate) with some of the energies of *amour propre* (cf.
54.372).

Remember that in this paper Madison is talking about a particular situation—the internal check on the most powerful governmental department, the legislature. The force that must be
controlled here is the democratic House of Representatives—as
we saw in Madison's other attempt to control the House by joint
veto of the President and the Senate. (This proposal is made on
the very next page, 51.350.) So the pluralists are offering us a
text that is aimed directly against them. The check referred to
has nothing to do with "free interplay" of interests out in the
electorate, or among the people's representatives in the more
popular chamber. It describes the check that those interests *run
up against* when senators combine private ambition with the dignity of their office to oppose those interests. This check, coming
from senatorial dignity, is meant to restrain the active jostling of
interests that may be reflected in the House. The House, which
should be the special arena for "the free play of interest," is just
what Madison does *not* trust.

Another passage from No. 51 seems, at first glance, to support the pluralists. It occurs in the second addendum to the paper, which returns to the scheme of representation presented in No. 10 (51.351–2):

> Whilst all authority in it will be derived from and dependent on the society, the society itself will be broken into so many parts, interests and classes of citizens, that the rights of individuals or of the minority, will be in little danger from interested combinations of the majority. In a free government, the security for civil rights must be the same as for religious rights. It consists in the multiplicity of interests, and in the other, in the multiplicity of sects (353).

Here, surely, multiplicity of interests is praised as beneficent, as protective of civil rights? Yet, even at first hearing, one catches an off-note, a word the pluralists would not themselves use, in that phrase "danger from interested combinations of the majority." A majority can win, so long as it is not *interested*. But surely the free play of interests is not meant to keep *all* interests from winning? That is the deadlock formula, not "let the best prevail." The best may be *moderated* interest, but it would still be an interest—unless interest itself is an evil thing.

Yet how can that be? Multiplicity of interests must be a good thing if it protects civil rights. Isn't the multiplicity of sects a good thing? Well, not really—not in itself. We know that religious freedom was a good thing for Madison; this is one of the earliest and most intense of his beliefs. It was good in itself, and should be adopted as respecting freedom of the mind. But Madison knew that such an argument would not carry far with many of his countrymen—most notably with sectarians themselves. He was a scathing critic of sects, which for him as for Hume were the prototypes of faction. But if people would not adopt religious freedom on its own merits, they might be forced to adopt it as an ironic offshoot of the zealotry expressed by the sects themselves. Since all wanted to prevail, *none* of them should. There would be no established church.

Now look back at Madison's paralleling of sects with interests. The sectarian controversy is not supposed to lead, ever, to one sect's prevailing, becoming the established church by *winning* the "competition." Sectarianism at the private level would just reinforce nonsectarianism at the public level. There was to be no communion between the two. The parallel does not mean that interests should compete to see which will *prevail* in the public arena; *rather, they are to be excluded so far as possible from the public arena.*

We must read in this light what should be the pluralists' favorite passage from No. 51:

> The policy of supplying by opposite and rival interests, the defect of better motives, might be traced through the whole system of human affairs, private as well as public. We see it particularly displayed in all the subordinate distributions of power; where the constant aim is to divide and arrange the several offices in such a manner as that each may be a check on the other; that the private interest of every individual, may be a centinel over the public rights. These inventions of prudence cannot be less requisite in the distribution of the supreme powers of the state (51.349).

We can understand, now, why Burns saw deadlock where the pluralists see healthy competition. The interests are to be mutually checked, mutually neutralized so that something quite different—public right—may prevail. Interests are only sentinels guarding the one good thing to be preserved, "the public rights." The interests are not to be treasured for themselves; and no one of them is to prevail over others, because that would mean it prevailed not only over other private interests but over the public good itself.

This reading of No. 51 is confirmed if we look back at No. 10. On three pages of that Number (10.59–61; cf. 49.313), interests are linked with passions as unruly, the things to be controlled by government, not to control it. Passions and interests are regularly paired by Madison (37.232, 42.283). The whole point of representation is to "refine and enlarge the *public* views" by choosing men "whose wisdom may best discern the true interest *of their country*" (10.62; italics added). These men turn their gaze from the partial and private interest to the public and common one, the invariable characteristic of "virtue" in Montesquieu and the other secular moral guides of the Enlightenment.

If a multiplicity and interplay of interests is encouraged, it is to *block them all;* so that, above their self-defeating squabble, the true interest of the entire body of the people may shine clear by contrast, for pursuit by virtuous men. This is the real meaning of "the greater security afforded by a greater variety of parties, against the event of *any* one party being able to outnumber and oppress the rest" (10.64; italics added). Only in this way can it be said that enlightened legislation "involves the spirit of party and faction in the necessary and ordinary operations of Government" (10.59)—as sects are involved in toleration, to make sure *they* do not get their way. Private disagreement stands "centinel" over public agreement.

At 10.64 Madison assumes it is the very nature of interest to "oppress the rest." Pluralist readings of Madison take "interest" as a neutral term; it may mean an illegitimate interest, but one cannot assume that from the outset. (Testing legitimacy is the very function of competition.) But in the eighteenth century the word still carried its original, technical, legal sense—a *partial* claim on something, part ownership *in* it. When Shakespeare's clown, in *As You Like It*, tells Audrey that a youth "lays claim to you," she answers, "he hath no interest in me in the world." That does not mean the youth is not fond, but that he has no claim, even partial, upon her (where the clown had said he "lays claim" to her, in fee simple as it were).

Thus, for Madison, assertion of a partial claim can never be on the same footing with regard for the *common* good. In fact, the mere assertion of a partial claim disqualifies one from judging: "No man is allowed to be a judge in his own cause" (10.59). So "interest," where not qualified by an adjective like "true" or "public," usually means a biased and private view, not to be taken as the public one. Hamilton says that the Constitution is opposed by "a spirit of interested and suspicious scrutiny" (15.97).

The transitive verb "to interest" means "to offer a stake in" or *engage*. It can be used neutrally to describe things: an interesting study (11.67), an interesting question. But it is used pejoratively by both Madison and Hamilton to describe the biased engagement of *humans* in a struggle. Madison says faction arises when some leaders' "fortunes have been interesting to the human passions" (10.59). Hamilton says "the great interests of society" are opposed by vain and obstinate men "who have credit [plausibility] enough to make their passions and their caprices interesting to mankind" (70.475). So Madison brands with one word the "*interested* combinations" of No. 51 (351).

It may seem that Hamilton is using "interested" in a favorable way at 71.481; but he is talking of engaging interest with office, the very thing Madison described at 51.349. One can give ambition a certain sentinel's role over the dignity of (in Hamilton's context) the presidency—as, in the constitutional literature, a king's pride was meant to coincide with the nation's (see 22.142, 75.505).

The political meaning of "interest" is best established by the eighteenth-century use of "disinterested" as a term of high praise for statesmen (*JM*, 9.249; cf. Hume, *History*, 2.13.56). That was certainly the attitude of Publius, whose last thought was to encourage interests (*or* religious sects) for their own sake. The disinterested man is "candid," and candor is a quality Publius cannot praise enough. The candid man comes to a discussion or decision with no prior commitment; he is "blank" of bias, ready to receive evidence impartially (*OED*, s.v., 3). "Every candid reader will make the proper reflections . . ." (38.242). In the regular coupling of virtue with wisdom (as the requisites of rule), candid can take the place of virtue, as talented or judicious can take the place of wisdom. Thus Madison speaks of "the candid and judicious part of the community" (36.230), which means the same as Hamilton's "impartial and judicious" (61.410). The conjunction "cool and candid" (41.269) means free of passion and bias. The new Constitution must be "examined with accuracy and candour" (45.314). In all these ways Publius is exalting the virtue that is the very opposite of interest.

TWENTY-FIVE

Party

Those who employ their pens on political subjects, free
from party-rage and party-prejudices, cultivate a science . . .

—Hume, 1.12.156

Not the least merit of Dahl and Burns, coming when they did,
was to show that Laski's liberal reading of The Federalist was no
truer to the text than was the conservative Publius damned by
Beard and cosmetically resurrected by Kendall. For Dahl's "polyarchy" is not pluralism of the free-market sort. He arrived at
his formula by arguing that majority rule is a meaningless concept and minority rule is dictatorship—which leaves only "minorities rule": As many *groups* of people should have as much say
as possible on as many things as possible. This plan shies away
from monarchy on one side, anarchy on the other—whence
"polyarchy."

Dahl admits that, by one very broad reading of Madison,
"some but not all minorites could be given an effective veto"
(*Preface,* 28), then adds: "As will be seen in Chapter Five,
something like this actually seems to operate in the American political system." His fifth chapter describes a polyarchal "American Hybrid." Those who do not (as they should) read patiently
on in Dahl might be tempted to ask what all the fuss is about if
Dahl thinks one reading of Madison consistent with his own pre-
sentation of the American system. Why Dahl's thorough demoli-
tion of Madison if partial agreement is possible?

But Dahl is right in seeing that a "polyarchal" view wrested
rather forcefully from one side of Madison's thought does not
save the whole structure. Dahl will have no truck with separation of powers (which he calls constitutional safeguards); in his

eyes, Madison's acceptance of that doctrine undermines the minority-veto concept Dahl finds lurking in one part of No. 10. (By the way, it isn't there.) As we saw earlier, the social pressures of Polybius' mixed government do not belong in a scheme of separated powers. *Social* pressure crosses the boundaries, breaks down separation. It is pressure exerted in all the legally or morally allowable ways.

For Dahl and Burns, the inadequacy of Madison's approach is demonstrated by the fact that only an extraconstitutional organizing principle—the party system—has kept the Constitution functioning through most of its lifetime. Parties are not official parts of the government or of the Constitution's machinery. They grew up to supply what that machinery had neglected. They come and go on private initiative. They organize interests, inform and scold, promote and punish candidates for office. They have, in effect, taken on some of the functions of "types" in the mixed-government theory—so that where Hume could present British constitutional history, at certain points, as a struggle between monarchy and republicanism (1.7.122–6), American historians shape conflict around parties—Federalists against Jeffersonians, Jacksonians against Republicans, Lincolnians against Whigs, New Deal Democrats against business Republicans, internationalist Democrats against isolationist Republicans. It does not matter that the parties, open to compromise, have been rather mild in voicing their antagonism most of the time. The mixed ideal was always to achieve a mean of means, a blend of previously tempered and moderate types.

What is important for the polyarchal analysis is that parties seek to extend their influence *throughout* the system, on state and federal levels, in both chambers of Congress, in the executive as well as the legislature. They, too, have no truck with separation doctrine so far as that affects their activity. (The judiciary is supposed to be nonpartisan; but in fact the party affiliation of a judge often affects his appointment or his confirmation prospects.)

The parties are (or have been in their healthiest days) loose arrangements for building coalitions, gathering support from different groups. In them the minorities forge larger alliances. They are a principal (if not the principal) channel of "minorities rule." Burns's lament in *The Deadlock of Democracy* resembles Bolingbroke's claim that Walpole's ministerial "influence" had divided the types from within, not letting them speak for their *own* interest in the constant barter, tending toward balance, of a mixed government. As placemen made Parliament speak with two voices, so, in Burns's time, the separation of powers split both Democratic and Republican parties into two—a presidential party and a congressional party. "Checks and balances" prevented the *real* interplay of interests from being voiced by strong parties. The logical opposition we saw between mixed and separated forms plays itself out in the modern fight between Burns and Madison.

Though Dahl has no kind words for John Calhoun (*Preface*, 29, 30, 92), his party rationale is a better expression of "concurrency" than Calhoun came up with. The logic of Dahl's scheme is coalition, not competition; he deals in more sophisticated social analysis than the crude political "market" of the pluralists. So Dahl is quite right to see Madison's separated-powers scheme as deleterious; it does, as Schattschneider said, tend to brake (if not break) the American party system along with more obviously dangerous "factions."

But for Madison, of course, party *was* faction. The term still meant, mainly, "party to" some transaction, principally legal. We have already come across this usage—as in Jefferson's "You are surrounded by British counsellors, but remember that they are parties" (*TJ*, 1.134). Judicial review is implied in the Constitution when it speaks of "controversies to which the United States shall be a party." Parties in this sense are, by definition, disqualified from decision making: "They would consequently be parties to the very question to be decided by them" (49.342; cf. 10.59). "Party" is sometimes used as an adjective, equivalent to "partisan"—"party-artifice" (67.453), "party-rage" (9.50; cf. Hume 1.12.156). The word always refers to a person or persons speaking *ex parte*, not judiciously (53.391). It is contrasted with "impartial guardians of a common interest" (46.318; cf. 60.404–6).

To let partial interest prevail in the national councils is, for Madison, to make the part greater than the whole (37.239; cf. Hamilton at 60.405–6). Hume, in setting his own standards of historical science, accuses Rapin de Thoyras of a "partiality" that destroys the historian's power to judge fairly (2.15.473). For Hume, organized opposition to a government degenerated too easily into faction, the subject of his two essays on partisanship, "Of Parties in General" and "Of the Parties of Great Britain." These essays, as Adair demonstrated, are the source of Madison's reflections on faction as the great menace to republics.

Hume divides factions into personal and real, though he admits there is an overlap, either when personal opposition makes enmity a principle, or when real disagreement descends to "personalities." Personal faction is given the longer treatment (1.8.128–30) because sociability figures so largely in Hume's thought on government. When government grows out of the affective life of the family and clan, that original force remains more important in politics than modern theory would make it.

Over against personal faction, Hume describes three forms of real faction—that from interest, including property (130, 132); that from principle, including religious sentiments (130–2); and that from affection (133). There are some obvious difficulties with this arrangement. How, for instance, does one distinguish "personal" parties from "real" parties based on affection? For personal parties Hume demands actual consanguinity or shared circumstance. Affection in real parties can attach followers to leaders "with whom they are no wise acquainted, whom perhaps they never saw, and from whom they never received, nor can ever hope for any favour" (133).

Hume considered affection automatic. It can give a paradoxically selfless aspect to mobilized "interests." In that case, the follower is generous even when the leader is selfish (1.9.135). This reflects the Humean doctrine of feelings as contagious:

> The propensity to company and society is strong in all rational creatures; and the same disposition, which gives us this propensity, makes us enter deeply into each other's sentiments, and causes like passions and inclinations to run as it were, by contagion, through the whole club or knot of companions (1.21.249).

The "social disposition of mankind" leads to paradoxes of generous action performed in a bad cause, ignoble ones in a good cause. Hume is thinking of the emotions for and against the Old Cause in Scotland.

Just as Hume distinguishes between principled followers and interested leaders (1.9.135), so he calls religious views principled in the pious followers and interested in the priests (132). And he says that, with time and common experience, any of the real factions may become a mere personal faction, as the original grounds of division fade into experienced mutual affronts (129). Madison keeps Hume's fourfold division, but slightly rearranges it. His first sentence (10.58–9) lists Hume's parties from principle (including religion), from affection, and from personal attachment. (As Adair pointed out, the distinction between the last two would be unclear without Hume's text to explain it.) His next sentence picks up what Hume said, in his first division, on the propensity to quarrel over trifles (personal faction). Hume put it this way:

> Men have such propensity to divide into personal factions, that the smallest appearance of real difference will produce them. What can be imagined more trivial than the difference between one colour of livery and another in horse races? Yet this difference begat two most inveterate factions in the GREEK empire, the PRASINI and VENETI, who never suspended their animosities, till they ruined that unhappy government (128; cf. AH, 4.183).

That becomes, in Madison:

> so strong is this propensity of mankind to fall into mutual animosities, that where no substantial occasion presents itself, the most frivolous and fanciful distinctions have been sufficient to kindle their unfriendly passions, and excite their most violent conflicts (10.59).

Madison saves till last the faction from principle, and centers it on property—which Hume tended to downplay as a reaction to Harrington and the "selfish systems" of Hobbes and Locke (1.8.130, 1.7.122; cf. Forbes, *Hume's Philosophical Politics*, 199, 207–9). So Madison does stress property more than Hume did (while keeping Hume's fourfold division). But Adair rightly says that Beard had to quote selectively, here, to make Madison an economic determinist. First, Madison's rephrasing of Hume on principled factions is drastically truncated by Beard—from "opinions concerning religion, concerning Government and many other points" (10.58) it becomes "opinions concerning government." Then it is given a wholly new interpretive context: "The theories of government which men entertain are emotional reactions to their property interests" (*Economic Interpr.*, 15–16, 157; see *Fame*, 86).

Not much has been written, outside Adair, of Madison's division of faction into four *types*. Most people are more concerned with his division of it into two *sizes:* minority and majority. Beard claimed Madison thought in the latter two categories because he wanted to protect the property of the few from the greed of the many. That view is still voiced, as when Dahl reads Madison's motive as wishing to "guarantee the liberties of certain minorities whose advantage of status, power, and wealth would, he thought, not be tolerated indefinitely by a constitutionally untrammeled majority" (*Preface*, 31). The assumption, throughout, is that Madison could have invented his scheme of things only out of some animus toward majorities as such.

For Madison the trouble with any party is that it is, literally, a part. It is only part of the sovereign people—no matter whether a small part or a large part—so it should not speak for the whole. I raised earlier the question: Why should a republican want to put limits on the people? The answer, of course, is that the crucial limits are those placed on "the sovereign," wherever sovereignty may reside. In the seventeenth century, constitutional theory was intent on limiting the monarch. The judging-own-cause norm was met by giving the House of Lords a judicial function when it came to judging the king's ministers (or, even, deposing the king). It is not, therefore, accidental that a separate judiciary arose in the eighteenth century when Parliament became the center of power. It, too, must not judge its own cause; and the executive-legislative division that had hitherto been exhaustive had to be supplemented with some mode for applying the law to parliamentary lawmakers. By Madison's time the question had "traveled" from "King in Parliament" as representing mixed types to a Congress representing the people through two channels. How does one keep government by the *people* limited, so that it will be a government of laws and not of men?

We have considered the principal check Madison imposed on

Congress, the bicameral arrangement that is his main point in
No. 51. But he thought even that check needed supplementing,
and he did not rest his main hopes for the republic on checks
and balances. His republican remedy for republican maladies
came from the doctrine of representation offered in No. 10. Yet
that paper, when it is not misread as dealing with "checks and
balances," is misread as dealing with the problem of majority
rule. (Dahl combines both misreadings.)

Madison begins with the fact that factions can rally minority
or majority support, and with the commonsense judgment that
majority factions will be harder to control. What is wrong, in either case, is the power of a group (no matter what its size) to
conduct the transaction to which it is a party. In a direct democracy, there is no way to evade this violation of constitutional
morality: The people *en bloc* will decide for the people *en bloc*.
This will be an unlimited constitution exactly as absolute monarchy was unlimited. It will be a government of men, not of
laws.

Yet who is going to speak for the interests of the whole people
if not the whole people? Madison seems, two thirds of the way
through No. 10, to have created a problem he cannot possibly
solve. No part, whether majority or minority, should speak for
the whole; yet the whole cannot speak for itself because that
would make it absolute, its mere whim law, its every adjudication irredeemably partial. It is a *totum* that can only act *ex parte*.

Madison considers representation the means of escape from
this legal solecism. The people do not directly judge their own
case; they delegate authority to others, who may judge between
contending interests. But what if the delegates *represent* interest
instead of judging it?

> Under such a regulation, it may well happen that the public voice
> pronounced by the representatives of the people, will be more con-
> sonant to the public good, than if pronounced by the people them-
> selves convened for the purpose. On the other hand, the effect may
> be inverted. Men of factious tempers, of local prejudices, or of sin-
> ister designs, may by intrigue, by corruption or by other means,
> first obtain the suffrages, and then betray the interests of the people
> (10.62).

What is left for Madison? He has eliminated direct democracy; and even representation, taken by itself, does not protect a people from lawmaking by partial interests. For representation to work well, Madison now claims, it must be conjoined with another principle—extent of territory.

TWENTY-SIX

Extent of Territory

At the same time, the parts are so distant and remote,
that it is very difficult, either by intrigue, prejudice, or
passion, to hurry them into any measures against the
public interest.

—Hume, 2.16.492

Most students of The Federalist have failed to do what Publius
said *must* be done. They have not consulted "the genius of the
people," on which all workable government is based. The genius
of the American people, we are repeatedly told by Publius, is republican; and we know that a republic requires virtue, defined
as regard for the common above the private good. Obviously, if
this commodity is so desperately required, one must have a
way of identifying, preserving, and using it. Like Montesquieu,
Madison and Hamilton assume that the presence of virtue can be
ascertained, as can the presence of honor (for monarchies) or of
fear (for despotisms). Otherwise, there is nothing to consult
when building a constitution.

The Enlightenment could afford to be proud of its virtue,
since Christian humility was not necessary to it—in fact, was
precluded by it (*Inventing,* 317–18). Men were to be *ostentatiously* devoted to the public cause, as Diderot and Rousseau assured the world *they* were. In America, Washington's wartime
service without personal recompense was constantly held up as
the signal of republican virtue. Franklin suggested, in Philadelphia, that all presidents of the United States serve without
pay.

So, though not everyone might be able to discern the public
good, true republicans can—from their own virtuous genius, looking to that good—identify the few men *outstanding* for wisdom

and virtue. If we accept that starting point, of virtuous reflection on the meaning of republicanism, then Dahl's problems with the definition of faction disappear. Madison wants to eliminate from office the citizens "who are united and actuated by some common impulse of passion, or of interest, adverse to the rights of other citizens, or to the permanent and aggregate interests of the community" (10.57). Dahl, unable to take very seriously *virtue* as the object of the quest, says the definition is useless because we are given no prior definition of citizens' rights or the community's true interest. The former would need some authoritative oracle of justice, the latter some rule that would fit all circumstances. Neither can be had. But one *can* tell which citizens do not look to the common good. Otherwise, one could not tell who does regard the common good above the private; virtue would be unidentifiable, and the republican form would have no basis.

Madison may be said to argue in a circle here. The virtuous will choose the virtuous because they are virtuous. In that case, why worry? There is no reason to check either the people themselves or the good men they have chosen to represent them. Yet Madison wants to do both, and this seems contradictory. To address this problem we must give Montesquieu and his followers some credit for common sense. They did not say that the qualities on which governments are built are eternal givens. The constitutional form is meant to preserve its characteristic *ressort*, whether honor, fear, or virtue. A failure to guard the forms of honor would of itself indicate a failure of honor. In the same way, the virtuous will be those readiest to adopt disciplines of virtue.

For that is how we must look at representation if we are to do justice to Madison's argument. He is looking for the ways men can *demonstrate* their virtue, their lack of interest in the private sense wherever public good is concerned. Representation is itself a sign of trust and surrender—the agent, the delegate, is put in charge of a man's affairs. There is a commitment *of* the agent to seek his *client*'s good; but in a scheme of republican virtue there is also a commission *to* the agent to seek the *public* good. The client authorizes his agent to arbitrate between contending interests, including his own, for the general ("aggregate") and true ("permanent") interest of all. But Madison says there is a *further* discipline where extent of territory is added to the scheme of representation. He constructs three levels of democracy—direct democracy, representation, and representation with extended territory—and says there is as great a difference between the last two as between the first two: "Hence it clearly appears that the same advantage, which a Republic has over a Democracy, in controling the effects of faction, is enjoyed by the Union over the States composing it" (10.64; cf. *JM*, 10.212–13).

What adds the extra discipline to be derived from extent of territory? Madison gives two preliminary answers and then the major answer, the one that "principally" renders factions harmless. His first answer is misstated at times, to make him say a larger territory will include more men of obvious virtue. That may be true in absolute numbers, but not proportionally. Madison's point, however, is that the more extensive the republic, the higher the ratio between constituents and delegates must become, if the assembly is not to be unmanageably large. Thus, with proportionally fewer offices to fill, but a proportionally stable pool of virtuous men to draw from, extent "will create a greater option, and consequently a greater probability of a fit choice" (10.63).

To see the force of his argument, we might recall Jefferson's scheme of public education in his *Notes on the State of Virginia* (*Inventing*, 147). This aimed at broad representation of the educational districts (or centuries). Each century would advance one boy of exceptional talent for further training. There is a clear sacrifice of merit to inclusiveness at this stage. Suppose one century has three boys of talent superior to that of anyone in the two neighboring centuries. Under Jefferson's plan, two of the superior boys in the first century will be excluded, while two of inferior ability are advanced. In Madison's scheme, contracting the number of representatives by increasing the scope of the territory represented would yield this result: From all three centuries, the one superior man first chosen would advance, but not the two inferior men. The quality of the assembled delegation would thus be improved. The demand on citizen virtue arises from the surrender of any guarantee that someone from one's immediate locale will be in the final delegation. One submits to the process for the common good.

Madison's second argument looks at the same process from the side of the electing people rather than the elected representative. As there will be a further winnowing in the number of agents, there will be an extension of the electorate calculated to break down narrow partisanship or "the vicious arts" by which such partisanship sways, influences, intimidates others. Return to the Jefferson parallel. If each of the three centuries is to send forward a candidate, the most powerful family in each century might be able, by favors or old ties or withheld work opportunities, to advance its family "heir" to the office. *Combine* the three, and those within the "realm" of each family will have greater leeway to choose a candidate based upon merit rather than the local heir. Public virtue has submitted to another discipline.

Dahl calls these two preliminary arguments "extremely dubious and probably false" (*Preface*, 16). He can say that because he does not share Madison's assumption that the aim of a republic is to assemble a panel of virtuous delegates. If one is representing "interests," each interest—no matter what its nature—should have a voice. If one is representing virtue, the obviously factious (narrowly partisan) interests should yield to the obviously virtuous candidate. In terms of Jefferson's plan for "representing" talent in the state schools, if the aim of representation is to give as many locales as possible a voice, then one boy should be advanced from all three centuries we have imagined. But if the aim is to achieve greater concentration of merit at the state level, one should adopt Madison's norm. Dahl, who does not recognize that norm, cannot see what Madison is up to. Not knowing where the target is, he finds the aiming operation a total mystery.

But Madison places most of his emphasis on a final argument that has been misunderstood to the point of rendering it nugatory or ridiculous. The heart of this last and principal defense against faction lies in one sentence:

Extend the sphere, and you take in a greater variety of parties and interests; you make it less probable that a majority of the whole will have a common motive to invade the rights of other citizens; or if such a common motive exists, it will be more difficult for all who feel it to discover their own strength, and to act in unison with each other (10.64).

That famous sentence has received dozens of readings, most of them making little if any sense. At the most foolish level, some suppose that extent of territory offers a mere logistical block to evil combinations. This view would derive human virtue from bad roads. And it would expose Madison's argument to refutation by the telegraph. Besides, as Burns and others have argued, mere problems of communication from sector to sector would impede good combinations as well as evil ones. The formula seems to be one for poor or little government, something comforting to libertarians but totally at odds with Madison's own ideal of a vigorous federal union. Let us pay Madison the minimal compliment of refusing to reduce him to this level if we can find any other plausible meaning for his sentence.

If the merely logistical problem of *communicating* evil schemes is not central to Madison's argument, what about the problem of forming a common *motive* for such schemes? Why does extent of territory make a common motive less likely? That might be true of local interests in the strict sense—the desire of each family in each century to have its own boy advance to the state level in Jefferson's scheme. But what of "interest" in the larger sense? Why shouldn't the three leading families in all three centuries support a plan that favors leading families in general? That would give them more strength at the state level than would squabbling for total control over each one's separate "turf."

Can one obviate that objection by saying Madison discussed truly *extended* territory, not the goings-on of three contiguous centuries in the state of Virginia? But extent is built up by the "marching" of sector with sector, and large interests could reach up and down the whole seaboard comprising Madison's America. The common motive does not have to be advancement of leading families in Virginia. It could be a banker's motive, as Beard suggested. That was not a merely regional interest, even in Madison's day; and there were many economic interests—regarding, e.g., shipping policy—that could assemble a majority of represented districts in the country. Unless we are to fall back on the "bad communications" reading of Madison's sentence, there seems no reason why protectionist or antiprotectionist motives could not assemble a majority; and either one might be a factious majority. How would this common motive be impeded in prosecution of its designs? If there was any difficulty at first, it would soon disappear. As the first interpretation of Madison was "refuted" by the telegraph, this second one would soon find its rebuttal in lobbyists.

Some have derived from Madison's sentence the idea of competing interests disciplining themselves in a "free market" of political competition, so that the best (not the factious) should prevail. But how can that reading fit Madison's words? He talks of *preventing* competition, of making it difficult to concert plans for competing, or even to form a common motive (or be conscious of it, or put it into execution). He is not trying to encourage competition but preclude it. If competition has any role, it should be self-*canceling*, as we saw in the parallel passage (51.351–2) on multiplicity of sects rendering the sects irrelevant for political purposes.

Is this last the real meaning of Madison—that extent of territory will make the interests self-canceling? If so, we still have not escaped the problem of distinguishing nonfactious from factious causes. What will make mere extent of territory protect the one while excluding the other? We are not talking directly of religious sects here, which could be entirely excluded from politics. We are dealing with expressly *political* views. What does extent of territory have to do with distinguishing these?

The obvious place to look for an answer to that question is in Madison's very next sentence. Yet that sentence looks so naïve that people seem to avert their eyes from it, out of regard for Madison.

> Besides other impediments, it may be remarked, that where there is a consciousness of unjust or dishonorable purposes, communication is always checked by distrust, in proportion to the number whose concurrence is necessary (10.64).

This sentence is almost enough to make one think Madison endorsed the naïve circularity of the argument that the republic will be virtuous because virtuous men will choose virtuous leaders. Isn't the present sentence just the reverse of that? Given enough time and numbers brought into their plot, evil men will undo themselves. They will either distrust (and therefore cripple) each other, or trust (and therefore undo) each other. In either case, why care about checks at all? Just give them enough rope.

So far we have considered only trivial reasons why "extent of territory" mattered so crucially to Madison, but these trivialities are often taken as his real point, and the text does not seem to yield anything *but* trivialities. Is it an advantage to have a dispersed and divided people? Then why form a federal union at all? How can Madison argue for a stronger *union* than the Articles afforded yet do so in terms of dispersal and division?

The great fault of all these interpretations is that they do not consider extent of territory primarily as qualifying *representation*. Madison does not prize a scattered quality in the electorate for its own sake—*any* bar to citizens interacting with each other. But he does want to keep *representative* bodies pure of selfish interest. The effect of territorial extent is to be tested in the national legislature, since Madison's aim is to "secure the national Councils" against faction (10.65). We must look to those councils, to see how views are "enlarged and refined" in them.

TWENTY-SEVEN

To Refine . . .

In a large government, which is modelled with mas-
terly skill, there is compass and room enough to refine
the democracy . . .

—Hume, 2.16.492

All three arguments Madison advances for representation in extended republics have this in common: They all weaken or exclude the possibility of *instruction*. As more districts are united
under a "single member" to represent them, it becomes impossible to register different interests in anything like their proportion
among the citizens. This, of course, is the argument against
nonproportional representation of any sort. What seems the
plan's flaw for others is its recommendation for Madison.

In his second argument, Madison says that inclusion of various
locales within a single representative's sphere will free voters
from undue local pressure, so they can vote for "the most
diffusive and established characters" (10.63). The system is
rigged to make constituents vote for the man of virtuous reputation, not for one who merely shares their interest. This solves the
problem of direct democracy, that it makes people judges in
their own case. Extent of territory means, at the minimum, this:
The farther off you send a delegate from his base, the less precise can his instruction be. He must cope with contingencies not
foreseen when he was dispatched. He will not have time or
means to clear all responses with his "home base."

Nor is this a problem that can be solved by the telegraph. The
assembling of the entire citizenry, to vote on each new issue that
comes up in the "national councils," is precluded by their occu-
pation at other tasks. (Representation involves, among other
things, a division of labor—the delegate is paid to spend his time

acquiring skill and knowledge, staff and allies, to cope with his peers in assembly.) True, bankers might co-ordinate their schemes by telegraph; a representative cannot counter those schemes by telegraphing each member of his constituency. In that sense, extent of territory might be thought to work in favor of faction.

But Madison's whole point is that factious schemes will have a hard time making their way in a national council of uninstructed delegates chosen for their judicious impartiality. Banker A in Sector A may succeed in getting a partial representative elected. But all his communings with bankers in sectors B, C, and D will not help him at the legislative level unless they can *all* get representatives elected with the same kind and degree of partiality. Madison argues that such co-ordination becomes less likely as the ratio of voters to representatives increases.

Yet none of this argument makes sense unless you agree that the aim of election is, precisely, the choosing of impartial adjudicators of the varying interests. The disappearance of that agreement, in the interval between Madison's time and ours, explains the difficulty modern readers have with Madison's meaning. (Hume showed how "extent of domain" can counter local interest where change of venue is called for; cf. *History*, 2.13.73.) It went almost without saying, at a time when men professed republican virtue with unembarrassed pride, that one was not electing a "stooge" for oneself, but a person of disinterested virtue—the model was Washington—who would consult the public good. The test for choice was simple: Was the candidate nonfactious? That is: Did he obviously, by profession backed up with conduct, look to the rights of *all* citizens and the *aggregate* interests of the community? Madison's "useless" definition of faction was actually his norm for voting.

The strength of a republic was, for Hume and Madison, public virtue. If men do not want that quality represented, first and foremost, in their national councils, then they have ceased to be republicans and that form of government must fail. This has been Publius' message throughout The Federalist, and it is Madison's message throughout No. 10. If this is not grasped as his main point, the paper falls into those separate absurdities Dahl has described.

The theme sounded throughout is the transcending of local and narrow interest, how to give hearing to "our most considerate and virtuous citizens" (57), how to fashion a scheme based on "candid review of our situation" (57), how to replace passion with rights, private interest with aggregate interests (57). The goal is to keep legislators from being "advocates and parties to the causes which they determine" (59); to make them consider "the good of the whole" instead of the "immediate interest which one party may find in disregarding the rights of another" (60); to prevent direct democracy from sacrificing "the weaker party, or an obnoxious [vulnerable] individual" (61). These phrases all occur in the preliminary part of No. 10, where Madison is defining the problem. But his meaning emerges principally from three sentences that, in this most studied Number of The Federalist, have been very little studied or understood. I shall devote the rest of this chapter to the first of these sentences, and the next chapter to the other two.

Having rejected direct democracy for its failure to meet the "judge-own-cause" standard of constitutional responsibility to laws and not to men, Madison introduces a discussion of indirect (representative) democracy—what he calls a republic—with this sentence:

> The effect of the first difference [between a democracy and a republic—namely, delegation] is, on the one hand to refine and enlarge the public view, whose wisdom may best discern the true interest of their country, and whose patriotism and love of justice, will be least likely to sacrifice it to temporary or partial considerations (10.62).

Douglass Adair was a graduate student in New Haven when he first grasped the point of this sentence—the way it combines representation, virtue, and (in the next paragraph) extent of territory. He grasped it all because he saw how Madison had derived the concepts and their inner connections directly from Hume— from that essay we have come across so often in this study, the "Idea of a Perfect Commonwealth." This is the part of his dissertation that Adair repeated in an important later essay; and in both places he introduced a quote from Hume's essay the same way: "It was Hume's next two sentences that must have electrified Madison as he read them" (diss., 252 = *Fame*, 99). It is safe to presume that Adair was himself "electrified" when he first saw the connection, a connection tested and confirmed by his own later work on both Madison and Hume. He had good reason to think he had discovered the central point in Madison's whole theory of representation in a virtuous republic.

Here are the key sentences Adair takes from Hume's essay:

> In a large government, which is modelled with masterly skill, there is compass and room enough to refine the democracy, from the lower people, who may be admitted into the first elections or first concoction of the commonwealth, to the higher magistrates, who direct all the movements. At the same time, the parts are so distant and remote, that it is very difficult, either by intrigue, prejudice, or passion, to hurry them into any measures against the public interest (2.16.492).

The image is of "refining," in which a substance is passed through several processes—Hume's successive "concoctions"—to reach a pure state. For Madison, the thing to be refined is virtue. It is present in the people, who are admitted to the first concoction; otherwise their genius would not be republican. But it is in an impure state there, mingled with private interest and local bias. Through several concoctions, the interest is purged, the distilled product rendered. That product is *dis*interest; *im*partiality; candor; clarity (through "liquidation"); virtue.

This is the goal of representation taken simply. What can extent of territory add to its action? When one has to send uninstructed delegates to a distant national council, where they will deal with representatives from other such distant areas, local pride as well as zeal for the public good dictates that one choose a worthy man, sure to win respect for one's area, trusted not only to act well but to convince his peers that he is acting well.

Madison had some experience of this process in his political life. As a young man he had followed the gathering and activity of the Continental Congress, called to respond to the crisis of the mid-seventies (*JM*, 1.159 ff.). The colonies chose their worthiest men for those conclaves. Virginia's own first delegation was clearly a "refinement" of all its political virtues and skills; it included Peyton Randolph, Benjamin Harrison, Edmund Pendleton, George Wythe, Richard Henry Lee, Patrick Henry, and George Washington (*Inventing*, 3 ff.). Randolph, the most powerful man in Virginia, was such a paragon of virtue that Jefferson's test, in a moral crisis, became: What would Peyton Randolph do? Wythe and Pendleton were the leading legal scholars from Virginia. If, during the period of the Articles, the Confederate Congress had declined in quality, that was because no real power was given it. Merit stayed in the state legislatures, where real work went forward. Madison realized that a basic shift of gravity was needed to make the national councils as weighty as they had been in the years when independence was declared. (Shifting the arena for virtuous ambition back to Congress had been Hamilton's plan in his June 18 speech.) Madison knew how important it was for the Constitutional Convention that George Washington attend. Not only would his acknowledged public virtue give "heft" to the body itself, and to any of its proposals; he was bound, as well, to give stature to the Virginia delegation, which would present the plan for a constitution Madison was already drafting.

It takes no great empathy to feel Madison's distress when Washington turned down the call to represent Virginia in Philadelphia. Washington had attempted to reform the Society of the Cincinnati by removing the hereditary feature from their membership. Met with a tacit rebuke from state chapters of the order, he pleaded sickness to avoid attending the 1787 national meeting in Philadelphia. (So much for the idea that Washington could not tell a lie.) After turning down his wartime comrades, he did not feel he could accept another proposal for going to Philadelphia at the very time the Cincinnati would be in session.

Madison would not take no for an answer; he patiently and repeatedly made the case for Washington's attendance and asked others (especially Governor Edmund Randolph) to press on Washington the importance of his participation at a moment so crucial for the republic. This appeal to his public *virtue* made him bring that virtue to bear on the proceedings at Philadelphia. His endorsement became, in time, one of the principal arguments for ratification of the Constitution. It was an endorsement made with full knowledge and influence since Washington had taken part in the construction of the draft; had, indeed, presided over the whole Convention. Luckily, we cannot know what effect his absence from the Convention might have had. Madison thought he knew, and made sure he would not have to learn that effect by experience. He needed Washington. The nation needed him. Here we have a striking instance, close to Madison's experience, of the motive for choosing virtuous delegates to deal with fellow citizens from distant areas having different priorities. Instruction cannot forecast the interplay of thought and motives among such delegates; so a trustworthy and impressive man must be sent into their midst.

Adair was able to establish Madison's meaning not only from the parallel with Hume, but from another passage in Madison. In his 1787 Notes (*JM*, 9.357), Madison wrote: "An auxiliary desideratum for the melioration of the Republican form is such a process of elections as will most certainly extract from the mass of the society the purest and noblest characters which it contains; such as will at once feel most strongly the proper motives to pursue the end of their appointment, and be most capable to devise the proper means of attaining it" (diss., 260 = *Fame*, 103). *Extraction* of a *pure* strain from the *mass* shows that some image of "concoction" is in Madison's mind here as well as in No. 10.

Adair did not notice that Madison had used a similar image in the convention debates of 1787. On May 31 he reported his own views thus: "He was an advocate for the policy of refining the popular appointments by successive filtrations, but thought it might be pushed too far" (Farrand, 1.50). He was arguing for popular election of the House, while keeping filtered (indirect) election for the Senate and *both* other departments of the federal government.

James Wilson, born and educated in Scotland, a student of the Swiss Hutchesonian Burlamaqui (*Inventing*, 250–1), used not only Hume's argument but his word: "A vice in the Representation, like an error in the first concoction, must be followed by disease, convulsions, and finally death itself" (Farrand, 2.10). Wilson, who was Madison's ally on many points, is here agreeing with him that the Senate should be given proportional, not equal, votes. After all, even with proportional representation, the states would not be effaced as functioning units; state legislatures would choose the senators, no matter what their number. The "chemistry" of Wilson's image is of successive concoctions, each meant to remove a different impurity. If all the later concoctions did their work, yet the first one had not removed the impurity it was meant to purge, the patient would be just as dead as if no impurities had been eliminated.

Others at the Convention used the refining image in a frankly aristocratic way—closer to Hume's mixed-government argument than to Madison's republican use of it, but establishing that Madison did, in fact, mean to "purify" the popular vote. John Dickinson said, "In the formation of the Senate we ought to carry it through such a refining process as will assimilate it as near as may be to the House of Lords in England" (ibid., 1.136). And Elbridge Gerry said, of state legislators appointing senators, "The elections being carried thro' this refinement, will be most likely to provide some check in favor of the commercial interest agst. the landed" (ibid., 1.152).

Before discussing the other two crucial passages in No. 10—crucial for showing the importance Madison gave to representation over extended territory—we should recognize what this passage, of itself, establishes. First, it should be noted that No. 10 is in no way meant to encourage competing interests, to give them a voice (any more than can be avoided) in the national councils, to protect their role. Madison said the causes of faction could not be removed (that would mean removing freedom), but the effects could be inhibited—not at the local level, perhaps, but in the national councils. And that would be done by purging narrow interest from the representatives, who are to be chosen indirectly through a series of concoctions, purifying them of partiality.

Second, insofar as local pride affects the choice of representatives, it should be a pride in the *virtue* of the man who embodies the district's good name before his peers in council. This scheme, inhibiting the expression of narrow interests, almost forces the voter to choose "established characters" for his agents (10.63). This resembles—though Madison does not make the point here—the way ambition coincides with the dignity of senatorial office to make bicameralism work (51.349). Ambition is the "interest" most cognate to virtue.

Madison's language on this subject is thoroughly Humean. In his debate with the critics of *luxuria*, Hume defended "refinement" and urbanity over the ideal picture of rough peasant virtue—especially in his essays "Of the Delicacy of Taste and Passion" and "Of Refinement in the Arts." The latter essay, standing second in his collection of economic works, praises commerce as civilizing. In the essay that follows it, Hume speaks of trade as enlarging men's views from purely parochial concerns to much greater ones: "But when men's industry encreases, and *their views enlarge,* it is found, that the most remote parts of the state can assist each other as well as the more contiguous, and that this intercourse of good offices may be carried on to the greatest *extent* and intricacy" (2.4.324; italics added). That presents, in economic terms, the very process Madison describes politically: Extent of territory assists refinement and enlargement of view. In the essay before that on refinement, Hume talks of the need for men to "enlarge their view" from the particular to the universal in discussing matters of trade (2.1.288). The complex of ideas around the notion of "concoction" is discussed entirely in Hume's terms.

TWENTY-EIGHT

. . . and Enlarge

> But industry, knowledge, and humanity, are not advantageous in private life alone: They diffuse their beneficial influence on the *public*, and render the government as great and flourishing as they make individuals happy and prosperous.
>
> —Hume, 2.2.302

Here is the second crucial sentence from No. 10:

> In the next place, as each Representative will be chosen by a greater number of citizens in the large than in the small Republic, it will be more difficult for unworthy candidates to practise with success the vicious arts, by which elections are too often carried; and the suffrages of the people being more free, will be more likely to centre on men who possess the most attractive merit, and the most diffusive and established characters (10.63).

I have cited Dahl's complaint that this preliminary argument makes no sense. Here I wish to focus on the passage's last clause. As local influence is escaped, the vote becomes *free* to seek out virtue. Since the health of the republic depends not only on the citizens' possessing virtue but on their being able to identify it, men must find representatives of "attractive merit"—merit that actually shines out and draws others.

I do not recall any commentary that treats the end of this sentence as very important; but if the search for virtuous men is the whole point of republican representation, then the meaning of these words is pivotal. Who are Madison's "most diffusive and established characters"? If character were to be taken in one modern sense—not men of character, but "fit characters" (Hamilton's use at 76.513 and 78.530) in the sense of personal *types*—

then "diffusive" could mean "bountiful" (*OED*, s.v., 1), perhaps "magnanimous" (*bonum est diffusivum sui*). But the other member in Madison's pairing is "merit," not a *person* (or persons), so we expect a *thing* here—character as reputation. That is how Madison uses the word at 63.422 and 423, Hamilton at 76.510, and Jay at 3.15, 64.433, 64.437 (and cf. *JM*, 9.355, 10.213). Hume had referred to a leader's "established character" in his *History* (5.72.407).

In this context "diffusive" must mean "general" or "widespread." Madison is saying that escape from local prejudice will allow men to vote for those whose reputation is not only established but reaches out across larger stretches of the extended republic. In terms of Jefferson's scheme for sifting scholars, choice would be extended, out from one's own "century," to other centuries, looking for candidates of truly continental stature. The model, of course, is Washington, the first choice for every office in the republic's early days.

Other words for diffusion help us determine what Madison meant by refining and *enlarging* the public views (10.62), and make us see the connnection of this "enlargement" with wider reputation. Madison in No. 56 answers the charge that choosing representatives from larger districts—so that they are "diffusively elected" (56.379); cf. 57.390, "a diffusive mode of chusing representatives"—will make the people's agents too ignorant of petty localities' concerns. He says that "a more diffusive knowledge of the circumstances of the state" can easily be checked against exceptions to it, while it is harder for mere local concern to mount toward widespread knowledge.

Madison is making rapidly the same point Hamilton made at greater length in No. 36:

> It has been asserted that a power of internal taxation in the national Legislature could never be exercised with advantage, as well from the want of a sufficient knowledge of local circumstances as from an interference between the revenue laws of the Union and of the particular States. The supposition of a want of proper knowledge, seems to be entirely destitute of foundation. If any question is depending in a State Legislature respecting one of the counties which demands a knowledge of local details, how is it acquired? No doubt from the information of the members of the county. Can-

not the like knowledge be obtained in the national Legislature from the representatives of each State. And is it not to be presumed that the men who will generally be sent there, will be possessed of the necessary degree of intelligence, to be able to communicate that information? Is the knowledge of local circumstances, as applied to taxation, a minute topographical acquaintance with all the mountains, rivers, streams, high-ways and bye-paths in each State, or is it a general acquaintance with its situation and resources—with the state of its agriculture, commerce, manufactures—with the nature of its products and consumptions—with the different degrees and kinds of wealth, property and industry? (36.224).

Hamilton illustrates diffusive knowledge in a diffusive language that lapses from grammar in the final sentence; but his meaning is clear, and is Madison's meaning at 56.379.

The role of a "diffusive character" in an extended republic is vital to Hamilton's view of the presidency:

Talents for low intrigue and the little arts of popularity may alone suffice to elevate a man to the first honors in a single state; but it will require other talents and a different kind of merit to establish him in the esteem and confidence of the whole union, or of so considerable a portion of it as would be necessary to make him a successful candidate for the distinguished office of president of the United States. It will not be too strong to say, that there will be a constant probability of seeing the station filled by characters pre-eminent for ability and virtue (68.461; cf. 75.506, 510).

The genius of a republican system is to raise men's eyes from local champions promoted only by local interest to the recognition of general reputation based on attractive merit.

The third passage I mentioned from No. 10 concerns the consciousness of bad faith in "interested" men:

Besides other impediments, it may be remarked, that where there is a consciousness of unjust or dishonorable purposes, communication is always checked by distrust, in proportion to the number whose concurrence is necessary (10.64).

I suspect others give this sentence the simplistic meaning I mentioned in Chapter Twenty-seven. The bad guys will undo themselves—a hope on which few would wish to build a political system. But Madison raises this point in reference to the one political system that depends on isolating and identifying public virtue and public vice (faction) through an election process of several "concoctions." If the voters of one district are unable, in the "first concoction," to identify a man of real virtue, the representatives of other districts should recognize that he is not their peer. By failing to co-operate with him, they in effect send him home; immobilize his efforts to the point where his constituents, no longer finding him useful, vote him out of office. Surely the select group of representatives will not send him on to higher office (in the Senate). Nor will the select group of presidential electors consider him.

This may indeed sound like a fairy-tale approach to politics when we consider what actually happens in the republic Madison thought he was explaining. We do have candidates, now, who openly profess this or that interest; are expected to do so, and punished if they do not; who belong to parties, and run as members of them. For Madison, all of these things were not only undesirable; their occurrence would spell, in his mind, the end of the republic. The norm of choice should be the *disinterested* arbitrator of competing claims. Legislators should be "cool and candid," chosen for their fairness.

This did not seem an impractical aim in the nation that so easily found its Washington for unanimous vote of the electoral college. In fact, Washington's own high ideals of fairness, which kept him from favoritism toward Virginians during the war and in his Administration, were expressed in a homely way that shows how deep was the principle of fair dealing in that world. Rather than haggle over price for the sale of his lands, Washington suggested that he choose an agent, the purchaser choose an agent, and the two agents choose an arbitrator (Flexner, *Washington,* 4.373). Even the first choice is thus made to depend on fairness; a narrow partisan would probably not choose a wise adjudicator, or get his own choice accepted by the other side. Only one confident of his own bid's basic equity will be ready to entertain such a proposal. We have here, in little, the concoction method of elections that Madison proposes in No. 10. It is the genius of this scheme that the winners at each successive level of election will be men of more established reputation, hesitant to soil that reputation by low arts or intrigue or unfair dealing.

Shame will inhibit them among their peers: "Honour is a check."

If this view reflects a wide-eyed innocence, then the practical Hamilton was equally wide-eyed. It is time to return to the principal question left over from No. 51. Madison relies on the bicameral check within Congress, where ambition will combine with office to prevent incursions on either chamber's dignity. But why should this check prevent a joint incursion on executive or judicial spheres? The answer is that the bicameral check is a final "concoction", in which is engaged the honor of men at the height of republican rewards for virtue. If one chamber should fail in its own professed aims of equitable dealing, the other will try to rescue *its* honor, at least, by opposition. That is clearly what Madison meant, and what Hamilton spells out when he considers the relations between the two chambers.

Hamilton looks first at the hypothesis that a haughty Senate might block reasonable expansion of membership in the House, an expansion caused by growth in the physical extent of the country and by popular demand for a just response to this growth. These very things will give the House extra strength in its opposition to the Senate's unworthy plan. The argument of virtue will be clear, and will force the factious to lie low if they do not wish to be branded for their narrowness of interest:

> This advantage must be increased by the consciousness felt by the same side, of being supported in its demands, by right, by reason, and by the constitution; and the consciousness on the opposite side, of contending against the force of all these solemn considerations (58.393).

This is, precisely, that inhibition on open conspiring that Madison predicted "where there is a consciousness of unjust or dishonorable purposes" (10.64). In a republic founded on and rewarding public virtue, public vice must hide, fear exposure, distrust comrades. And if the honor of the House gives it strength in some encounters, the honor of the Senate will come into play in others:

> These questions will create no difficulty with those who reflect, that in all cases the smaller the number and the more permanent and conspicuous the station of men in power, the stronger must be the interest which they will individually feel in whatever concerns the

government. Those who represent the dignity of their country in the eyes of other nations, will be particularly sensible to every prospect of public danger, or of a dishonorable stagnation in public affairs (58.395).

It is the job of earlier concoctions to make sure that narrow interest does not "find its way into the national councils" (Hamilton at 60.404; cf. Madison at 10.65). If it should find its way there, the last concoction engages the honor of men at the very pinnacle of republican "character." In any final concoction, that reputation for established merit must be relied on. If virtue fails there, then it has probably departed the republic altogether and a change of governmental mode becomes inevitable.

Even those who do not consider this plan of government naïve may well find it repulsively elitist, even aristocratic. That would not have bothered the three Publii. Once you take away mere inheritance as the source of privilege, all the founders believed in a kind of meritocracy for virtue and talent. Jefferson's plan for "universal" education was meant to give everyone the rudiments of knowledge; but after that the "best geniusses will be raked from the rubbish" (*Notes*, 146). Besides, seen in context, Madison's plan reflects no contempt for the people. The *original* virtue must reside in them; the same virtue is only purified by successive concoctions through representation. Washington proposes an agent-arbitrator scheme, not because he lacks virtue, but because he is conscious of it. If the people are "checked," so are their representatives, even at the very top, where Madison's principal "check" of bicameralism is to work.

It is illustrative to contrast Madison's attitude toward the people with Montesquieu's. Montesquieu opposes democracy because the people are incapable of caring for their own affairs (*Esprit*, 11.6.24). Madison, though he agreed with Hume that mobs must be treated, in general, as made up of knaves (55.374; cf. Hume 1.6.118), shared as well Hume's generally optimistic view of man as sociable and acting from a moral sense. The genius of the people is virtuous. In No. 10, he does not exclude people from direct handling of their affairs because they are stupid or vicious. Even if they were neither, direct democracy would be wrong because it violates the constitutional norm, "No man is allowed to be a judge in his own cause" (10.59). No king, no legislature, no body at all should be put in a situation where interest has no overseer. The virtuous man will not want to be put in that situation. He welcomes the scrutiny of fair men. His virtue is not private, but public; on display, and asking to be tested. The war for independence had been waged by men with these ideals, drawn from many sources in the Enlightenment (*Inventing*, 317–18). Was it too much for Madison to hope that a government could be built on them? If so, it was a noble failure, which made sense in its own terms and its own day, if not in ours.

TWENTY-NINE

Diffusive Character

The stomach digests the aliments: The heart circulates
the blood: The brain separates and refines the spirits.
—Hume, 1.15.198

There is good reason to think of the American Constitution as a
triumph of Enlightenment interest in social mechanics—as an intricate machine kept in equipoise by the arrangement of multiple "counterpoises" (*Inventing*, 98–110, 288–9). There is ample
language from the Philadelphia Convention and the states' ratifying panels to justify this interpretation. The Federalist itself uses
the imagery of mechanics—even of celestial mechanics (15.97,
18.112). As Montesquieu spoke of social *ressorts*, we hear of various governmental "springs" (Madison at 20.127 and 58.396, Hamilton at 65.443 and 70.477), of the "engines" for ruling or ruin-
ing states (Madison at 18.111, 38.245, and 58.395; Hamilton at
16.99, 29.186, 59.400, and 83.562), and of the social machinery
(19.121), sometimes in terms of clockworks (15.98), sometimes
of hydraulics (21.134).

But another Enlightenment tradition made thinkers rely on
chemical (as well as mechanical) analogies when discussing social laws. Doctors like John Arbuthnot were types of the *médecin-
philosophe* (*Inventing*, 95). So was Dr. Benjamin Rush of Philadelphia. And William Petty, a physician by profession, combined
the mechanical and medical skills in a dazzling way (*Inventing*,
133–9). Chemistry was not only the basis of experimental medicine by the mid-eighteenth century (part of a revolt against
Boerhaave's mechanical approach to medicine). It was also considered a liberal art with Priestley and Lavoisier for heroes. Samuel Johnson was famous for the experiments he conducted in his
chambers. Public lectures and demonstrations were widely at-

tended. Jacques-Louis David painted *Lavoisier and His Wife* (1788) as the union of political, domestic, and scientific virtues. When Dr. Rush had to define chemistry for his Philadelphia students, he wrote: "Chemistry is that science which teaches the effects of heat and mixture, to improve our knowledge in nature and the arts" (see *Chymia* 4, 1953, 50).

The concept of equipoise was as important to doctors as to "mechanicians" like Rittenhouse. Greek medicine had from the time of Alcmaeon considered health as an "equal portioning" (*isonomia*) of the bodily powers. It was easy for a balanced constitution to become both the sign and the cause of good health in society. We have seen that Polybius created a nosology for the various types of human society (*Histories*, 6.18.7–8). Rush had studied at Edinburgh under William Cullen, whose fame was based on his extensive nosological tables (*Transactions and Studies of the Philadelphia College of Physicians*, 1965, 122–3). Rush diagnosed whole societies as Cullen had individual men and women. In the Revolution, he found specific diseases corresponding to excesses of loyalism or patriotism. To the Tory's symptoms, corresponding in part with what we would call paranoia, he gave the name of a proper disease, revolutiana (*Medical Inquiries and Observations*, 1794, 1.273–4). Excessive patriotism led to manic symptoms, which he called anarchia.

It is not surprising that Publius would, in a less technical way, take a physician's approach to social ills. When Hamilton (of all people) argued against the minority's ability to check a majority, he reminded his audience that "what at first sight may seem a remedy, is in reality a poison" (22.140). As Madison had mocked the closet philosopher of government, so Hamilton warns against "the reveries of those political doctors, whose sagacity disdains the admonitions of experimental instruction" (28.176). This was one point on which Jefferson would have agreed with Hamilton —the Virginian's admiration for Dr. Rush was based on what he saw as the latter's modest empiricism (*Inventing*, 187).

Yet one must know when to trust political physicians. To make this point, Madison gives us an extended use of the analogy:

A patient who finds his disorder daily growing worse; and that an efficacious remedy can no longer be delayed without extreme danger; after cooly revolving his situation, and the characters [reputations] of different physicians, selects and calls in such of them as he judges most capable of administering relief, and best entitled to his confidence. The physicians attend: The case of the patient is carefully examined: a consultation is held. They are unanimously agreed that the symptoms are critical, but that the case, with proper and timely relief, is so far from being desperate, that it may be made to issue in an improvement of his constitution. They are equally unanimous in prescribing the remedy by which this happy effect is to be produced. The prescription is no sooner made known however, than a number of persons interpose, and without denying the reality or danger of the disorder, assure the patient that the prescription will be poison to his constitution, and forbid him under pain of certain death to make use of it. Might not the patient reasonably demand before he ventured to follow this advice, that the authors of it should at least agree among themselves, on some other remedy to be substituted? and if he found them differing as much from one another, as from his first counsellors, would he not act prudently, in trying the experiment unanimously recommended by the latter, rather than in hearkening to those who could neither deny the necessity of a speedy remedy, nor agree in proposing one? (38.243).

The most famous medical reference in The Federalist occurs at the beginning and end of No. 10, where Madison looks for a Polybian "proper cure" (10.56) to "the diseases most incident to Republican Government" (10.65). There are other medical-chemical images in the same paper. One of the many traces of Hume that Adair found in No. 10 was the use of "aliment" to describe the nourishing of faction:

The fine Latinity of the word "aliment" apparently caught in some crevice of Madison's mind . . . This word is not a common one in eighteenth-century political literature. Outside of The Federalist and Hume's Essay I have run across it only in Bacon's works. To the man of the eighteenth century even the cognate forms "alimentary" (canal) and "alimony," so familiar to us in common speech, were still highly technical terms of medicine and law (Fame, 104).

Adair is right, as usual, about words. But we should remember that philosophes read many technical works of medicine and the law.

"Aliment" was everywhere in the medical and chemical literature. Arbuthnot wrote a treatise *On Aliments*. Hume used the word generically in his essay "Of Parties in General":

> If mankind had not a strong propensity to such divisions, the indifference of the rest of the community must have suppressed this foolish animosity, that had not any aliment of new benefits and injuries, of general sympathy and antipathy, which never fail to take place, when the whole state is rent into two equal factions (1.8.129).

It was Madison who gave this word a specifically chemical use, popular in the 1780s because of experiments connected with Priestley's and others' phlogiston theory:

> Liberty is to faction, what air is to fire, an aliment without which it instantly expires (10.58).

Dr. Rush, a good friend of Priestley, began all his chemistry courses with the discussion of heat as the principle of chemical change. The great popularizing texts of the Enlightenment reflected a general fascination with the "new" science of chemistry (see Diderot's *Encyclopédie* s.v. "Chymie"). The 1771 Britannica had an engraved chart for all the retorts and alembics through which David sent and bounced light in his portrait of *Lavoisier and His Wife*.

Given this background of general knowledge widely disseminated among philosophes, we should expect a skillful use of chemical images by the men of Madison's generation. Yet the texts I have so far cited on the "purification" of the democracy seem vague or conflicting when we ask exactly what chemical operations they refer to. At the Philadelphia Convention, Madison spoke of "successive filtrations" (Farrand, 1.50), a sieving process that does not (of itself) involve heating. Yet in No. 10 he talked of refining and enlarging public views by "passing them through the medium of a chosen body of citizens" (10.62)—which is clearly not mere sieving. Filtration passes material through a baffle. But in Madison's case the "chosen body" is not a mere screen, but itself the first product of the process.

Messrs. Dickinson and Gerry referred vaguely to the "refining" of the Senate and of elections (Farrand, 1.136, 152). Only Hume and James Wilson seem specific in their references

to a "first concoction" (2.16.492; Farrand 1.10)—a technical term
familiar to educated audiences in the eighteenth century, but
one which must seem a little odd to modern readers. The reference is to the canonical three concoctions of digestion theory—a
matter much studied and debated in the Enlightenment. Digestion raised taxonomic questions of an almost metaphysical di-
mension, challenging the very concept of a "chain of being."
Mere vegetable life, mere grain, could be raised by digestion
into animal life. Some men considered this an act of generation
or vivification, one that broke down (dis-gested) the original
substance to fashion an entirely new one, while purging away
the experiment's "dregs" (*faeces*). Edinburgh was a special center for digestive studies, and great ingenuity was used to extend
observation from vivisected animals to living humans. When, in
1784, a troupe of entertainers came to Edinburgh with a young
performer who swallowed stones as part of his act, Edward Stevens persuaded him to swallow a perforated silver ball with a
live leech in it. He wanted to disprove the vivification thesis that
digestion will not act on living animals—the leech was evacuated
entirely digested inside the ball.

Dr. Rush's own Edinburgh dissertation was on digestion: *De
Coctione Ciborum in Ventriculo* (1768). To prove that the first
coction was a fermentation process producing acid, he vomited
various foods under controlled conditions and wrote up his results in the required Latin form. When students challenged his
theories, Rush would answer: "I shall not yield to Dr. Spallan-
zani, Dr. Stevens, Dr. Goss, etc., until they have taken as many
emetics to establish their theory as I have done." Rush held that
the addition of bile refined the acid ferment into "chyle" (or
"chyme"), the regular term for the first coction's issue. The second coction absorbed chyle into the blood (see Hume's description at the head of this chapter), and a third coction produced
the rare liquids, humors, or "spirits" of the body.

Digestion was thought to involve many chemical processes—
analysis, solution, maceration, trituration, fermentation, refining.
But the controlling process was most often thought of as distillation—digestion produced, ultimately, the body's "spirits." Chemical analogies were endless, leading Dr. William Hunter to com-
plain in 1784: "Some physiologists will have it, that the stomach

is a mill, others that it is a fermenting vat, others, again, that it is a stew-pan; but, in my view of the matter, it is neither a mill, a fermenting vat nor a stew-pan; but a stomach, gentlemen, a stomach" (*Two Introductory Lectures*, 95). Nonetheless, the debate over digestive processes went fiercely on, and was widely reported. (There is a very full discussion in Ephraim Chambers's 1741 *Cyclopaedia;* and see the *Encyclopédie* s.vv. "Chylification," "Coction," and "Digestion.")

When James Wilson argued for proportional representation in the Senate, his use of "first concoction" could mean any first stage in a heating operation—e.g., the removal of poisons from a medical potion. Coction simply means "cooking," and concoction a "cooking-with" something else. But when a *numbered* coction (or concoction) is used alone in the eighteenth century, the audience was bound to think of the digestive sense:

> If equality in the 2d branch [the Senate] was an error that time would correct, he should be less anxious to exclude it being sensible that perfection was unattainable in any plan; but being a fundamental and perpetual error, it ought by all means to be avoided. A vice in the Representation, like an error in the first concoction, must be followed by disease, convulsions, and finally death itself (Farrand, 2.10).

We can be sure of Wilson's meaning from his repetition of the figure in 1788, when he applied it to the election of virtuous representatives:

> For, believe me, no government, even the best, can be happily administered by ignorant or vicious men. You will forgive me, I am sure, for endeavouring to impress upon your minds, in the strongest manner, the importance of this great duty. It is the first concoction in politics, and if an errour is committed here, it can never be corrected in any subsequent process: the certain consequence must be disease (*Works*, 2.778).

Indigestion was a serious matter, defined by the Chambers *Cyclopaedia* as "a crudity, or want of due coction, either in a food, a humour of the body, or an excrement." Lack of proper coction in the first stage would yield "crude humours"—"those which want of that preparation and elaboration which they ordinarily receive from a thorough digestion" (ibid., s.v. "Crude"). This would result in "a disorderly exercise of the functions," and upset the entire animal "oeconomy":

> But chiefly [is crudity recognized] from a fault in the quantity or quality of the humours; both those still circulating, and those secreted; as of sweat, tears, mucus of the nose, saliva, sputum, the bile, urine, ichor, pus, blood, menses, lochia, milk, aphthae, &c. That state of the disease, wherein the *crude* matter is changed and rendered less peccant, and laudable, is called *digestion, concoction,* or *maturation* (ibid., s.v. "Crudity").

The "error" in first concoction was usually blamed on lack of sufficient maceration of the food—either by the teeth's mastication, or by trituration (the peristaltic action of the stomach walls). Some thought trituration the principal agent in digestion. But even those who attributed digestion to other causes—e.g., Dr. Rush (to fermentation and bile)—acknowledged that some maceration was necessary to the proper performance of the first coction. Rush himself said: "I would sooner go without my dinner than contend over a Goose with a carving knife. It is unfriendly to health, because the Carver to avoid the singularity of sitting long after the rest of the company are done is obliged to swallow his victuals before it is sufficiently masticated" (Lecture, December 9, 1796; see *Bull. Hist. Med.,* 1962, 345).

In Wilson's argument, proportional representation in the Senate would grind and process the delegations to fit the living heft of each state, its contribution to the whole. But equal delegations, unrefined and arbitrarily uniform, would be so many unassimilable lumps, bearing no relation to the absorptive capacities of the government and the circulation of living "humours." Such lumps clog the system at the outset, convulse it and make later correction impossible. This is a medical image vivid and appropriate—and unlikely to be used except in a center of enlightened medical practice like Philadelphia, where Drs. Rush and the Shippens and John Morgan had lectured to the public.

Edinburgh was *the* medical center of the time. Rush was always grateful to his teachers there: "The whole world does not afford a set of greater men than are at present united in the college of Edinburgh" (*Letters,* 1.41). It was from Edinburgh that

Hume wrote his description of digestion in the individual (1.15.198) and in the body politic:

> In a large government, which is modelled with masterly skill, there is compass and room enough to refine the democracy, from the lower people, who may be admitted into the first elections or first concoction of the commonwealth, to the higher magistrates, who direct all the movement (2.16.492).

Only the higher distillates can manage all the body's movement: "The brain separates and refines the spirits" in society's third concoction.

Was Madison, who drew so heavily on Hume, basing his "refining and enlarging" image of No. 10 on the digestive process? If so, he chose a set of words that does not really accord with any Enlightenment explanation of digestion. And there is no reason to think Madison followed Hume slavishly here. Even when he picked up the hint of "aliment" from Hume, he elaborated it with a specificity all his own. At 10.62 Madison is not describing digestion—nor any process of simple filtration or distillation. The peculiarity of Madison's description is that "the public views" are passed through a select body of men itself taken from the substance to be purified. A kind of self-purification is being described, one especially well suited to the treatment of virtue in a self-governing republic.

There is only one process familiar to Madison's educated readers that would correspond with Madison's words—the self-enriching form of distillation known in English as rectification, in French as *cohobation*. Madison's peers were familiar with the fine brandies produced by this chemical action; and descriptions of it are found in all the popular scientific reference works. According to the Chambers *Cyclopaedia:*

> *Rectification* is a reiterated depuration of a distilled matter, e.g. brandy, spirits, or oils; by passing them again over the faeces [dregs], or marc [lees], to render them more subtile, and exalt their virtues.

Madison meant to exalt virtues of a different sort, but by an analogous process. Diderot's *Encyclopédie* has this entry:

> La cohobation est une opération chimique qui consiste à reporter

les produits volatils d'une distillation . . . sur le résidu dont ils ont été séparés . . .

In brandy rectification, alembic necks were designed to trap part of the fumes and send them back down as cooling vapors, through which the heated ones must rise. Makers of rum in the West Indies accomplished the same thing by taking the first liquid distillate from the condensing coils and putting it back into the retort. New fumes coming over from the still pot reheated this liquid and passed through its fumes into the cooling "worms." Thus two separate distillations from the same substance were combined to form a third thing, the enriched liquor.

Madison's image is marvelously apt. Under the Constitution as it was originally framed, electoral distillations were to be both successive and overlapping, starting again from the original substance (the general body of the electorate) in the choice of presidential electors, House representatives, and state legislatures; and these returns to the experiment's first substance interacted with choices made solely or in conjunction with the prior distillates (e.g., state legislatures or the United States Senate).

Madison's figure is further suitable because, in this context, even "enlarge" has a chemical meaning, as does "diffusive." The spirits that rise from the distillation process are only a part of the original substance, and the subtlest part at that; but they tend to fill greater space. They are paradoxically enlarged by growing little—subtle, yet expansive and penetrating; the "higher spirits" that pervade and govern man in digestion's third coction. Chambers had discussed "diffusion" in digestive terms:

To conceive the nature of chemical *Digestion*, it may be necessary to show how the particles of bodies can, by this process, be diffused every way, and sustained in the menstruum [solvent].

But other entries connect the phenomenon with Madison's image of a distillate:

EXPANSION: Spirit of wine, with a heat less than that of boiling water, expanded it self by one twelfth part of its bulk.

RAREFACTION, *Rarefactio,* in physics, the act whereby a body is rendered *rare;* that is, is brought to possess more room, or appear under a larger bulk, without any accession of new matter . . . Our more accurate writers restrain *rarefactio* to that expansion of a mass into a larger bulk, which is effected by means of heat—All expansion from other causes they call dilatation.

DILATATION, in physics, a motion of the parts of a body whereby it expands, or opens itself to a greater space.

The ready use of chemical images in politics can be seen even when James Wilson wants to *attack* one form of electoral "processing," the election of state senators by specially chosen electors. Speaking ironically of those who had proposed this measure for Pennsylvania, Wilson said: "They must certainly know well the purifying virtues of those political alembicks, through which they wish to see our senators sublimated and refined" (*Works*, 2.793). But this assault on excessive indirection does not mean that Wilson rejected electoral refining of "character" in Madison's terms. In 1788, he praised the ratified Constitution in these terms:

> If the people, at their elections, take care to choose none but representatives that are wise and good, their representatives will take care, in their turn, to choose or appoint none but such as are wise and good also. The remark applies to every succeeding election and appointment. Thus the characters proper for publick officers will be diffused from the immediate elections of the people over the remotest parts of administration (ibid., 2.778).

According to Madison's science of representation, the same process that refines public views also enlarges them, frees them from captivity to local interest or narrow aims. The higher spirits of governance in the digestive body politic are like the freed fumes of an enriched brandy—or like the diffusive character of George Washington, which pervades the entire republic.

THIRTY

The Third Publius

A man who loves only himself, without regard to
friendship and desert, merits the severest blame; and a
man, who is only susceptible of friendship, without
public spirit, or a regard to the community, is deficient
in the most material part of virtue.
—Hume, 1.3.106–7

I come at last to the forgotten Publius—come to him, appro-
priately, here; because, brief as his contribution was, he demon-
strates how widely shared was that view of elections Hume
called a concoction.

Jay was the most distinguished man, in 1787, to take up the
pen of Publius, the man Hamilton most wanted for the task.
They had known each other since Hamilton's arrival in the Livingston circle at Elizabethtown, where Jay was engaged to Livingston's daughter. Slight, a dandy, touchy of his honor, studious
of the law, Jay had been a gentleman rebel at King's College—instant reassurance, to Hamilton, that polish could be acquired
outside Nassau Hall. The two men had things in common despite
the ten years' difference in their age. Jay, who was sometimes
condescending to inferiors, had the good sense to see at once the
rough genius of this West Indian arrival; any condescension to
Hamilton would have ended their friendship before it began.

Hamilton had reason to feel complimented when his own
Farmer Refuted was mistaken for Jay's work; and to feel proud
of Jay's collaboration in the fight to make New York ratify the
Constitution. Jay's injury cut short his contribution—which became a blessing for us. It would be revealing to have papers on
the judiciary written by the man who became first chief justice
under the Constitution. But it is hard to see how Hamilton's

work in Nos. 78 and 81 could be bettered; and Madison would not have contributed so heavily if Jay had remained close to the project.

Yet Jay's five Numbers repay study. Nos. 3 and 4 are particularly impressive. He begins in No. 3 the discussion of federal government as an inhibition on war. Most authors addressing a popular audience would, in our day, say that union makes for strength against the unjust bellicosity of foreigners. But so naturally did political questions become a test of one's *own* virtue, in the founding period, that Jay begins with a concern to prevent bellicosity on the part of Americans themselves. The union of the states will not, in the first place, *repel* aggression so much as *repress* it. The questioning of "interest" in general makes Jay argue that the united continent will have less interested motive for inflicting war on innocent neighbors (including, very specifically, the Indian tribes).

Jay begins by inquiring "whether so many *just* causes of war are likely to be given by *United America,* as by *disunited* America; for if it should turn out that United America will probably give the fewest, then it will follow that, in this respect, the Union tends most to preserve the people in a state of peace with other nations" (3.14). Here the emphasis on virtue no longer seems naïve, even in our terms; it is more realistic than the romantic view later Americans would take of their wars as automatically just. Jay starts with the assumption that war will be unjust and tries to prevent injustice from arising.

But how will union make for more just treatment of potential enemies? Jay's answer is in full accord with Madison's view of representation as distilling virtue into the national councils. Jay takes account of the fact that young America could not be isolated: Spanish and British territories marched on American soil. Grievances were bound to arise at the chafing points; but *parties to the grievances should not judge their own cause:*

> The bordering States if any, will be those who, under the impulse of sudden irritation, and a quick sense of apparent interest or injury, will be most likely by direct violence, to excite war with those nations; and nothing can so effectually obviate that danger, as a national Government, whose wisdom and prudence will not be di-

minished by the passions which actuate the parties immediately interested (3.17).

Even if disputes arise, the national council is not expected to act as a partisan agent for any American state against foreigners. It should show disinterest, possessing in its second concoction the impartiality of Washington's adjudicator chosen through different men's agents:

> But not only fewer just causes of war will be given by the national Government, but it will also be more in their power to accommodate and settle them amicably. They will be more temperate and cool, and in that respect, as well as in others, will be more in a capacity to act advisedly than the offending State. The pride of States as well as of men, naturally disposes them to justify all their actions, and opposes their acknowledging, correcting or repairing their errors and offences. The national Government in such cases will not be affected by this pride, but will proceed with moderation and candour to consider and decide on the means most proper to extricate them from the difficulties which threaten them (3.17).

This Number, written before any contributed by Madison, offers us, already, a "Madisonian" constellation of values and terms. Social men must act "amicably"—with "confidence and affection," as Jay puts it at 5.24, not with sour "jealousy." They must trust their affairs to representatives who are "temperate and cool," who rise above the "pride of [directly interested] States," men whose special capacity it is to act "advisedly." The whole doctrine is in this string of words: "proceed with moderation and candour to consider and decide on the means most proper."

The council of esteemed reputation can act with proud magnanimity, not from petty vanities:

> Besides it is well known that acknowledgments, explanations and compensations are often accepted as satisfactory from a strong united nation, which would be rejected as unsatisfactory if offered by a State or a Confederacy of little consideration or power (3.17).

Such a spirit will prevent sudden war at the slightest provocation.

Because such violences are more frequently caused by the passions and interests of a part than of the whole, of one or two States than of the Union [another of the hastily written Numbers' faulty sentences]. Not a single Indian war has yet been occasioned by aggressions of the present Foederal Government, feeble as it is, but there are several instances of Indian hostilities having been provoked by the improper conduct of individual States, who either unable or unwilling to restrain or punish offenders, have given occasion to the slaughter of many innocent inhabitants (3.17).

For more than a century, in the history of the republic Jay was arguing for, condemnations of fellow Americans for slaughtering Indians would be rarely heard and harshly received. The virtuous republic disappears when people no longer question their own virtue.

Jay, like Madison, thought the republic itself should imitate the conference that proposed its plan. The federal Convention was "composed of men, who possessed the confidence of the people, and many of whom had become highly distinguished by their patriotism, virtue and wisdom, in times which tried the minds and hearts of men" (2.10)—a discreet reference to that "Big Bertha" of the Constitution's proponents, the president of the Convention, General Washington. Anything pondered with candor by these patriots should be given "sedate and candid consideration" (2.11) by the people they were trying to serve. If this communication of public purpose succeeds, it will result in a return of distinguished men to the national councils, authorized to legislate for the people:

Because when once an efficient national government is established, the best men in the country will not only consent to serve, but also will generally be appointed to manage it; for altho' town or county, or other contracted influence may place men in state assemblies, or senates, or courts of justice, or executive departments; yet more general and extensive reputation [Madison's "diffusive character"—10.63] for talents and other qualifications, will be necessary to recommend men to offices under the national government—especially as it will have the widest field for choice, and never experience that want of proper persons, which is not uncommon in some of the States [Madison's "greater option"—10.63]. Hence it will result, that the administration, the political counsels, and the judicial decisions of the national Government will be more wise, systematical and judicious, than those of individual States, and consequently more satisfactory with respect to other nations, as well as more *safe* with respect to us (3.15).

This government "will regard the interest of the whole, and the particular interests of the parts only as connected with that of the whole" (4.21).

Jay was assigned these early papers on national defense because of his diplomatic experience—an experience that would become far more extensive, and would be condemned as too *little* "interested" in the dispute over "Jay's treaty" with England. Because of the same expertise, Hamilton brought Jay back to the project to discuss the treaty-making power in No. 64.

There is an age requirement for those with power to make treaties (thirty-five for President and thirty for senators) and they are appointed by a "second concoction" in each case—by a "select" body of electors for the President, and by state legislatures for the Senate. So, if virtue is ever distilled in our system, says Jay, it will be at this level:

> As the select assemblies for choosing the president, as well as the state legislatures who appoint the senators will in general be composed of the most enlightened and respectable citizens, there is reason to presume that their attention and their votes will be directed to those men only who have become the most distinguished by their abilities and virtue, and in whom the people perceive just grounds for confidence. The constitution manifests very particular attention to this object. By excluding men under thirty five from the first office, and those under thirty from the second, it confines the electors to men of whom the people have had time to form a judgment, and with respect to whom they will not be liable to be deceived by those brilliant appearances of genius and patriotism, which like transient meteors sometimes mislead as well as dazzle (64.433).

It was a commonplace in Jay's time that kings chose ministers of talent because it was to the king's own interest to have a brilliant body of advisers. Jay saw the choice of the nation's agents in the same light, but with the "select" men of the concocting process standing warrant for the delegates they finally commission:

If the observation be well founded, that wise kings will always be served by able ministers, it is fair to argue that as an assembly of select electors possess in a greater degree than kings, the means of extensive and accurate information relative to men and characters, so will their appointments bear at least equal marks of discretion and discernment. The inference which naturally results from these considerations is this, that the president and senators so chosen will always be of the number of those who best understand our national interests whether considered in relation to the several states or to foreign nations, who are best able to promote those interests, and whose reputation for integrity inspires and merits confidence. With such men the power of making treaties may be safely lodged (64.433).

Trust in the adjudicating power of men eminent for virtue rests on the commonsense realization that they will grasp the relation of legitimate local interest to the "aggregate and permanent interests" of the community to which they also belong, and whose "character" has been committed to their care:

In proportion as the United States assumes a national form, and a national character, so will the good of the whole be more and more an object of attention; and the government must be a weak one indeed, if it should forget that the good of the whole can only be promoted by advancing the good of each of the parts or members which compose the whole. It will not be in the power of the president and senate to make any treaties, by which they and their families and estates will not be equally bound and affected with the rest of the community; and having no private interest distinct from that of the nation, they will be under no temptations to neglect the latter (64.437–8).

If Madison was naïve in his hope of distilling virtue from the electorate through successive concoctions, it was a naïveté held by older and more experienced men, men like the third Publius, a worthy partner of the other two.

THIRTY-ONE

Accuracy

> As one form of government must be allowed more per-
> fect than another, independent of the manners and hu-
> mours of particular men; why may we not enquire
> what is the most perfect of all, though the common
> botched and inaccurate governments seem to serve the
> purposes of society, and though it be not so easy to es-
> tablish a new system of government, as to build a ves-
> sel upon a new construction?
>
> —Hume, 2.16.480

If my argument has been a sound one, the reading of No. 10 has
been subject to misunderstanding of Madison's language and
Enlightenment assumptions. Interpretations vary; but regard for
No. 10 is uniform. It survives thorough attack (like Dahl's) as
well as misguided defense (like Kendall's). The paper has a
weightiness of language, an authoritative bearing, that awes the
reader. It is a masterpiece of neoclassical prose, the style drawing mainly on Hume and Bolingbroke but showing traces as well
of Addison and Dr. Johnson. Madison has indeed "concocted"
his argument into a pure form. He recommends electoral distillation in words that have themselves been distilled, refined, enlarged.

The words show constant pressure of intellect on them, a sensible control. We can see this in the way the final sentences echo
the first, rounding things off, "concluding the whole." The opening section states a problem and seeks a cure; the end states the
cure and dismisses the problem. The ring is closed.

> Among the numerous advantages promised by a well constructed
> Union, none deserves to be more accurately developed than its
> tendency to break and control the violence of faction. The friend of

popular governments, never finds himself so much alarmed for their character and fate, as when he contemplates their propensity to this dangerous vice. He will not fail therefore to set a due value on any plan which, without violating the principles to which he is attached, provides a proper cure for it (10.56).

The scientific air of Madison's "modern" politics is signaled in the use of "well constructed." We have seen how the clockwork engineers of enlightened research sought formulae for the *société bien organisée*. Thus Madison asks what "may be expected from a well constituted senate" (62.419). Hamilton, too, seeks the "well ordered constitution of civil government" (30.189) and "a well constituted court for the trial of impeachments" (65.439). A constitution is, precisely, an *ordering*, a proper articulation into parts; a machine for living. For Hamilton, the scientist of government must adjust a quantity of energy to the mass that must be moved:

> When the dimensions of a State attain to a certain magnitude, it requires the same energy of government and the same forms of administration; which are requisite in one of much greater extent. This idea admits not of precise demonstration, because there is no rule by which we can measure the momentum of civil power, necessary to the government of any given number of individuals; but when we consider that the island of Britain, nearly commensurate with each of the supposed confederacies, contains about eight millions of people, and when we reflect upon the degree of authority required to direct the passion of so large a society to the public good, we shall see no reason to doubt that the like portion of power would be sufficient to perform the same task in a society far more numerous. Civil power properly organised and exerted is capable of diffusing its force to a very great extent; and can in a manner reproduce itself in every part of a great empire by a judicious arrangement of subordinate institutions (13.80–1).

Madison takes the same mechanical approach to the problem of limiting the number of representatives, keeping a high ratio between them and their constituents. The idea that the more delegates there are, the better the representation, is a delusion:

> The countenance of the government may become more democratic; but the soul that animates it will be more oligarchic. The machine

will be enlarged, but the fewer and often the more secret will be the springs by which its motions are directed (59.396; cf. 10.63).

The algebra of government—the proper equations between extent of territory, size of government, number of representatives—reflected a favorite concern of the Enlightenment (cf. *Esprit,* 18.8, and *Inventing,* 155, on Cesare dí Beccaria).

Hume's essay, "Idea of a Perfect Commonwealth," that essay whose traces we have found throughout The Federalist, opens with a consideration of accuracy:

> It is not with forms of government, as with other artificial contrivances; where an old engine may be rejected, if we can discover another more accurate and commodious (2.16.480; on the age's passion for accuracy, see *Inventing,* 105–10, 128–31; and Hume, *History,* 2.23.482, 6.70.259).

Though Hume admits that governments cannot be easily corrected, he thinks that a clear vision of a perfect form would help improve "the common botched and inaccurate governments" (ibid.). So, in the opening sentence of No. 10, Madison brings up the aspect of well-constructed unions that "deserves to be more *accurately* developed" if the friends of popular government are to protect its reputation. All these notes are sounded again in the conclusion, but in the major key as it were. What began as a cause for anxiety becomes the ground for confident boasting:

> In the extent and proper structure of the Union, therefore, we behold a Republican remedy for the diseases most incident to Republican Government. And according to the degree of pleasure and pride, we feel in being Republicans, ought to be our zeal in cherishing the spirit, and supporting the character of Federalists (10.65).

The phrases chime responsively. The opening's "well constructed Union" becomes the ending's "proper structure of the Union." The "proper cure" being sought becomes "a Republican remedy." A republic's "propensity to this dangerous vice" becomes "the diseases most incident to Republican Government." The "friend of popular governments" becomes what "we feel in being Republicans." But the "alarm" felt by republicans at the outset yields to the "pleasure and pride" of the same men in the last sentence. The danger to the "character" of a republic is resolved in the proud "character" finally adopted by republicans. The prior condition for any cure—that it be effected "without violating the principles to which he [the republican] is attached" receives triumphant vindication when Madison says that the adoption of representation with extent of territory allows people to boast equally of being republicans *and* federalists.

The density of Madison's style comes from neoclassical thought patterns, which are ultimately derived from the organizing of Greek prose, everywhere, by antithetical particles (*men . . . de*) or correlating ones (*te . . . kai*). Antithesis and correlation are evident in almost every sentence of No. 10, and in the larger blocks of words and thoughts. Take, for instance, the basic values to be protected from faction. These are disjunctive yet correlative, inclusive yet distinguishable—private right and common good: "the rights of citizens . . . the permanent and aggregate interests of the community" (10.57). Those values keep reappearing under same/different guises:

- public and private faith (10.57)
- public and personal liberty (ibid.)
- rules of justice and the rights of the minor party (ibid.)
- distrust of public engagements and alarm for private rights (ibid.)
- justice and the public good (10.60)
- the rights of another or the good of the whole (ibid.)
- both the public good and the rights of other citizens (ibid.)
- the public good and private rights (10.61)

Other couplings—of virtue and wisdom, of passion and interest—are repeated and varied with similar skill. The result is a density of weave, a sense of complex relations properly maintained, in the constant adjustment of complementary and conflicting pairs. An air of scientific method is sustained by the bifurcative approach Madison favors, imitating Hume. Alternatives are posed, and one is eliminated. Then the surviving thing is divided, and one of *its* components eliminated. Two methods of cure for faction—removing causes or inhibiting effects (58). Two methods of removing causes—but one undesirable and the other impracticable. Two kinds of faction—majority and minority (60). Two forms of control for majority faction—preventing its occasion or enfeebling its operation (61). The forms of faction are given in Hume's division and subdivision (58–9).

The overall strategy of the Number is that of exhaustive enumeration and elimination. Factions are undesirable but unavoidable (58–60). Majority factions pose the great problem (60–61). Direct democracy is helpless against this (61–62). Representation offers a partial solution (62). Extent of territory, together with representation, offers the entire cure (62–4).

The hinge on which the whole Number turns is often given slight notice, since it falls within the first major section in logic, but sets up a solution that will not appear for several pages. In discussing the undesirability of faction, which lets *ex parte* opinion speak for the whole, Madison introduces his concept that legislation should be quasijudicial, a form of disinterested *arbitration:*

> No man is allowed to be a judge in his own cause; because his interest would certainly bias his judgment, and, not improbably, corrupt his integrity. With equal, nay with greater reason, a body of men, are unfit to be both judges and parties, at the same time; yet, what are many of the most important acts of legislation, but so many judicial determinations, not indeed concerning the rights of single persons, but concerning the rights of large bodies of citizens; and what are the different classes of legislators, but advocates and parties to the causes which they determine? Is a law proposed concerning private debts? It is a question to which the creditors are parties on one side, and the debtors on the other. Justice ought to hold the balance between them. Yet the parties are and must be themselves the judges; and the most numerous party, or, in other words, the most powerful faction must be expected to prevail. Shall domestic manufactures be encouraged, and in what degree, by restrictions on foreign manufactures? are questions which would be differently decided by the landed and the manufacturing classes; and probably by neither, with a sole regard to justice and the public good. The apportionment of taxes on the various descriptions of property, is an act which seems to require the most exact impartiality; yet, there is perhaps no legislative act in which greater opportunity and temptation are given to a predominant party, to trample on the rules of justice. Every shilling with which they over-burden the inferior number, is a shilling saved to their own pockets (10.59–60).

Madison goes on in the next sentence to say that we cannot count on enlightened statesmen invariably being present to "adjust these clashing interests." But how can he say this and then propose, two pages later, his plan "to refine and enlarge the public views, by passing them through the medium of a chosen body of citizens, whose wisdom may best discern the true interest of their country, and whose patriotism and love of justice, will be least likely to sacrifice it to temporary or partial considerations" (10.62)? The passage on page 29 is part of the preliminary discussion on faction's evil, before proposals are considered for its cure. Madison obviously means that "enlightened statesmen" will not be on hand by mere accident. Measures must be taken to distill virtue and purge interest; to create a judicial aspect to the legislature by sending uninstructed delegates, from an extended territory, through successive processes of choice, thus making it harder for interest to invade the national councils, to mobilize itself brazenly on a large scale, to confess its *ex parte* nature among men who have been sworn to impartiality. Adair summed up Madison's "proper cure" to the republican malady in 1943:

> Compound various economic interests of a large territory with a federal system of thirteen semi-sovereign political units, establish a Humian scheme of indirect elections, which will functionally bind the extensive area into a unit while "refining" the voice of the people, and you will have a stable republican state (diss., 269).

Adair would later put less emphasis on economic interests; and his reference to "semi-sovereign" states would later be less confident. But it is amazing how quickly he identified, in 1943, the basic argument of No. 10. It is equally amazing that his solution has recieved such widespread neglect.

As we have seen, Adair found further evidence for Madison's approach in his "Notes on the Confederacy." But there is more evidence still, not only in the Convention debates (Farrand, 1.50), but in other Numbers of The Federalist itself. Madison reminds us in No. 43 that he sees the legislative task as semijudicial or adjudicating:

> In cases where it may be doubtful on which side justice lies, what better umpires could be desired by two violent factions, flying to

arms and tearing a State to pieces, than the representatives of confederate States not heated by the local flame? To the impartiality of
Judges they would unite the affection of friends (43.294).

The heat of passion must yield to cool and candid decisions—as
Jay described the solving of border disputes with foreigners in
No. 3. In No. 55, Madison assures doubters that the House of
Representatives can maintain a level of public virtue and impar-
tiality:

> I am equally unable to conceive that there are at this time, or can
> be in any short time, in the United States any sixty-five or an hun-
> dred men capable of recommending themselves to the choice of the
> people at large, who would either desire or dare within the short
> space of two years, to betray the solemn trust committed to them
> (55.376).

He gives, as warrant for his argument, the performance of the
wartime Congress, which had extraordinary powers yet did not
abuse them: "We know by happy experience that the public
trust was not betrayed; nor has the purity of our public councils
in this particular ever suffered even from the whispers of
calumny" (55.377). Madison ends this Number with criticism of
"jealousies" that slander the nature of man as incapable of republican virtue.

In No. 57, Madison gives us a "rerun" of his argument in No.
10, confirming what was intended there:

> The aim of every political constitution is or ought to be first to ob-
> tain for rulers, men who possess most wisdom to discern, and most
> virtue to pursue the common good of the society; and in the next
> place, to take the most effectual precautions for keeping them virtu-
> ous, whilst they continue to hold their public trust (57.384).

He argues that the makeup of the House of Representatives—the
part of the government he feared most, remember—would render
its circumstances "impartial to the rights and pretensions of
every class and description of citizens" (385). Men will be recommended to the electorate in terms of virtue and ability, not
birth or wealth: "Who are the objects of popular choice? Every
citizen whose merit may recommend him to the esteem and
confidence of his country" (ibid.). All the incitements to virtuous
ambition and benevolent legislation will exist in this form of
election:

If we consider the situation of the men on whom the free suffrages of their fellow citizens may confer the representative trust, we shall find it involving every security which can be devised or desired for their fidelity to their constituents.

In the first place, as they will have been distinguished by the preference of their fellow citizens, we are to presume, that in general, they will be somewhat distinguished also, by those qualities which entitle them to it, and which promise a sincere and scrupulous regard to the nature of their engagements.

In the second place, they will enter into the public service under circumstances which cannot fail to produce a temporary affection at least to their constituents. There is in every breast a sensibility to marks of honor, of favor, of esteem, and of confidence, which, apart from all considerations of interest, is some pledge for grateful and benevolent returns. Ingratitude is a common topic of declamation against human nature; and it must be confessed, that instances of it are but too frequent and flagrant both in public and in private life. But the universal and extreme indignation which it inspires is itself a proof of the energy and prevalence of the contrary sentiment [a standard argument for the moral sense; see *Inventing*, 225–6].

In the third place, these ties which bind the representative to his constituents are strengthened by motives of a more selfish nature. His pride and vanity attach him to a form of government which favors his pretensions, and gives him a share in its honors and distinctions [cf. Hamilton's talk of "emoluments" to bind men to the federal government at *AH*, 4.180]. Whatever hopes or projects might be entertained by a few aspiring characters, it must generally happen that a great proportion of the men deriving their advancement from their influence with the people, would have more to hope from a preservation of the favor, than from innovations in the government subversive of the authority of the people (57.385–6).

That last sentence tells us exactly how his scheme of representation would prevent large-scale faction, carrying its partial nature on its face, from appealing to bias instead of impartial judgment.

Such will be the relation between the House of Representatives and their constituents. Duty, gratitude, interest, ambition itself, are the cords by which they will be bound to fidelity and sympathy with the great mass of people (57.387).

And if these preservatives of public virtue are present even in the first concoction of popular choice, they are bound to be even

more evident in the successive concoctions that give the republic
its President, its Senate, and its Supreme Court.

Speaking of the bicameral check in No. 58, Madison tells us it
will force obviously factious men to lurk ineffectually rather than
strut and prevail:

> This advantage must be increased by the consciousness felt by the
> same side, of being supported in its demands, by right, by reason,
> and by the constitution; and the consciousness on the opposite side,
> of contending against the force of all these solemn considerations
> (58.393, a gloss on the "consciousness of unjust or dishonorable
> purposes" at 10.64).

We learn more of the mechanics of the bicameral check, from
ambition and pride united with right of office, at 58.394:

> But will not the house of representatives be as much interested as
> the senate in maintaining the government in its proper function,
> and will they not therefore be unwilling to stake its existence or its
> reputation on the pliancy of the senate? Or if such a trial of
> firmness between the two branches were hazarded, would not the
> one be as likely first to yield as the other? These questions will
> create no difficulty with those who reflect that in all cases the
> smaller the number and the more permanent and conspicuous the
> station of men in power, the stronger must be the interest which
> they will individually feel in whatever concerns the government.
> Those who represent the dignity of their country in the eyes of
> other nations, will be particularly sensible to every prospect of
> public danger, or of a dishonorable stagnation in public affairs
> (58.394–5).

So there is ample confirmation of Madison's meaning, in both
No. 10 and No. 51, from his other Numbers.

But, more important, Hamilton also makes the argument he
had first doubted when he heard it from Madison's lips at the
Convention. At that time, he wrote in his notes:

> Maddisons Theory—
>   Two principles upon which republics ought to be constructed—
>   I that they have such extent as to render combinations on the
> ground of Interest difficult
>   II By a process of election calculated to refine the representation
> of the People—

Answer—There is truth in both these principles but they do not conclude so strongly as he supposes.

The Assembly when chosen will meet in one room if they are drawn from half the globe—& will be liable to all the passions of popular assemblies.

If more *minute links* are wanting others will supply them. Distinctions of Eastern middle and Southern states will come into view; between commercial and non commercial states. Imaginary lines will influence &c. Human mind prone to limit its view by near and local objects. Paper money is capable of giving a general impulse. It is easy to conceive a popular sentiment pervading the E states.

Observ: { large districts less liable to be influenced by factions demagogues than small

Note — This is in some degree true but not so generally as may be supposed. Frequently small portions of the large districts carry elections. An influential demagogue will give an impulse to the whole. Demagogues are not always *inconsiderable* persons. Patricians were frequently demagogues. Characters are less known & a less active interest taken in them (*AH*, 4.165–6 = Farrand, 1.146–7).

The first thing to notice about these impressions, written on the spot during a first hearing of Madison's theory, is that they are in only partial disagreement: "There is truth in both these principles . . . This is in some degree true . . ." Hamilton feels that Madison does not go far enough in eliminating interest; that faction will still mobilize itself across extent of territory, and local views will not be transcended in elections.

But he supports Madison on both points in The Federalist. In No. 60, he says that factions will not be mobilized, for the reasons given in No. 10; and in No. 68, he says that public virtue will be distilled in the "refining" process of elections. Is Hamilton insincere in this? I know no way of testing that. He may have concluded, on longer reflection, that Madison was right; or that the limited agreement he first felt was too cautious; or that the principles looked more effective in the final Philadelphia draft than in the inchoate scheme of June 6. He may have persuaded himself in the effort at persuading others—a common enough human propensity. But even the limited agreement registered on June 6 is enough to absolve him from total inconsistency in arguing for principles that he thought true, so far as they went, even when he first heard Madison expound them. Remember that his own preferred scheme was presented as impracticable from the outset, an ideal but not a goal—and one with enough similarity to Madison's plan in No. 10 to make *it* the practical goal.

At 60.404, Hamilton says that extent of territory will make unlikely "a concert of views, in any partial scheme of elections." And he, like Madison, finds a further check or concoction in bicameralism—though Hamilton allows, more than Madison would, for a workable check between legislative and executive departments:

> The house of representatives being to be elected immediately by the people; the senate by the state legislatures; the president by electors chosen for that purpose by the people; there would be little probability of a common interest to cement these different branches in a predilection for any particular class of electors (60.405).

Hamilton, himself an example of honorable ambition, speaks with convincing warmth when he describes the distillation of virtue into the higher offices of the union:

> This process of election affords a moral certainty, that the office of president, will seldom fall to the lot of any man, who is not in an eminent degree endowed with the requisite qualifications. Talents for low intrigue and the little arts of popularity [No. 10's "the vicious arts, by which elections are too often carried"] may alone suffice to elevate a man to the first honors in a single state; but it will require other talents and a different kind of merit to establish him in the esteem and confidence of the whole union, or of so considerable a portion of it as would be necessary to make him a successful candidate for the distinguished office of president of the United States. It will not be too strong to say, that there will be a constant probability of seeing the station filled by characters preeminent for ability and virtue (68.460–1).

This is indeed a Madisonian Hamilton speaking, repeating the doctrine of No. 10. Extent of territory helps to eliminate partial interest and distill impartial virtue. This is the authentic teaching of all three Publii.

Epilogue

The reader may well observe, at this point, "If that is Madison's explanation of America's government, then Madison was cock-eyed." I said at the outset that Madison's explanation, in the varying interpretations that have been made of it, itself needed explaining. It is fair for anyone to object that my interpretation (or, rather, Adair's) needs most explaining of all.

The text of Madison seems, on this reading, at odds not only with everything we have been told about the Constitution but with everything we can observe about our government's actual operation. We have been told that Madison distrusted the people, and power, and rulers. But it is clear from the text that Madison expected a great deal from the people, from central power, and from their rulers. The people, since *they* were virtuous, would choose wise and virtuous rulers who would exercise power benignly—so long as America remained a republic.

We have been told that Madison pitted interest against interest in a constructive process of self-correction. The texts I have looked at say that interest is to be eliminated from the political arena, distilled out of the process, just as religious sects are. The aim of the electoral "refining" process is to produce *dis*interested men at the top of the ruling structure.

We have been told that the Constitution is a kind of Lockean bargain made to protect contending property interests. Yet Adair found the most direct influence on The Federalist in Hume's conception of government as a utilitarian division of labor within a generally benevolent set of social ties.

We have been told that Madison's aim was to check governmental powers in general; but he argues for a vigorous central government, and wants only to check partial and "interested" voices from speaking for the whole.

We are told that, though Madison had a dark view of human nature, he still wanted the people to have the final say. That was true so far as legislative supremacy went, but not when it came to judging their own interests. A common modern assumption would be that they should have *most* say in that situation. Madison says (in No. 49) they should have *least* say then. And he gives us his reason: Even the sovereign power must be limited in a constitutional government lest it be a judge in its own case.

We are told that Madison wanted decentralized power, divided sovereignty, and strict construction. On all three points his words say the opposite.

We are told that he, like other founders, believed in Country ideology on matters like the corruption of the British constitution. Instead, he agreed with the principal critic of that ideology.

Popular misconception on one or two of these matters might be conceivable, but how could it be wrong over the whole range of issues? Or, to put it another way, how could I be so perverse as to think so many people so wrong on so many points that affect The Federalist? That is what seems to need explaining now.

First of all, we should remember that Madison himself was wrong in his expectations of the way our government would work. He thought the executive would be weak and vulnerable, that the veto provided in the Constitution would prove useless unless strengthened by combination of the President with either the Supreme Court or the Senate; that the House would be the radical branch of Congress, and the Senate would be obstructionist; that the legislature would be the most powerful branch, and the House the more powerful chamber. On all these matters he proved wrong as a prophet. And we have not considered the most important thing he left out. He thought the political process could operate without organizations for openly stated partisan interest. He thought that parties not only would not but should not come into existence; and believed that their activity would spell the ruin of his whole scheme.

It seems likely that if Madison was so wrong in a predictive sense, it was because his analysis did not fit later conditions or suppositions. Yet we have kept trying to make it do so, for two reasons. We have assumed that The Federalist is a faithful exposition of the Constitution as it was drafted in Philadelphia; and we have assumed that our government works in general accord with the prescriptions of that Constitution. But we could be wrong on both counts. The Constitution may not reflect Madison's theory of representative government. It may, in fact, reflect no single theory, but a combination of views hammered out by way of practical compromise. Throughout this book, I have been considering not what the Constitution itself says, but what Madison says it says. The authoritative enactment of the Constitution was effected by the separate ratifying conventions, whose procedures will have to be studied if we want to understand the Constitution as a separate document. That is the subject I propose to study in my next book. But here we look only at the theory of Publius, to see if it is internally consistent and expressed clearly.

Nor should we assume too quickly that our government, in its evolution over two centuries, though it may conform with an amended Constitution, has the shape that Constitution envisaged. This does not mean that our government as a whole is unconstitutional, or anticonstitutional. But much of it may be extraconstitutional; may exist in ways that the Constitution's ratifiers did not have in mind; may have grown up outside the Constitution's purview. Consider, for instance, the political party system. That is not unconstitutional (though it is un-Publian; we see here how The Federalist can differ from the Constitution). The Constitution neither forbids nor encourages parties. They are not illegal; in that sense they are "constitutional." But they were not specifically provided for by the framers and ratifiers; in that sense they are extraconstitutional.

By assuming the identity, or near-identity, of The Federalist, the Constitution, and our political system, we have encouraged a series of mental shortcuts and theoretical abbreviations. We tend to read all three things anachronistically, considering them outside their three separate times, joining them in some abstract state of timeless accord and mutual explication.

If we follow the clue of Madison's "wrong" predictions, I think the most adequate explanation for his general "error" is not stupidity, bad luck, or the freaks of history. He would be bound to err if his analysis was based on different cultural realities than the ones that succeeded his age—all those cultural changes that have taken place between his time and ours. He was observing a world different from ours, living in that world, responding to it. And much of that world has disappeared, or been so changed as to mislead more than it would have by simple disappearance.

His was the world of the American Enlightenment—a world of the classical virtues reborn, of optimism about man's effort to order society rationally, of a new science of man. Error, it was felt, would yield to truth; superstition would be defeated by curious inquiry, candid and unfettered research, personal and societal integrity. It was the world of the Encyclopedists, of the Scottish social scientists—it would become a new age free of cant and restored to republican simplicity, a kind of secular Eden.

In that world, the concept of public virtue had a hard and clear meaning, a heft and weightiness of the real, no longer apparent to us. We do not even pretend that we choose our politicians for their virtue. That kind of talk would look sappy or insincere in our political discourse. But it was no such thing for Madison and his contemporaries. When Joseph Warren gave the Massacre Day oration in 1775, he stopped at the door of Old South Church and put on a toga before mounting the pulpit. He did not refer to that toga as he spoke, and no one thought it either odd or funny that he should wear it. Of *course* he would invoke the ancient republican values when defending his age's reborn virtue. Benjamin Franklin was often portrayed as a Roman senator. Jefferson wanted Houdon to sculpt Washington in a toga, as he had sculpted Voltaire.

We have seen that private names, of classical origin, were given to members of Princeton's secret societies. It was the job of modern statesmen to play the role of a Brutus or a Cato; and yet the role-playing was deadly serious. Men died to sustain their role—Joseph Warren himself at Bunker Hill, or Nathan Hale becoming Cato in his final moments. The public good—*res publica*, common weal—was a shining new ideal to those who swept away priestly and kingly power and put the people in command of their own fate. The French Revolution's cult of Rome appeared first in America. We gave the world its Cincinnatus. We not only admired Washington; we dared to think of him as the product of our new political science—the virtuous ruler serving not for private gain but out of pride in his own virtue; impartial; not consulting any interest but the "permanent and aggregate interests of the community." That is the vision of The Federalist.

Was it unrealistic? Perhaps. But extraordinary men made the vision a reality, at least for a while. They were a privileged few, but they insisted on honest performance within their meritocracy. The most virtuous man *did* lead Virginia into war—Peyton Randolph. The most virtuous man *did* conduct that war and form the nation and rule it without Napoleonic excess—George Washington. A galaxy of distinguished men devoted themselves to public service, and launched the first new nation of the Enlightenment, the first successful modern republic formed on a rational plan. States *did* surrender their sovereignty to form a nobler whole. We cannot suppose the experiment they undertook was bound to succeed. What kept us from falling back into monarchy, as France did after her great burst of revolutionary energy? Madison would not have hesitated one minute in answering that question. The public virtue kept us republican. It is the only thing that can.

Simply to describe those ideals is to show how distant we are from them. If you think not, ask the current President of the United States to put on a toga the next time he gives a televised speech to the nation. Our world is different, in many ways improved. The deferential society that made for a monopoly of talents has yielded to a more equal and just one. Slavery is abolished. Education is more common. Frank partisanship has been expressed in our politics, but tamed there as well. We did not destroy the republic, though we took some steps that Madison thought were bound to do that. Perhaps they would have if we had maintained the culture of the Enlightenment. But the nation changed, and then changed again.

So: What good is Madison's explanation if it applies to a different world from ours, differs, even, from the Constitution as that document has actually done its work in our midst for two hundred years? Well, if nothing else, Madison explains himself in The Federalist—not a minor thing. Without him and his like, without their ideals, their virtuous labors for the common good, there would have been no America to be preserved and passed on through the necessary changes of the centuries. In that sense, he does explain America—in explaining himself he tells us what Washington meant to his peers and friends and followers, what Jefferson meant. America has to be explained, historically, in terms of the Enlightenment, of the code of public virtue espoused without embarrassment by its most distinguished leaders. And the place to begin that effort is, indeed, with "Publius," the man of the people, the public man.

Key to Brief Citations

The Federalist is referred to by number and page in Jacob Cooke's edition (Wesleyan University, 1961).

Hume's political essays are referred to simply by part (1 or 2), essay number, and page (e.g., "Honour is a great check upon mankind," 1.6.119) in volume I of *Essays Moral, Political, and Literary*, edited by T. H. Green and T. H. Grose (London, 1882).

Adair, diss.	Douglass Adair, "The Intellectual Origins of Jeffersonian Democracy: Republicanism, the Class Struggle, and the Virtuous Farmer" (Yale diss., 1943).
Adair, *Fame*	—*Fame and the Founding Fathers*, edited by Trevor Colbourn. Norton, 1974.
AH	Alexander Hamilton, *Papers*, edited by H. C. Syrett, J. E. Cooke et al. Columbia, 1961– .
Brant	Irving Brant, *James Madison*. Volumes 1–6. Bobbs-Merrill, 1941–61.
Farrand	Max Farrand, *The Records of the Federal Convention of 1787*. Volumes 1–4. Yale, 1911.
Giarrizzo	Giuseppe Giarrizzo, *David Hume, Politico e Storico*. Torino, 1962.
Gwyn	W. B. Gwyn, *The Meaning of the Separation of Powers*. Tulane, 1965.
Hume, *Enquiry*	David Hume, *An Enquiry Concerning the Principles of Morals*, edited by T. H. Green and T. H. Grose. London, 1882.
Hume, *History*	—*History of England*. Volumes 1–8. Boston, 1863.
Hume, *Treatise*	—*A Treatise of Human Nature*, edited by L. A. Selby-Bigge. Oxford, 1888.
Inventing	Garry Wills, *Inventing America: Jefferson's Declaration of Independence*. Doubleday, 1978.
JM	James Madison, *Papers*, edited by W. T. Hutchinson, W. E. Rachal et al. University of Chicago, 1962– .
Mitchell	Broadus Mitchell, *Alexander Hamilton*. Volumes 1–2. Macmillan, 1957–62.

Rotwein   Eugene Rotwein, Introduction to *David Hume: Writings on Economics*. University of Wisconsin, 1955.

Schatz   Albert Schatz, *L'Oeuvre économique de David Hume*. Paris, 1902.

TJ   Thomas Jefferson, *Papers*, edited by Julian Boyd et al. Princeton, 1950– .

Vile   M. J. C. Vile, *Constitutionalism and the Separation of Powers*. Oxford, 1967.

Topic Outline of The Federalist

42. Diplomatic and interstate
43. Miscellaneous
44. Powers superior to states' not obliterative of states

C. Separation of powers
47–48. Not absolute
49–50. Not guaranteed by oversight panels
51. *The* check: bicameralism

D. House of Representatives
52. Mode of election
53. Length of term
54. State apportionments
55–56. Electors-representative ratio
57. Qualification of representatives
58. Changing the ratio
59–61. House power to regulate elections AH

E. Senate
62. Makeup JM
63. Length of term JM
64. Treaty power JJ
65–66. Trying impeachments

F. Executive department
67–69. Republican, not monarchic, office
71–72. Length of term
73. Limits on office
74–77. Powers: pardon, treaty, appointments

G. Judiciary
78. No judicial supremacy
79. Conditions of tenure
80. Limited powers—
81. —but final in their sphere
82. Federal and state courts
83. Civil jury trial: not precluded

H. Miscellaneous objections
84. No bill of rights
85. Conclusion

JM (AH in Albany)

AH (JM in Virginia)

May 28, 1788: *Federalist II* published in book form

Index to Federalist Numbers

Index to Phrases (No. 10)

an aliment: 21, 74, 240–41
— *Imposes uniformity: impracticable* (p. 58)
    his opinions and his passions: 24–33
— *Ignores faction's range* (pp. 58–59)
    opinions concerning religion: 212
    attachment to different leaders (59): 21, 212
    interesting: Glossary, 206–7
    the most frivolous and fanciful distinctions: 212
    unequal distribution of property: 212–13
    distinct interests: Glossary, 205
    interfering: Glossary
— *Faction's evil: judges own cause* (pp. 59–60)
    a judge in his own cause: 114, 206, 210, 225, 258
    his interest: Glossary— "advantage" here, not "group" as in the three earlier uses
    impartiality (60): 114, 210
Control effects?
— *Minority faction by majority principle* (p. 60)
    convulse: cf. *Inventing,* 262–63; *Explaining,* 228
— *Majority faction by:*
    a) preventing impulse: impossible in republic (pp. 60–62)
        the public good and private rights (61): 257
        by one of two: 22, 257

no cure for the mischiefs: 240, 256, 259
obnoxious individual: Glossary, 225
patronized: with the meaning "recommended" (OED 1 c); but it means "adopted" at 26.164
their opinions and their passions (62): 24–33
b) preventing opportunity: possible in republic (p. 62)
    promises the cure: 240, 256, 259
    nature of the cure: 240, 256, 259
    refine: 226–30, 241–46
    and enlarge: 230, 246–47
    passing them through the medium: 241–42
    true interest: 205
    wisdom . . . and patriotism: 186, 225
    partial considerations: 210, 225
    effect may be inverted: 214
c) preventing conjunction of impulse and opportunity (pp. 62–65)
    fit characters (63): Glossary
    a greater probability: for probability theory in government, cf. *Inventing,* 139–48; *Explaining,* 218
    greater number of citizens: 218–19
    being more free: 231
    most diffusive: 231–33, 246–47

Glossary

"Your argument is obnoxious, but it will be liquidated once its specious character is discovered." That sentence would not be considered friendly if spoken today. But its terms were not hostile in the eighteenth century. We need to translate: "Your argument, though exposed to malice, will become clear when its attractive distinction is revealed." Minor misunderstandings can, cumulatively, become major if we forget the many small differences in usage between Publius' time and our own. Though I have dealt with more crucial eighteenth-century concepts and terminology in the text of this book, experience in reading The Federalist with students convinced me that a Glossary of slighter inconcinnities would be useful. The words of Publius are listed by essay and page in Cooke's edition. Wherever possible, I illustrate Enlightenment usage from Johnson's *Dictionary* (J plus definition number) and from that other touchstone of style, Hume's *History of England* (H plus volume, chapter, and page according to the Boston edition of 1863).

accommodation (7.38, 22.141): legal settlement (J 4). The more usual eighteenth-century term was "composition."

address, n. (63.429): skill (J 4, H 4.44.181). The word more frequently meant "bearing," to which Hume gives the special meaning of "strategy" at 3.39.446: "by treachery and dissimulation, which she called address."

artificial (43.290): feigned (J 2)

awful (20.128, 15.98, 65.441): intimidating (J 1)

barely (62.418): only (J 4, "by reading barely the Scripture")

casual (67.453, 456): random (J 1)

casualty (42.286, 55.377, 65.443): accident (J 1)

cause (10.59, 82.554): legal case (J 3)

character (10.56, 10.63, 15.91, 44.300, 63.422 and 423, 64.433, 76.510): reputation (H 5.42.56, 5.44.183). With Madison's men of "the most diffusive and established characters" (10.63) compare Hume 5.62.407: "His established character for truth and sincerity stood him in great stead." Elsewhere in The Federalist *character* means "defining trait" (11.66, 69.462, 83.569), "title" (10.65, 63.426), "role" (64.437, 81.544—cf. H 1.8.326), or "type" (2.9, 10.63, 76.513, 78.531—cf. H 5.54.9)

civilian, n. (9.56): expert in civil

(not canon or common) law (H 2.16.206)

cognizance (23.149): jurisdiction (J 1)

complacency (66.449): deference (J 1, "rudeness and want of complacency")

complaisance (71.482, 78.529): subservience (H 1.4.227, 1.8.323, 3.19.299)

to comprehend (43.289, 67.455): include (H 3.32.182, 3.39.434)

to conciliate (27.173, 70.472, 72.492): recruit (J 1)

confidential (49.342, 65.442): trusted (OED 4)

congenial (62.416): accordant (OED 2)

considerate, adj. (1.3, 10.57, 78.528, 79.533—adv. 42.284): wisely cautious (J 1)

delicate (43.298, twice): difficult (OED 9)

devotion (49.483): disposal (J 9, H 2.17.236, 3.31.124)

discoloured (49.341): discredited (OED 1 b 1483)

eligible (11.68, 30.188, 38.241, 74.501, 79.531–2, 81.543 and 548, 83.568): desirable (J 1). But "available" at 57.388, 69.463, and 72.487

to embark (73.498): engage (J 1)

to evince (1.5, 40.258, 79.531): prove (J 1)

experimental (72.487): experiential (J 1)

extraordinary (68.461): supplementary (OED 2)

fangled (43.290): contrived (OED 1)

genius (12.75, 16.101, 18.114, 21.129, 22.137, 35.222, 39.250, 55.375, 60.404, 62.418, 63.426, 70.471, 75.507, 82.555, 83.574): ethos (J 5, H 2.13.31, 2.16.179)

handle, n. (39.253): use (J 2)

immediate (74.501): primary (J 1)

to insult (43.289): invade (OED 4). But "deride" at 46.322 (twice)

interest (10.59 [three times], 10.63 [twice], 10.64): group or band with common aim (H 3.39.443, 3.40.535)

interested (1.4, 10.64, 15.97, 51.351, 59.397): biased (H 4.42.69). But "involved" at 7.39. At 71.481 (twice), "interested in" means "committed to."

interesting (1.3, 11.67, 14.84, 24.155): crucial (H 3.39.430). But "compelling" at 10.59 and 70.475; "engaging" at 49.340.

interfering (10.59, 37.237): self-crippling (from the first use, of a horse striking one leg with another, J 3)

jealous (9.52, 24.153–4, 25.159, 63.428): suspicious (J 6, H 1.6.118). But "protective" at 38.240 (J 4, H 6.68.152)

job (44.301): theft (J 2)

to liquidate (37.236, 78.525, 82.553): clarify (OED 1)

maxim (22.139, 48.332, 66.445, 83.559): rule (H 4.52.450)

mediocrity (62.416): middle term (J 1)

to modify (76.510): restrain (OED 1)

municipal (53.364): domestic, as opposed to foreign (OED 1). But "corporate" at 45.309 (OED 2)

obnoxious (10.61): vulnerable (J 4, H 2.25.509). But "resented" at 38.245 and 42.286

police (17.105): self-government (J 1, "the regulation and government of a city or country, so far as regards the inhabitants," H 2.16.218–19). Cf. *Inventing*, 332

policy (43.293, 46.319): practical wisdom (J 2, "consists in a certain dexterity of managing business for a man's secular advantage")

popular (10.57, 10.61, 83.574): democratic (J 4)

primitive (14.86, 24.154): original (J 1)

to result (48.335): revert (J 1)

to retort (54.369): return (J 2)

revolution (19.122, 20.128, 39.250, 52.356, 55.376, 63.429, 63.431): reform (J 3, H 2.7.292, 3.38.387). This was the normal political use in the eighteenth century (cf. *Inventing*, 49–64). It is Madison's favored meaning in The Federalist—he glosses the word with "reform" three lines above at 19.122, and applies it to gradual *de*formation at 63.429 and 431 But he *opposes* revolution to reform at 38.240. *See* next entry.

revolution (16.104, 23.150, 26.164, 28.177, 60.404): forcible overthrow (J s.v. *revolt*). Hamilton favored this use, glossing the word with "revolt" nine lines above at 60.404 (cf. *Inventing*,

51). But Hamilton uses the word as well for the Glorious Revolution (26.165–6) and for the period of the American Revolution (24.156).

to revolve (38.243, 45.310): consider (J 2)

satisfactory (31.196): sufficient (OED 4)

scruple, n. (21.131, 40.265, 43.290): objection (OED 4, H 4.44.154)

to scruple (63.425): hesitate (J 1, H 3.40.539)

specious (10.57, 49.342, 59.400): attractive (H 3.38.417). But *"deceptively* attractive" at 18.116 and 35.218

story (70.471): history (J 1)

topic (10.51): argument (J 1, H 3.37.335, 337, 338)

undertaking (62.421): investment (J 1)

unsophisticated (1.195): uncorrupted (J s.v. *sophisticate*, 1)

virtual (79.533): implied (OED 4)

wilfully (63.426): by design (J 2)

Index to Proper Names